CONGRESS AND
THE POLITICS OF
U.S. FOREIGN POLICY

CONGRESS AND THE POLITICS OF U.S. FOREIGN POLICY

JAMES M. LINDSAY

THE JOHNS HOPKINS UNIVERSITY PRESS
BALTIMORE AND LONDON

To Marci

2 November 1986

© 1994 The Johns Hopkins University Press
All rights reserved. Published 1994
Printed in the United States of America on acid-free paper
03 02 01 00 99 98 97 96 95 94   5 4 3 2 1

The Johns Hopkins University Press
2715 North Charles Street
Baltimore, Maryland 21218-4319
The Johns Hopkins Press Ltd., London

ISBN 0-8018-4881-4
ISBN 0-8018-4882-2 (pbk.)

Library of Congress Cataloging-in-Publication Data will be found
at the end of this book.
A catalog record for this book is available from the British Library.

CONTENTS

PREFACE AND ACKNOWLEDGMENTS

Complaints about Congress abound, and the literature on foreign policy is no exception. One can wade through the popular and scholarly commentaries on U.S. foreign policy and find few kind words said on behalf of Congress and its members. Most of what has been written agrees that Congress has failed in the exercise of its foreign policy powers and disagrees only on the exact nature of the failure. On one side of the debate stand the Irreconcilables, who complain that members of Congress pandering to the transitory passions of their constituents are usurping the president's rightful leadership role in foreign policy. On the other side stand the Skeptics, who complain that a lack of political incentives leads to episodic and superficial congressional interest in foreign policy. Whichever telling of the story one prefers, the ultimate lesson is the same: Congress is ill-suited to be involved in decision making on foreign policy.

This book challenges the arguments of both Irreconcilables and Skeptics, and it presents a more balanced and positive assessment of Congress's role in foreign policy. In doing so the chapters that follow explore the motivations for congressional activism, the means by which members try to turn their policy preferences into policy outcomes, and the circumstances under which they succeed. My basic argument is that while politics invariably colors congressional behavior, it does not make members of Congress inherently unfit to decide foreign policy. Instead, politics often drives members to address the substance of foreign policy—although in ways that sometimes irritate Irreconcilables and Skeptics alike—and thereby to discharge Congress's constitutional duty to oversee U.S. foreign policy.

In arguing that Congress contributes, on balance, to the making of U.S. foreign policy, I am not blind to the institution's flaws. Congressional activism is not cost-free, and it does not guarantee that the country will choose wisely in foreign affairs. Quite the contrary. As critics from across the political spectrum like to point out, Congress can be inefficient, it can miss the significant in a rush for the trivial, and it can place self-interest before the national interest. Moreover, if Congress actually did run U.S. foreign policy, as the more extreme Irreconcilables sometimes claim, its shortcomings no doubt would imperil the national interest.

But Congress does not control foreign policy. Rather it is a subsidiary, though still important, actor in a decision-making process that continues to be led by the president. And in that decision-making process Congress and its members play the valuable role of critic and legitimizer. Members bring different values and perspectives to bear on policy debates, views that provide a useful (if sometimes lengthy) political scrub for administration proposals. In this regard the supposed vices of Congress are often virtues, a point critics tend to forget—until, of course, the president begins to pursue a policy they oppose.

Several colleagues helped me in writing this book. Randall Ripley encouraged me to write on Congress and foreign policy, and, as Chapter 7 shows, he greatly shaped my approach to the question of congressional influence. Ellen Collier and Jim McCormick helped me to locate information I knew I needed but could not find. Robert Art read the entire manuscript and graciously offered advice on how to improve it. Dan Neppl and Maile Solis were diligent research assistants.

My family also deserves credit. James and Collette Lindsay, Peter and Nancy Nottonson, Robert and Rose Dieda, Frank and Madge Shemanski, and Henry Dieda all provided love and encouragement. Phoebe and Zooey Lindsay helped me to refine my arguments during our many walks together. Ian Alexander Nottonson Lindsay debuted when the book was at its midpoint and immediately began pushing me to do twice as much work in half the time. Marci Lindsay has been my source of strength and inspiration since we first met. I owe her the world for showing me that dreams do come true.

CONGRESS AND THE POLITICS OF U.S. FOREIGN POLICY

INTRODUCTION

THE IRAN-CONTRA HEARINGS gripped the American public in the summer of 1987. The Reagan administration found itself accused of violating U.S. law, and many wondered if the country would revisit the travails of the Watergate era. Yet before the hearings closed, it was Congress that found itself on trial. Several witnesses used their testimony to criticize Congress's handling of foreign policy, none more passionately than Lt. Col. Oliver North: "Plain and simple, the Congress is to blame because of the fickle, vacillating, unpredictable, on-again-off-again policy toward the Nicaraguan democratic resistance. . . . In my opinion, these hearings have caused serious damage to our national interests. Our adversaries laugh at us, and our friends recoil in horror."[1] Many Americans apparently agreed; almost overnight the little known North became a national celebrity.

North's complaint about Congress, if true, is deeply troubling. In marked contrast to the deference Capitol Hill frequently accorded presidents in the 1950s and 1960s, Congress today involves itself in a dizzying array of foreign policy issues. Some sense of the extent of congressional activism can be gleaned from a simple statistic about current legislation on foreign policy. The 1960 edition of *Legislation on Foreign Relations* ran 519 pages; the 1990 edition ran 5,483 pages and spanned four volumes. Nor does Congress shy away from major issues. Whereas Lyndon Johnson pushed the Gulf of Tonkin Resolution through Congress with only two dissenting votes, George Bush saw the resolution authorizing the use of force against Iraq pass by only five votes in the Senate.

Moreover, congressional activism on foreign policy promises to continue in the coming years. The collapse of the Soviet Union opened debate over what will replace containment as the lodestar of U.S. foreign policy. With the disappearance of the Soviet threat the rationale for many foreign policy programs evaporated, and the scrutiny accorded to spending on foreign affairs is increasing accordingly.[2] The alarm felt in many quarters of Capitol Hill over the press of economic and social problems at home will only intensify congressional activism as members try to shift resources away from foreign policy and toward domestic policy. At the same time, growing global interdependence is blurring the line separating domestic affairs from foreign affairs. Issues such as drug trafficking, immigration, global warming, and trade inevitably push Congress into the fray on foreign policy because they involve important domestic interests.

The extent of congressional activism on foreign policy is clear. But what role does Congress play in the making of foreign policy? Are we witnessing "foreign policy by Congress" as some have alleged? Or is congressional debate more smoke than fire? Who in Congress wields power on foreign policy issues? Do members of Congress simply follow the political winds on foreign policy? Does Congress undermine the national interest when it ventures beyond the water's edge?

As important as these questions are, answers are in short supply. The study of Congress and foreign policy is a backwater field of political science; most systematic studies of the subject are now more than a quarter of a century old.[3] Although popular commentary abounds, most of it argues about Congress's constitutional prerogatives, debates whether Congress is gaining power relative to the president, or claims that Congress harms U.S. foreign policy. The crucial questions of what members of Congress do and why they do it—questions that by all logic should precede any effort to assess the vices and virtues of Congress's involvement in foreign affairs—draw little study.

The chapters that follow try to fill the glaring gap in our knowledge of the role Congress plays in the making of foreign policy. Given the tremendous changes that overtook Capitol Hill and the world in the two decades after Vietnam, such a study is long overdue.

THREE FALLACIES

Everyone agrees that Congress is more active in foreign policy today than at any time since the 1930s. The dispute arises over the consequences of congressional activism. At one extreme in the debate lie the Irreconcilables. So named because they are as opposed to congressional involvement in foreign policy as their Senate forebears were to the Treaty of Versailles, Irreconcilables warn that "overreaching" by an "imperial Congress" has created a "fettered presidency."[4] They yearn for the good old days when the president ran the show. Not surprisingly, those who sound the tocsin most vigorously on the perils of foreign policy by Congress tend to be administration officials and their supporters.

At the other extreme in the debate lie the Skeptics. They argue that congressional activism is more show than substance. Congress, in their view, operates on the margins of foreign policy, so much so that the author of one recent article felt compelled to title his article "Why the President (Almost) Always Wins in Foreign Affairs."[5] If Irreconcilables count among their number many administration officials, the Skeptics predominate in academia. Perhaps the best evidence of how the Skeptic's view prevails among academics is the scant attention the scholarly literature pays to Congress and foreign policy.

Although Irreconcilables and Skeptics dominate the debate over congressional activism in foreign policy, neither describes Congress's role accurately. Irreconcilables grossly exaggerate the extent and effect of congressional activism. Although members of Congress challenge the White House far more than they did during the heyday of the imperial presidency, they by no means control foreign policy. The president and his subordinates in the executive branch continue to lead in policy making. Skeptics, on the other hand, err by equating influence with the ability to write policy preferences directly into law. Skeptics are right to note that many hotly contested legislative initiatives die on Capitol Hill. Yet even when members of Congress fail to dictate the substance of foreign policy, they frequently influence it indirectly.

But more than misjudging the extent of congressional influence, Irreconcilables and Skeptics both perpetuate three common fallacies about Congress and foreign policy: the electoral fallacy, the technocratic fallacy, and the adversarial fallacy.

The Electoral Fallacy

Most discussions of Congress and foreign policy emphasize that senators seek reelection every six years and representatives every two years. This banal observation draws so much attention because foreign policy analysts deeply distrust the American public. They believe that because the public has little knowledge of or interest in foreign affairs, members have few reasons to master foreign policy issues and every reason to cater to the passions of the moment. What results, in the words of former undersecretary of state William D. Rogers, is that "Congress is beholden to every short-term swing of popular opinion. The temptation to pander to prejudice and emotion is overwhelming."[6]

No one can deny that members of Congress worry about reelection. To repeat Rep. Frank Smith's (D-Miss.) oft-quoted quip: "All members of Congress have a primary interest in being re-elected. Some members have no other interest."[7] Even members with safe seats fear their margins of safety will evaporate if they take their constituents for granted.[8] In many respects, life in the Senate and (especially) the House *is* a perpetual campaign. And as Sen. Frank Church's (D-Idaho) infamous denunciation of the Soviet brigade in Cuba in the fall of 1979 attests, members sometimes place their self-interest before the national interest, with significant consequences for the country.[9]

Yet the preoccupation with the pathologies of reelection leads to the electoral fallacy, the belief that the electoral connection makes members of Congress inherently irresponsible on foreign policy. While members act irresponsibly at times, responsible congressional action is by far the norm. On most foreign policy issues voters know and care little about specific policy choices, thereby giving members considerable freedom to vote their consciences. Where electoral incentives exist, they frequently encourage members to delve into the substance of a foreign policy issue. David Mayhew, whose seminal work on the electoral connection is approvingly cited by those who fret about congressional pandering, emphasizes that members work policy issues "when somebody of consequence is watching, when there is credit to be gained for legislative maneuvers."[10] Sometimes the credit comes from the average voter. More often it comes from interest groups, especially so-called advocacy groups. Because interest groups span the ideological spectrum, members who choose to work foreign policy issues can make their efforts electorally worthwhile.

At the same time, the electoral fallacy rests on an impoverished conception of legislative motivation. For all the importance attached to reelection, it is only one of the motives driving congressional behavior. Most members also want to advance their personal conceptions of good public policy. Of course, it is chic today to deride members of Congress as politicians bereft of commitment to anything or anyone but themselves. Yet far more than is commonly recognized, members hold views about what role the United States should play in the world, views they want to see translated into policy. It is this clash of ideas, as much as if not more so than material interests or constituency pressures, that drives congressional debate on foreign policy.

The Technocratic Fallacy

Closely related to the electoral fallacy is the technocratic fallacy, the (usually implicit) belief that the work of Congress should be an "eat your peas and spinach" endeavor. Many observers seem comfortable only with the member of Congress who acts as a "lonely gnome who passes up news conferences, cocktail parties, sometimes even marriage in order to devote his time to legislative 'homework.'"[11] Robert Art, for instance, argues that "policy oversight requires disciplined analysis, hard work, perspective, time to reflect, and detachment from the agency one oversees. All of these are commodities in short supply in the harried and increasingly specialized Congress of today."[12] Howard Wiarda objects that "the system of hearings has been so politicized that it sometimes resembles a circus rather than a serious effort to arrive at sensible policy."[13]

These portraits of legislative behavior do Congress a disservice. Far more than the critics acknowledge, members of Congress and their staff do engage in proactive and systematic review of bureaucratic behavior, or what political scientists are now fond of calling police-patrol oversight.[14] Each year the foreign policy and defense committees hold hearings and issue reports on topics such as political reform in Eastern Europe, America's services trade deficit, and the environmental impact of World Bank lending. Most such efforts go unnoticed in academia and in the wider political community precisely because they attract no media attention.

By the same token, it is just as inaccurate to contend that members of Congress always act as lonely gnomes. For every member such as Sen. Sam Nunn (D-Ga.) who builds a reputation by working quietly within the institution, there are others whose first instinct in any situation is to find a television camera. And because members want to be reelected, they have strong incentives to be seen addressing salient political issues. Not only is taking a position electorally valuable when constituents share a member's views, but simply being seen on television or mentioned in the newspapers may well enhance a member's electoral prospects.

But contrary to the technocratic fallacy, legislative work and self-promotion are not mutually exclusive endeavors. Despite all the praise that scholars lavish on police-patrol oversight, it often represents a waste of time and effort. Because government agencies comply with congressional intent most of the time and because the ability of members to review agency behavior is inherently limited, police patrols may fail to discover an agency's shortcomings—even when they exist. In contrast, responding to what voters or other political actors define as a problem not only offers the opportunity to reap electoral reward, it increases the likelihood that members will actually uncover problems with how agencies operate.

Moreover, for any member of Congress seeking to change policy, publicity is an invaluable weapon. A member who wants to mobilize his or her colleagues must first capture their attention and second persuade them. The media are an invaluable tool for accomplishing both goals. At the same time, members know that gridlock on Capitol Hill makes it difficult to pass legislation and that presidents respond to public opinion. That knowledge encourages members to use legislative debate, oversight hearings, and media appearances to influence the terms of public debate and, in turn, administration policy. Thus, much of what critics dismiss as self-promotion or grandstanding is a concerted effort by members to push public and elite opinion in a direction that favors their policy preferences and undermines the administration's. These efforts might at times resemble circuses, but they are circuses with very real substantive objectives.

The technocratic fallacy, then, fails to recognize that Congress is a political institution and not a bureaucratic one.[15] Time and resource constraints combine with the electoral imperative to encourage members of Congress to conduct their legislative work in ways that help their electoral chances. To expect members to act as if they worked for an idealized bureaucracy that dispassionately and proactively analyzes policy poses a standard of judgment that Congress will never meet, and it directs attention away from the ways in which members make their preferences felt on foreign policy.

The Adversarial Fallacy

A third fallacy found in most writings on Congress and foreign policy is the adversarial fallacy, a preoccupation with the conflictual side of executive-legislative relations. Such a preoccupation is understandable. Executive-legislative conflict is deeply rooted in constitutional theory and historical practice. The 1980s, in particular, saw presidents Reagan and Bush struggle with Congress over several major foreign policy issues: aid to the Nicaraguan contras, arms control with the Soviet Union, most-favored-nation status for China, and the use of force against Iraq, to mention just a few. And these struggles had a strongly partisan flavor as Republicans in the White House consistently squared off against Democrats in Congress.

As understandable as the preoccupation with executive-legislative conflict may be, it misses much of the interaction between the White House and Capitol Hill. Issues such as aid to the contras notwithstanding, Congress's dealings with the president are marked more by cooperation than by conflict. During the Reagan years the White House and Congress cooperated on policy toward Afghanistan, China, India, Libya, and the Persian Gulf, among others. The first year of the Bush administration saw executive-legislative cooperation on what had been a source of intense conflict, namely, policy toward Nicaragua. And lost amidst the debate over whether to use force against Iraq was the fact that President Bush's initial decision to send U.S. troops to defend Saudi Arabia was widely applauded on Capitol Hill.

If most presidential initiatives in foreign policy never become an issue in Congress, some do. But the extent of conflict should not be exaggerated simply because Congress takes a vote. When presidential policies do appear on the legislative agenda, Congress often reaffirms them resoundingly. To take just one example, representatives opposed to the Pershing II missile offered numerous amendments to kill the program but never garnered the support of more than a third of the House. And sometimes Congress considers foreign policy legislation at White House request. When the Reagan administration wanted to punish New Zealand for its nuclear-free weapons policy but did not want to be seen doing so, it encouraged a senior Republican in the House to introduce punitive legislation.[16]

Even when Congress and the White House become locked in conflict, more is usually occurring than meets the eye. Though it is convenient to treat Congress and the executive branch as "its"—a convenience I will indulge in as well—both institutions are actually "theys."[17] Congress clearly is not a monolith; every vote testifies to the ideological, partisan, and regional divisions within the institution. But division also marks the executive branch. No one familiar with the literature on bureaucratic politics would mistake the Defense Department for a unified bureaucracy or overlook the rivalries between the State Department and the staff of the National Security Council. The splits within the executive branch mean that losers in executive branch decision making frequently turn to Congress for help in changing policy.

Examples of alliances—some explicit, some tacit—that cut across the two branches of government are not hard to find. The most obvious are those between presidents and their supporters on Capitol Hill. But alliances between congressional opponents and disaffected executive branch officials also abound. Critics of the second Strategic Arms Limitation Talks (SALT II) drew considerable support from officials in the Defense Department.[18] In the mid-1980s, officials in the State Department encouraged congressional interest in the Philippines as a way of putting pressure on President Reagan to end support for Ferdinand Marcos.[19] When Secretary of Defense Dick Cheney canceled the V-22 Osprey, the marines lobbied on Capitol Hill to save the plane. And when President Bush began to consider a Defense Department proposal to sell advanced weaponry to Saudi Arabia after the Gulf War, State Department officials opposed to the plan told the media the sale would damage the Middle East peace talks.[20]

Once the prevalence of cross-cutting alliances on foreign policy is recognized, the normative aspects of executive branch conflict take on a new light. Most commentators urge members of Congress to follow the lead of the White House on the grounds that the executive branch possesses greater technical expertise and better comprehends the national interest (a result of the president having been elected in a national election). But on many occasions the experts in the executive branch disagree among themselves over which policies serve the national interest. In circumstances such as these, then, it is hardly surprising that many members regard presidential initiatives with skepticism. By the same token, on most every issue, some group in the executive branch welcomes congressional involvement. As one congressional staffer put it when asked if foreign policy officials obeyed the directives laid down by the appropriations committees: "Sure they'll do it. *Someone* there wants to!"[21]

The electoral, technocratic, and adversarial fallacies each distort our understanding of Congress and foreign policy. In particular, the three fallacies prompt pessimistic conclusions about the congressional role in foreign policy. My goal in this book is to challenge these conclusions and to present a more balanced assessment of Congress's role in foreign policy. The chapters that follow show that while politics invariably colors congressional debates, it does not make members of Congress inherently unfit to decide foreign policy. Indeed, politics often drives members to address the substance of foreign policy—although in ways that sometimes irritate Irreconcilables and Skeptics alike—and thereby to discharge Congress's constitutional duty to oversee the making of U.S. foreign policy.

In trying to provide a more balanced assessment of Congress's role in foreign policy, I am not claiming that congressional activism is cost-free or that it guarantees that the country will choose wisely in foreign affairs. As critics from across the political spectrum like to point out, Congress can be inefficient, it can miss the significant in a rush for the trivial, and it can choose bad policies. Yet the deficiencies of congressional activism should not blind us to its virtues or lead us to overlook the vices that attend congressional deference to the executive branch. Contrary to what both Irreconcilables and Skeptics claim, U.S. foreign policy on balance benefits from congressional activism.

ORGANIZATION OF THE BOOK

The chapters that follow explore Congress's role in the making of foreign policy. I should emphasize that I use the term *foreign policy* to encompass the entire array of policies that affect the U.S. role in the world. An all too common failing is to equate foreign policy with crisis policy or national security policy. As Chapter 7 discusses at greater length, such a limited conception of foreign policy channels the discussion to precisely those areas where presidential power is the strongest and congressional influence the weakest. Conversely, studies that focus on decisions to use force miss an entire class of issue areas such as foreign aid, human rights, and trade where congressional activity and influence is extensive.

By the same token, I use *foreign policy* to include defense issues. Although defense and foreign policy are often treated as distinct policy domains, it is far more difficult to disentangle the two than the different labels might otherwise suggest. During the heated debates in the 1980s over the MX missile and the Strategic Defense Initiative, for example, what was at stake was not only the future of specific weapons systems but also the means by which the United States would deter the Soviet Union and (if the Reagan administration was to be believed) the course of the Strategic Arms Reduction Talks (START). Likewise, the decisions being made today about the size, composition, and purpose of U.S. military forces after the cold war both flow from and place significant limits on America's role in the world.

The first three chapters begin the examination of Congress's role in the making of foreign policy by exploring the whats, whys, and whos of congressional activism. Chapter 1 traces the history of congressional involvement in foreign policy and reviews the developments that have encouraged members of Congress to become more active since the end of the Vietnam War. Chapter 2 examines the constraints and incentives that individual members face when dealing with foreign policy. While it is often assumed that electoral pressures discourage sustained legislative interest in foreign policy, members have personal and political incentives to undertake detailed substantive work. Chapter 3 discusses the roles played by committees, the floor, party leaders, and congressional staff. Although critics make much of the fact that many committees claim jurisdiction over some aspect of foreign policy, the real power remains in the hands of the traditional foreign policy committees. The distribution of power among these committees, however, has changed dramatically.

Chapters 4, 5, and 6 review the tools that members of Congress use to make their preferences felt in foreign policy. Chapter 4 surveys efforts to dictate the substance of foreign policy through legislation. Because of the limitations inherent in substantive legislation, members often are less interested in passing a bill than they are in using it as a lever to force the administration to change its policy. Chapter 5 shows how members use procedural legislation to design decision-making processes that incorporate congressional preferences into executive branch decisions. Chapter 6 analyzes several nonlegislative means that members use to influence foreign policy. Much of what commentators dismiss as congressional posturing turns out on closer inspection to be attempts to use the media to change the terms of debate and thereby the content of policy.

The final two chapters examine Congress's impact on foreign policy. Chapter 7 addresses the question of influence. It explores how Congress's importance varies across the different types of foreign policy, ranging from almost none in crisis policy, to a modest amount in strategic policy, to a substantial influence in structural policy. Nonetheless, Congress remains a junior partner to the president. It is by no means a coequal of the president and it does not control foreign policy. Chapter 8 concludes the study by assessing the vices and virtues of congressional activism. The conventional wisdom holds that Congress unnecessarily politicizes foreign policy and hampers the ability of presidents to carry out their duties as the representative of the nation. On closer inspection, these criticisms fall short.

1

FOREIGN POLICY ON CAPITOL HILL

WHEN GEORGE BUSH became president, he set out to restore comity to an executive-legislative relationship on foreign policy that had become frayed during the Reagan years. Disturbed by the fact that Congress and the White House had come to challenge not only each other's policy proposals but also each other's motives, Bush used his inaugural address to call for "a new engagement between the Executive and the Congress." He reminded his audience of a time when America's political differences "ended at the water's edge," and he concluded that the "old bipartisanship must made new again."[1]

President Bush never achieved the new engagement he hoped for. Although Congress and the White House cooperated on some foreign policy matters, his decisions on the Gulf War, China's trade status, aid to El Salvador, and other issues came under sharp attack on Capitol Hill. Yet the failure to establish a new engagement owed less to a lack of effort on the part of the president or members of Congress than to the premise on which the idea rested. For all the president's nostalgia about politics stopping at the water's edge—a nostalgia shared by Irreconcilables and Skeptics alike—conflict between the president and Congress is deeply rooted in both constitutional theory and historical practice. The Constitution divides foreign policy between the executive and legislative branches, thereby creating, in Edward Corwin's famous phrase, "an invitation to struggle for the privilege of directing American foreign policy."[2] And while that invitation does not preclude cooperation where Congress and the president share the same policy preferences, where they do not members of Congress have gladly tried to put their own mark on foreign policy.

Of course, when presidents and pundits wax nostalgic about the White House and Congress working hand in hand on foreign policy they long not for the one hundred fifty years preceding World War II but for the two decades that followed it. Yet the memories of what one Irreconcilable calls "the golden years from Pearl Harbor to the Tet Offensive" are highly selective.[3] Although the first postwar decade saw Congress and the White House cooperate on drafting the Marshall Plan and the Atlantic Charter, it also saw the two bitterly contest U.S. policy in Asia as well as the president's authority to send troops abroad and sign executive agreements. Executive-legislative relations turned more harmonious as the second postwar decade began, but only because members of Congress abdicated much of their responsibility to oversee foreign policy. Deference, not cooperation, came to characterize executive-legislative relations in the late 1950s and early 1960s.

Whatever the merits of congressional deference—and they are by no means as obvious as Irreconcilables have claimed—the extreme willingness with which members of Congress followed the president's lead during the second postwar decade was a historical oddity occasioned by the near-unanimous belief that communism threatened the United States. The Vietnam War shattered that consensus. Members, as well as the broader public, came to doubt both the severity of the threats facing the United States and the claim that the national interest is best served by giving the president the maximum possible discretion. No longer deterred from action by beliefs about their inherent inferiority, Congress rejoined the struggle for the privilege of directing American foreign policy. In some instances this struggle has led to cooperation and compromise; in others it has led only to conflict and confrontation.

THE CONSTITUTIONAL BLUEPRINT

Americans are fond of casting political disputes in constitutional terms. The debate over Congress's proper role in foreign policy is no exception. Irreconcilables argue that the framers of the Constitution intended the president to reign supreme in foreign affairs and that in recent years Congress has claimed powers that do not belong to it. An important question then presents itself: What precisely are the foreign policy powers of Congress?

A literal reading of the Constitution hardly supports the position staked out by Irreconcilables. The Constitution gives the president relatively few specific (or enumerated) powers in foreign policy. Article 2, Section 2 designates the president "Commander in Chief of the Army and Navy of the United States" and specifies that, subject to the approval of the Senate, the president has the power "to make Treaties" and "appoint Ambassadors."

Article 2, Section 3 stipulates that the president "shall receive Ambassadors and other public Ministers." Other than these clauses, the Constitution stands silent on the question of the president's authority in foreign affairs. And while Irreconcilables insist that the position of commander in chief confers a broad range of special foreign policy powers on the president, the framers saw the position simply as an office and not as an independent source of decision-making authority.[4]

In contrast to the limited grant of specific authority to the president, the Constitution allocates considerable foreign policy powers to Congress. Article 1, Section 8 assigns Congress the power "to provide for the common Defence," "to regulate Commerce with foreign Nations," "to define and punish Piracies and Felonies committed on the high Seas," "to declare war," "to raise and support Armies," "to provide and maintain a Navy," and "to make Rules for the Government and Regulation of the land and naval Forces." Article 2, Section 2 specifies that the Senate must give its advice and consent to all treaties and ambassadorial appointments. And Congress's more general powers to approve government spending and cabinet officials give it potentially great influence over foreign policy.

Of course, no analysis of the text of the Constitution can by itself settle the issue of what powers Congress exercises in foreign policy. As Louis Henkin observes, "The Constitution enumerates, and allocates to the political branches, some foreign affairs powers . . . but many powers that are indisputably foreign affairs powers (and were surely intended for the federal government and denied to the states) are not mentioned."[5] Which branch of government has the power to make peace, to abrogate treaties, or to extend political recognition to other states are all questions that cannot be answered by reading the text of the Constitution. The answers to these and other constitutional questions have been shaped by over two centuries of political practice and case law.

Yet even if the Constitution dealt with foreign policy in greater depth, we would still not know exactly how foreign policy powers are divided between the president and Congress. Despite having written the Constitution, the framers themselves squabbled almost immediately over what the document meant in practice. In 1793, George Washington declared the United States neutral in the war between Great Britain and France. Pro-French members of Congress immediately charged him with exceeding his authority and exercising a power that properly rested with Congress. The resulting political furor prompted Alexander Hamilton and James Madison to address the question of how the Constitution allocates authority on foreign policy between the president and Congress.

In theory, Hamilton and Madison knew the Constitution better than anyone. Both had served at the Constitutional Convention and (along with John Jay) had written the Federalist Papers. Yet Hamilton and Madison offered radically different interpretations of the Constitution. Writing under the pen name Pacificus, Hamilton argued that foreign policy is by its very nature the province of the executive branch and that the powers delegated to Congress in the Constitution are "exceptions out of the general 'executive power'" that "are to be construed strictly, and ought to be extended no further than is essential to their execution." Writing as Helvidius, Madison condemned Hamilton's argument as unsupported "by any general arrangements, or particular expressions, or plausible analogies, to be found in the constitution."[6] Madison argued instead that Congress enjoyed wide latitude in the exercise of its legislative powers in foreign affairs.

Two hundred years after the Pacificus-Helvidius debate, the exact allocation of constitutional powers on foreign policy remains in dispute.[7] Hamilton's broad interpretation of the president's powers in foreign affairs has had great appeal over the past half-century, and presidents (and their lawyers) have repeatedly invoked passages from Pacificus to buttress their own expansive reading of presidential authority. But while recognizing the practical force of Hamilton's arguments, legal scholars also recognize that Congress retains formidable powers in foreign affairs, powers that may at times conflict with those of the president.

In short, the Constitution provides for the executive and legislative branches to share authority over foreign affairs. At times, members of Congress may, as Irreconcilables fear, try to exercise powers that in fact belong to the executive. But because Congress possesses considerable authority to act in foreign affairs, such instances of congressional aggrandizement are rare. Instead, most complaints about congressional activism in foreign policy turn on objections to the substance of Congress's actions and not their constitutionality.

CONGRESS IN AN ISOLATIONIST AMERICA

One can find much in the first one hundred fifty years of the American republic to support Hamilton's view of a strong presidential role in foreign policy. George Washington established that the president had the right to initiate the conduct of foreign policy, to represent the United States in its foreign relations, to negotiate international agreements, and to extend polit-

ical recognition to other states. Thomas Jefferson espoused a strict construc-
tionist interpretation of the Constitution but secretly ordered the navy to
fight the Barbary pirates. James Polk maneuvered the country into a war with
Mexico. Theodore Roosevelt sent the U.S. fleet around the world and dared
members of Congress to deny the navy the funds it needed to stay afloat.
Franklin Roosevelt concluded the famed destroyers-for-bases deal, even though
he doubted that he had the legal authority to do so.

Yet if presidents from Washington through Franklin Roosevelt acted in
ways that presidents in the second half of the twentieth century would use to
justify the expansion of the foreign policy powers of the presidency, the same
historical record provides ample evidence of a strong congressional role in the
making of foreign policy. Hamilton's expansive claims about executive power
notwithstanding, Washington ultimately conceded that neutrality was a
congressional prerogative. The "war hawks" in the House of Representatives
played an instrumental role in pushing a reluctant James Madison into the
War of 1812.[8] When James Monroe proposed what would later become
known as the Monroe Doctrine, many on Capitol Hill charged him with
overstepping his authority, and Congress refused to consider a resolution
endorsing the Doctrine.[9] The House of Representatives responded to the
Mexican-American War by adopting a resolution (later killed in conference)
declaring that the war had been "unnecessarily and unconstitutionally begun
by the President of the United States."[10]

Congress's role in foreign policy grew more marked after the Civil War, so
much so that the latter half of the nineteenth century has been called an era of
"congressional government," "congressional supremacy," "government-by-
Congress," and "senatorial domination."[11] Congress's say in foreign policy
making was exercised primarily through the Senate's treaty-making power.
Between 1871 and 1898 the Senate refused to approve every major treaty
submitted to it, with the votes often falling along party lines.[12] When the
United States emerged victorious from the Spanish-American War, the soon-
to-be secretary of state John Hay wrote that he "did not believe another
important treaty would ever pass the Senate" and that "the man who makes
the Treaty of Peace with Spain will be lucky if he escapes a lynching."[13]

President McKinley escaped a lynching, however, when he steered the
Treaty of Peace with Spain through the Senate, thereby breaking the long
string of treaty defeats. Yet even this victory, which came with only one vote
to spare, attested more to the strength of the Senate than to the strength of
the White House. Just as the war hawks had forced war on Madison in 1812,
Congress had pushed a reluctant McKinley into war with Spain. Moreover,
the Senate approved the treaty in large part because McKinley, adopting a

practice initiated by Madison and used sporadically in the intervening decades, named three senators to the commission that negotiated the treaty. As one senator observed at the time, "The treaty would have been lost, if Senator Gray, one of the Commissioners who made it, who earnestly protested against it, but afterwards supported it, had not been a member of the Commission."[14]

The ability of the Senate to use treaties to shape the direction of foreign policy reached its zenith during Woodrow Wilson's presidency. While a professor Wilson had criticized the Senate's prominence in foreign affairs. In 1885, he complained that the Senate's "irresponsible exercise of . . . semi-executive powers in regard to foreign policy" had transformed its treaty-making power into a "treaty-*marring* power."[15] Two decades later, he charged that the Senate had come to "desire to rule rather than be merely consulted" and had "shown itself particularly stiff and jealous in insisting upon exercising an independent judgment upon foreign affairs." He advised future presidents to be "less stiff and offish" and to establish "intimate relations of confidence with the Senate on his own initiative, [and] not carrying his plans to completion and then laying them in final form before the Senate to be accepted or rejected."[16]

Whatever the merits of the advice offered by Wilson the scholar, Wilson the president ignored it. He promulgated his Fourteen Points without consulting leading members of Congress, and he refused to include any senators in the U.S. delegation to the Paris peace talks. When the Treaty of Versailles was signed in 1919, it enjoyed considerable support on Capitol Hill, though not in the form it in which it was submitted. Wilson, however, refused to accept the modified language that would have secured the two-thirds majority needed for approval. As a result, the Senate rejected the treaty on three separate occasions, with well-known consequences for U.S. foreign policy.[17]

In the decade after the defeat of the Treaty of Versailles, conflict between the White House and Congress was muted. Members fought efforts by Calvin Coolidge and Herbert Hoover to cancel the wartime debts of European allies, and the Senate refused to consent to the Geneva Protocol of 1925, but on most foreign policy issues the two ends of Pennsylvania Avenue shared the same policy preferences. As tensions escalated in Europe in the early 1930s, however, congressional efforts to influence foreign policy took on new vigor. Disillusioned by the failure of World War I to accomplish the lofty aims Wilson set for it, many in Congress (and the country) had come to believe that he had been far too eager to plunge the United States into war and had far too much power to see his wishes through. Led by archisolationists such as Sen. William E. Borah (R-Idaho), a majority in Congress believed that the United States could be kept at peace only by keeping the president on a short leash in foreign affairs. [18]

Just how willing members of Congress were to seize the reins of foreign policy soon became clear. In January 1935, Franklin Roosevelt asked the Senate to approve a treaty under which the United States would join the World Court. The treaty itself was more than a decade old. Both Harding and Coolidge had urged the Senate to approve U.S. membership, but the treaty had foundered, first over isolationist opposition to the Court's connection to the League of Nations and then when other members of the Court objected to the limitations the Senate placed on U.S. membership. Still the treaty enjoyed considerable popularity. At the time Roosevelt revived it, both the Democratic and Republican party platforms had endorsed the treaty. Nonetheless, the Senate refused to go along, rejecting the proposal by seven votes.

The debate over the World Court was only a preliminary event. The main tool members used to limit the president's foreign policy flexibility was neutrality legislation. When Mussolini threatened war with any country that interfered with his plans to conquer Ethiopia, members of Congress, worried that Roosevelt might risk a war with Italy, hurried to pass the Neutrality Act of 1935. The law required the president to embargo arms sales and shipments to all belligerents whenever he found a state of war. In 1936, Congress added to the neutrality laws by forbidding all loans to belligerents. In 1937, Congress first banned the shipment of weapons to both sides in the Spanish civil war (the Neutrality Act of 1935 did not apply to civil wars) and then revised the neutrality legislation to require that all goods destined for belligerent countries be paid for before shipment.

Another effort in 1937 to limit the president's discretion (as well as that of Congress) was the Ludlow Amendment, which sought to amend the Constitution to require a nationwide referendum before the United States could go to war. The idea of a national referendum had enjoyed some popularity in the early 1920s; both the Democratic and Progressive parties endorsed the idea during the 1924 elections. Rep. Louis Ludlow (D-Ind.) revived the proposal in 1935, and by late 1937 public opinion polls showed that more than two-thirds of the country favored the so-called Peace Amendment. [19] Despite Franklin Roosevelt's vigorous opposition, the Ludlow Amendment came within twenty-two votes of passage in the House.

For all the energy members of Congress expended on rewriting the neutrality laws and debating the Ludlow Amendment, the march toward war continued. By mid-1939 the Roosevelt administration had concluded that a war in Europe was imminent, and it asked Congress to rewrite the neutrality laws. Many on Capitol Hill, however, dismissed the possibility of war. In

July, Senator Borah confidently predicted, "We are not going to have a war. Germany isn't ready for it. . . . I have my own sources of information."[20] When Germany and the Soviet Union signed their mutual nonaggression pact on 23 August 1939, Rep. Sol Bloom (D-N.Y.), chair of the Foreign Affairs Committee, told a State Department official that the crisis was not serious; Hitler had come to terms with the Soviets to ensure himself a place of refuge when he eventually lost control of Germany.[21] A week later the war in Europe began.

With the outbreak of war, the balance of power shifted away from isolationist forces on Capitol Hill.[22] Yet while Congress began to pass measures that gradually committed the United States to the Allied cause, the measures provoked intense debate and passed by small margins. In November 1939, Congress repealed the ban on selling arms to belligerents, despite vociferous objections by isolationists. When Roosevelt proposed the Lend-Lease Act in January 1941, Congress was consumed by two months of debate, "which for bitterness and passion has rarely been equalled in American history."[23] In August, the House approved by a single vote a measure extending the length of military service for men drafted under the year-old Selective Service Act. This slimmest of victories came only after Representative Bloom physically prevented one member from changing his vote on the bill from yes to no.[24] It would not be until the bombing of Pearl Harbor that the split within Congress over the direction of U.S. foreign policy would be closed.

CONGRESS AND THE
IMPERIAL PRESIDENCY

Alexis de Tocqueville speculated in the 1840s that Congress's relative strength in foreign policy was the result of the country's isolation from external threat. "If the Union's existence were constantly menaced, and if its great interests were continually interwoven with those of other powerful nations, one would see the prestige of the executive growing, because of what was expected from it and of what it did."[25] The rise of the imperial presidency in the wake of World War II proved Tocqueville right.[26] As Americans became increasingly convinced in the late 1940s that hostile communist states threatened the United States and the rest of the free world, the president's foreign policy powers grew while those of Congress faded.

Yet the demise of congressional influence over foreign policy was more gradual than is sometimes supposed. Congress did not cease to be significant with the close of World War II, nor did deference immediately replace confrontation in Congress's dealings with the White House. For the first decade after the end of the war, executive-legislative relations were marked by a mix of cooperation, deference, and hostility.[27]

The cooperation between Congress and the White House during the late 1940s had its roots in the war. When the Roosevelt administration decided in 1943 to use an executive agreement to commit the United States to the United Nations Relief and Rehabilitation Administration (UNRRA), members of Congress from both sides of the aisle rebelled. They objected both to specific provisions in the agreement and to the fact that the White House was making the first major policy decision for the postwar era without including Congress. Roosevelt eventually acceded to congressional demands. The UNRRA agreement was revised and the plan submitted to Congress for approval.[28]

The debate over UNRRA established a pattern of consultations between senior administration officials and senior members of Congress that carried over to many other foreign policy issues. Senior members of the House Foreign Affairs and Senate Foreign Relations committees served as delegates to several major international conferences, including those that drafted the United Nations Charter, the peace treaties for the Axis satellite states, and the Rio Treaty. The State Department also consulted extensively with the senior members of the Foreign Relations Committee during the drafting of the NATO treaty. "Indeed, many changes were incorporated in the draft treaty as a result of this informal consultation until the members of the Foreign Relations Committee were satisfied."[29]

Cooperation between the two branches on foreign policy almost always gave way to congressional deference during a crisis. Executive-legislative consultations were minimal during the crises over Azerbaijan in 1946 and Berlin in 1948. In June 1950, President Truman informed members of Congress after the fact of his decision to send U.S. troops to repel the invasion of South Korea. Whereas only fifteen years earlier a majority in Congress had fought tooth and nail to prevent Franklin Roosevelt from taking any step that might entangle the United States in war, few members disputed Truman's authority to order U.S. troops into combat. Indeed, when it was suggested to Truman that he might strengthen his political hand by asking Congress to pass a resolution endorsing his decision to defend South Korea, the Senate majority leader and several other senior members argued that such a resolution was unnecessary and might prompt a damaging and divisive debate.[30]

The cooperation and deference that marked executive-legislative relations on some aspects of foreign policy did not extend to U.S. policy toward the Far East.[31] Congress was split on the wisdom of Truman's policy toward China from the start. In 1948, Congress rewrote the administration's foreign aid package to China, adding money for military supplies but cutting funds for economic aid. When the Nationalist Chinese government collapsed the following year, U.S. foreign policy became enveloped in a rancorous debate over who "lost" China. The administration enjoyed a brief respite from criticism during the early months of the Korean War, but when the fighting began to go badly, both Truman and Secretary of State Dean Acheson became the targets of bitter attacks. Korea became "Truman's war," and House Republicans offered one resolution demanding Acheson's resignation and another cutting off his salary.[32]

At stake in the debate over who lost China was the wisdom of U.S. policy and not the question of the proper allocation of power between the executive and legislature. The question of constitutional authority, however, was at the heart of the so-called Great Debate of 1951.[33] The debate was triggered when Truman announced in late 1950 that he had decided to send four army divisions to Europe. The president's unilateral decision grated on many conservatives, who had come to rue the precedent set by Korea. In January 1953, Rep. Frederic R. Coudert, Jr. (R-N.Y.) introduced a sense-of-Congress resolution declaring that U.S. troops could not be sent abroad "without the prior authorization of the Congress in each instance."[34] Truman categorically rejected the Coudert Resolution; he insisted that as commander in chief he had the authority to send troops anywhere in the world.

The Great Debate promised to settle the question of which branch of government controlled the movement of troops. In the end, however, it produced only a sense-of-the-Senate resolution that, as Acheson described it, "had in it a present for everybody."[35] Proponents of the Coudert Resolution claimed victory because the Senate resolution stipulated that the president could send more troops to Europe only with the approval of Congress. Opponents, on the other hand, noted that sense-of-the-Senate resolutions are not legally binding on the president. Yet if the Great Debate of 1951 did not settle a fundamental constitutional issue, it did provide a historical irony: among the senators defending Congress's prerogatives on troop deployments was Richard Nixon (R-Calif.), who some twenty years later would reverse course and bitterly resist congressional efforts to limit the president's authority to send troops abroad.

The controversy over the president's authority to send troops abroad soon gave way to another constitutional dispute, this time over his authority to make binding international commitments through executive agreements. The dispute over executive agreements was rooted in a series of Supreme

Court rulings in the 1930s and 1940s that elevated executive agreements to the same constitutional status as treaties and in the extensive use Franklin Roosevelt made of executive agreements during World War II. From the perspective of Capitol Hill, executive agreements had a singular deficiency: they were as binding as treaties but did not require the approval of two-thirds of the Senate.

To protect the Senate's prerogatives, Sen. John Bricker (R-Ohio) introduced a proposal in 1953 to amend the treaty-making provisions of the Constitution.[36] Although the Bricker Amendment appeared in several different versions—at one time attracting as many as sixty-three sponsors—the general thrust of the legislation was to give Congress the power to annul executive agreements. After a year of intense debate both in committee and on the floor, the Bricker Amendment fell well short of the two-thirds majority needed for passage. However, a modified version known as the George Substitute (after Sen. Walter George, the senior Democrat on the Foreign Relations Committee), came within just one vote of passage in a Republican Senate, despite the fervent opposition of President Eisenhower.

The Bricker Amendment has been called "the last hurrah of conservative isolationism."[37] It might equally be called the last hurrah of congressional assertiveness. Following the defeat of the amendment, executive-legislative consultations on foreign policy became more and more infrequent, and it would be another fifteen years before members of Congress would again seriously challenge presidential authority in foreign policy. Less than half a decade after pillorying Truman for his handling of Korea, most members of Congress had come to see their role in foreign policy as legitimizing rather than criticizing presidential decisions. The diminished conception that most members had of Congress's role is evident in a speech Rep. William Colmer (D-Miss.) gave in 1957 on the floor of the House: "We cannot make foreign policy in the Congress of the United States; that would be impossible. You know where that would lead to. So we must rely on the Chief Executive and those who would advise him. In fact . . . it is the constitutional duty of the President to make our foreign policy."[38]

None of this is to say that Congress slavishly followed the lead of the White House on foreign policy in the years from the defeat of the Bricker Amendment until the Tet Offensive. Members could be counted on to quibble with the details of the annual foreign aid budget, and from time to time they demanded that more be spent on defense.[39] But much of the scant congressional activity on foreign policy addressed marginal issues. Even rarer still were attempts to challenge the president's authority in foreign affairs or

to demand a greater say for Congress. Deference had replaced both cooperation and confrontation as the chief characteristic of executive-legislative
relations.

The deference members extended to the president inevitably diminished
their ability to influence foreign policy.[40] Nowhere was the decline of congressional influence more visible than in the case of the war power. Although
Truman's unilateral decision to defend Korea had eroded Congress's constitutional authority to declare war, the precedent was not necessarily permanent.
Dwight Eisenhower accorded greater respect to Congress's powers than did
his predecessor, and he refused to use force abroad without explicit congressional sanction. When the People's Republic of China threatened in 1955 to
attack the Pescadores and Formosa (Taiwan), Eisenhower immediately asked
Congress to authorize him to use U.S. troops to defend Formosa. Thus, the
debate over the Formosa Resolution presented members with an opportunity
to reverse the precedent set by Truman in Korea and to reassert the constitutional powers of Congress.

Yet rather than restoring Congress's war powers, the debate over the
Formosa Resolution enhanced the powers of the president. The resolution
passed with only three dissenting votes in each house. Many senior members
openly doubted the need for congressional authorization. Speaker of the
House Sam Rayburn (D-Tex.) went so far as to say that "if the President had
done what is proposed here without consulting Congress he would have had
no criticism from me." Moreover, the authority delegated to the president
was unprecedented in its scope. Unlike its predecessors, "the Formosa Resolution ordered no action and named no enemy, except as the President might
thereafter decide. Rather it committed Congress to the approval of hostilities
without knowledge of the specific situation in which the hostilities would
begin."[41]

In 1957, Eisenhower returned to Congress to request authority to use
U.S. troops as he saw fit to counter potential communist threats in the
Middle East. This time the Senate struck from the administration's draft
resolution language explicitly authorizing the use of force, a revision that
technically reduced the Joint Resolution to Promote Peace and Stability in
the Middle East to a simple declaration of policy. But senators made the
change not because they wished to reclaim lost congressional powers but
because they feared that the country might be harmed if presidents came to
believe they could use force only if they first obtained the approval of Congress.[42] Nor were members of Congress eager to hold Eisenhower to the
terms of the revised resolution. When he sent fourteen thousand troops to
Lebanon some sixteen months later, he based the decision on his powers as

commander in chief and not on the Middle East resolution. Despite the institutional slight, few members complained that Eisenhower had exceeded his authority.

The decline of Congress's war powers accelerated once the Democrats returned to the Oval Office. John Kennedy did not share his predecessor's belief that the White House needed to have Congress legitimate its decisions to use force abroad. He included only one member of Congress in the discussions that led up to the Bay of Pigs operation. When Kennedy imposed a naval quarantine on Cuba during the missile crisis, he did so on his own authority as commander in chief and without congressional approval or consultation.[43] Likewise, Congress played no role in his decisions to increase the number of military advisers in South Vietnam from eight hundred at the time of his inauguration to more than fifteen thousand at the time of his death.[44] For the most part, members of Congress shared Kennedy's expansive view of presidential authority. When the Bay of Pigs operation failed, for example, only one member complained publicly that the president had exceeded his authority.[45]

Kennedy's decision to increase U.S. troop presence in South Vietnam set the stage for what in retrospect was the nadir of congressional influence over foreign policy, the passage of the Gulf of Tonkin Resolution. Unlike either the Formosa or the Middle East resolution, debate on the Gulf of Tonkin Resolution was minimal. The House voted unanimously to support Lyndon Johnson after only forty minutes of discussion. Debate in the Senate lasted ten hours, and the resolution passed with only two dissenting votes.[46]

The speed with which members of Congress passed the Gulf of Tonkin Resolution raises doubts about the oft-supposed virtues of congressional efficiency. But what is most remarkable about the resolution is its assumption that the war power rested with the White House. Whereas the Formosa Resolution explicitly authorized the president to use force to defend U.S. interests, the Gulf of Tonkin Resolution simply stated that "the Congress approves and supports the determination of the president, as Commander in Chief, to take all necessary measures to repel any armed attack against the forces of the United States and to prevent further aggression."[47] As Jean Smith argues, "The change in wording reflected more than presidential predilections; it involved a fundamental shift in the role of Congress from one of ultimate authority to one of subordinate support."[48]

By the mid-1960s, then, members of Congress had ceded much of their authority over foreign policy to the president. Unlike the first postwar decade, few members were willing to protect Congress's prerogatives or to demand that the president consult with Congress. Members for the most part were content merely to legitimate decisions made by the White House. As Sen. Gaylord Nelson (D-Wis.) complained in 1965, members generally responded to even the most far-reaching presidential decisions on foreign affairs by "stumbling over each other to see who can say 'yea' the quickest and the loudest."[49]

CONGRESS RESURGENT

The era of congressional deference came to a crashing halt with the souring of opinion on the Vietnam War. In the 1970s, Congress passed legislation such as the War Powers Resolution and the Hughes-Ryan Amendment that sought to curtail the imperial presidency. In the 1980s, Congress and the White House fought bitterly over the MX missile, the nuclear freeze, and aid to the Nicaraguan contras, among other issues. Congressional activism could even be seen in instances in which Congress approved administration requests. Congressional support for such programs as arming the Afghan rebels and building cruise missiles reflected genuine cooperation with the executive branch rather than the acquiescence typical of the late 1950s and early 1960s.

The resurgence of congressional activism has correctly been attributed to the Vietnam War. Members of Congress deferred to the executive branch in the 1950s and 1960s in large part because of a widespread consensus that the United States and its allies faced a grave threat from hostile, expansionist communist states and that U.S. interests would be best served if the president had maximum discretion in foreign affairs. As the prospects for victory in Vietnam became dimmer and dimmer, however, and as it became increasingly clear that successive administrations had misled Congress and the American public on key points about U.S. involvement in Southeast Asia, the consensus broke down on both points. Suddenly there was disagreement over both the threats facing the United States and how best to meet them. With the ends and means of foreign policy once again legitimate topics for debate, a resurgence of congressional activism was inevitable.

In shattering the consensus on the threats facing the United States and how best to deal with them, Vietnam also changed the electoral calculus on Capitol Hill. During the 1950s and 1960s, members who opposed a presidential decision in foreign affairs frequently swallowed their objections because they calculated that challenging the White House entailed daunting political costs, especially if they wanted the president to pursue a less belligerent policy. The deference given to the president became self-perpetuating; potential critics declined to challenge the president because they believed that few of their colleagues would follow their lead. As Sen. J. William Fulbright (D-Ark.), the longtime chair of the Foreign Relations Committee, explained his reluctance to challenge the Defense Department: "I have been under the feeling that it was utterly useless and futile, that nothing could be done . . . no matter what I did."[50]

By shattering the public as well as the elite consensus on the means and ends of foreign policy, Vietnam made it far less costly for members to challenge the president. The boundaries of acceptable political debate were widened, and members—especially those on the liberal end of the spectrum—could advocate policies that in the 1950s and 1960s would have meant sure electoral death. Indeed, for members hailing from very dovish or very hawkish constituencies, challenging the president on foreign policy became an electoral plus. With less to fear from constituents, and in many cases with the prospect of something to gain, members took a greater interest in foreign policy.

As important as Vietnam is in explaining the end of congressional deference, it falls short of a complete explanation. Three other factors, some an indirect consequence of Vietnam, also contributed to the resurgence in congressional activism: a persistent gap in executive-legislative preferences, the demise of the "textbook" Congress, and the growth of interest group activity on foreign policy.

The Persistent Gap in Executive-Legislative Preferences

In the first two decades after the end of World War II, divided government was the exception rather than the rule in American politics. From 1945 to 1968, the same party controlled both houses of Congress and the presidency for sixteen out of twenty-four years. Moreover, because divisions on foreign policy cut across rather than along party lines, there was substantial agreement between the president and a majority in Congress even when partisan control was divided.[51] Dwight Eisenhower discovered, for example, that while the Democrats controlled Congress during his last six years in office, his harshest foreign policy critics were members of his own party. Indeed, Eisenhower grew so exasperated with the staunch support his fellow Republicans gave to the Bricker Amendment that "he indulged in private musings about forming a third, moderate party dedicated to implementing his legislative program."[52]

In the wake of the Vietnam War, split-ticket voting gained ascendancy in American politics. In 1969, Richard Nixon became the first president in 120 years to face a Congress in which both houses were controlled by the opposition party. From 1969 to 1992, the same party controlled both Congress and the White House for only four out of twenty-four years. Moreover, demographic shifts and the legacy of Vietnam combined to make each political party more homogeneous on foreign policy, with the result that ideological differences on foreign policy began to fall along partisan lines.[53] The disparity between congressional and executive preferences reached its zenith during the Reagan years. On issues as varied as the Strategic Defense Initiative, U.S. relations with Central America, and the utility of international organizations, the Reagan administration rejected not only the foreign policy preferences of most Democrats but the preferences of the foreign policy establishment as well.

The extent to which the gap in executive-legislative preferences determines the level and intensity of congressional activism can be seen in the evolution of U.S. policy toward Nicaragua during the 1980s.[54] Throughout the Reagan years, proposals to send military aid to the contras were bitterly contested, with administration officials impugning the patriotism of their critics and the critics in turn questioning the morality of the administration. George Bush, however, lacked a deep commitment to the contras. Within two months of coming to office, he signed a Bipartisan Accord on Central America with the congressional leadership that barred military aid but permitted humanitarian aid to the contras. By moving closer to the views of the majority on Capitol Hill, the compromise effectively removed Nicaragua as an issue in American politics.

Demise of the Textbook Congress

A second factor that facilitated congressional activism on foreign policy was the collapse of what has been called the textbook Congress. Throughout the first two decades after World War II, congressional decision making on foreign policy was an inside game, a closed system where major decisions were made by a relatively small number of senior members, and especially the chairs of the various committees concerned with foreign policy and defense.[55] These senior members generally could be expected to speak on behalf of Congress. During the days leading up to the Bay of Pigs Operation, for instance, the Kennedy administration felt it had adequately consulted with Congress because it had solicited the views of Senator Fulbright.[56] Likewise, when a constitutional showdown loomed in 1962 over congressional efforts to force the Kennedy administration to build the B-70 bomber, the matter was resolved (in the administration's favor) in one afternoon when President Kennedy and Rep. Carl Vinson (D-Ga.), the chair of the House Armed

Services Committee, met for a private chat and walk in the Rose Garden.[57]

The immense power of the committee chairs was due to their near-total control over committee business. By virtue of congressional rules, the chairs had the power to create subcommittees, set committee agendas, choose committee staff, and manage bills on the floor. Because committee chairs had so many ways to penalize anyone who refused to follow their lead, they received great deference from other members. For example, in the 1940s a junior member dared to ask Representative Vinson in the middle of a public hearing when he would get to ask a question. Vinson tartly replied, "You just have. Sit down." And Lyndon Johnson sat down.[58] The floor showed much the same deference to the committees. Attempts to overturn committee decisions seldom occurred, and when they did they garnered little support.

The ability of a small group of senior members to set the tone of congressional debate mattered because these men—and they were all men—believed that success in foreign policy required strong presidential leadership. If anything, Fulbright, Vinson, and others worried that Congress had too much say in foreign policy. Fulbright wrote in 1961: "It is my contention that for the existing requirements of American foreign policy we have hobbled the President by too niggardly a grant of power. . . . the price of democratic survival in a world of aggressive totalitarianism is to give up some of the democratic luxuries of the past."[59] Motivated by their belief that only a strong president would enable the United States to stem the communist threat, senior members used their powers to squelch challenges to presidential authority.

The ability of senior members to speak for Congress began to fade at the beginning of the 1970s. Prodded by Vietnam, Watergate, and the election of new, more individualistic members, both the House and the Senate adopted internal reforms that reduced the power of committee chairs. New subcommittees were created and given permanent jurisdictions and staff. Junior members won the right to prize committee slots as well as to a larger personal staff. With power more equitably distributed within Congress, members found it less costly to influence committee decisions from within and far easier to challenge them from without.

The rules changes that the House and Senate adopted in the 1970s meant the end of the textbook Congress as the inside game gave way to an outside game.[60] Although the defense and foreign policy committees remain the most important congressional actors on foreign policy, considerable congressional activity bypasses the traditional channels of influence within the committees. As has already been mentioned, floor debate on defense and foreign policy has grown enormously since the 1970s. Often the challenges are led by junior members with no committee assignment in foreign affairs. For example, the effort to punish China for the Tiananmen Square massacre was led in the House by Rep. Nancy Pelosi (D-Calif.), a two-term member who sat on the commerce and ethics committees.

The Rise of Foreign Policy Interest Groups

Interest groups have always been part of American politics. Foreign policy is no exception. Whether it was the Women's International League for Peace and Freedom lobbying to keep the United States out of World War I, or America First trying to keep the United States out of World War II, or the Committee of One Million pressing in the 1950s and 1960s to keep the United States committed to the defense of Nationalist China, organized groups have long sought to influence congressional attitudes on foreign policy.

Yet while foreign policy lobbies are not new, they have grown tremendously in number and in scope.[61] The rapid increase in interest group activity on foreign policy is due to several factors. As global interdependence has grown, more and more government decisions in foreign affairs have come to affect domestic interests. The civil rights and antiwar protests of the 1960s demonstrated the power of interest group politics and provided examples for new groups to emulate. Improvements in computer and communications technology made it far easier for groups to mobilize supporters with mailings and phone calls. The intense politicization of foreign policy during the Reagan years pushed people to organize on behalf of their favored causes. And the growth of interest groups proved to be self-reinforcing. As some groups succeeded in influencing policy, their very success prompted other groups, especially opposition groups, to form.

The interest groups most visible on foreign policy are those dedicated to advancing economic and ethnic interests. With the growing integration of the United States into the global economy, both American business and organized labor have moved aggressively to shape policy in their favor. At the same time, the widely perceived success of the so-called Jewish and Greek lobbies has encouraged other ethnic groups to follow suit. Today nearly every major ethnic group in the United States has a sizable organization representing it in Washington.[62]

There also has been tremendous growth in the number of advocacy groups that champion values rather than economic or ethnic interests. Many advocacy groups formed in the wake of the Reagan defense buildup to demand (or criticize, as the case may be) arms control and lower defense spending. Other groups arose to address issues such as global environmental degradation, human rights, and immigration. In addition to the appearance of new organizations, groups that traditionally focused on domestic issues have increasingly joined the fray on defense and foreign policy. The debate over the MX missile, for example, involved not just traditional arms control groups, such as the Council for a Liveable World and the Union of Concerned Scientists, but also groups such as the American Baptist Churches, Americans for Democratic Action, Common Cause, and the United Church of Christ.[63]

Another source of interest group activity is foreign governments. Before the mid-1970s, most foreign governments conducted their business through the State Department rather than Congress.[64] As legislators became more active on foreign policy, however, foreign governments took a sudden interest in attitudes on Capitol Hill. Much of a foreign government's lobbying is handled by its embassy, but foreign governments also have taken to hiring lobbyists and public relations firms to advance their interests. After Iraq invaded Kuwait, for instance, the Kuwaiti government secretly bankrolled the creation of a group known as Citizens for a Free Kuwait. This group in turn hired Hill and Knowlton, one of the country's largest public relations firms, to help persuade Congress that the United States should use force to liberate Kuwait.[65] In 1992 the governments of Croatia and Bosnia hired the public relations firm of Rudder-Finn Inc. to help build congressional support for their wars with Serbia.[66]

The growth of interest group activity on foreign policy has altered the political map in Congress. With more groups active on more foreign policy issues, members find themselves under greater pressure to address foreign policy. At the same time, the rise of interest group activity means that suddenly members stand a good chance of benefiting politically by undertaking detailed legislative work on foreign policy. It is perhaps not surprising that congressional activism has surged as a result.

THE RESURGENT CONGRESS
IN HISTORICAL PERSPECTIVE

The Vietnam War, the persistent gap in executive-legislative preferences, the demise of the textbook Congress, and increased interest group activity all have combined to push executive-legislative relations on foreign policy back toward historical norms. But congressional activism today differs in three ways from that typical during the one hundred fifty years before World War II.

One difference is the sheer breadth of congressional activity. Before World

War II, conflict between Capitol Hill and the White House was at times titanic, yet the range of issues precipitating executive-legislative conflict tended to be small. For the most part the United States had a relatively low profile overseas, and domestic policy issues far exceeded foreign policy issues in both number and political importance. With few foreign policy programs to oversee, members had fewer opportunities to delve into foreign affairs. And while members of Congress might have had opinions about pogroms in Russia or dictators in Latin America, America's low profile overseas meant they seldom had the opportunity or the means with which to influence events abroad.

All that changed when the United States assumed the mantle of a superpower after the end of World War II. Once the United States acquired a global array of military bases and foreign policy commitments, members of Congress suddenly had both many more programs to oversee and new tools (however crude they might be at times) with which to influence foreign affairs. The result is that members of Congress now regularly weigh in on everything from arms control agreements with Russia to famine in East Africa to human rights abuses in Asia. The tremendous breadth of congressional activity in turn has meant tremendous growth in legislation on foreign policy: as the Introduction noted, the number of pages of foreign policy legislation grew more than tenfold between 1960 and 1990.

The second difference in congressional activism is that the treaty power has given way to the appropriations power as Congress's primary tool for shaping foreign policy. The Senate is less able today than in the nineteenth century to influence foreign policy by granting or withholding its advice and consent. Although presidents continue to negotiate treaties, most international agreements are now handled as executive agreements: between 1980 and 1990 the executive branch concluded 3,851 executive agreements but only 170 treaties.[67] Because executive agreements often do not require congressional approval, their use diminishes the say Congress has over which international commitments the United States will make.

In place of the treaty power, Congress has come to rely on its power of the purse. The switch to the policy of global containment led to a tremendous expansion in the number and size of defense and foreign policy programs, each of which must be approved by Congress. In the 1950s and 1960s, the appropriations power lay largely unused because members of Congress agreed with the White House on many policy matters and were often willing to defer to the executive branch when they disagreed. But when the foreign policy consensus collapsed after Vietnam, members of Congress used appropriations decisions to make their preferences felt. As Chapter 8 discusses at greater length, Congress has become so involved in budgetary details that critics now complain that members are guilty of trying to micromanage foreign policy.

The diminished importance of the treaty power and the increased importance of the appropriations power has in turn produced the third major change in congressional activism, namely, the more prominent role of the House of Representatives. So long as treaties were the main tool by which administrations made foreign policy, representatives operated on the margins of policy making. With no large foreign policy establishment to oversee, the House found its foreign policy agenda occupied mostly by trivia and marginalia. In the 1920s, for instance, the House Foreign Affairs Committee devoted one week to debating "the question of authorizing a $20,000 appropriation for an international poultry show in Tulsa. This item, which . . . [was] finally approved, was about the most important issue that came before the Committee in the whole session."[68] In 1929 the Foreign Affairs Committee devoted considerable time and effort to debating whether the United States should switch to a proposed thirteen-month calendar.[69]

The creation of a large defense and foreign policy establishment has created many more opportunities for representatives to weigh in on foreign policy. The potential influence of the House lay unrealized for much of the 1950s and 1960s because most representatives preferred to defer to the president's judgment. Since that deference ended, however, the House has come to rival the Senate in congressional decision making on foreign policy. Indeed, when the Republicans controlled both the White House and the Senate during the first half of the 1980s, the efforts to rewrite the Reagan administration's defense and foreign policies were led by representatives and not by senators.

CONCLUSION

For much of the past two hundred years, Congress and the president have struggled over the direction of foreign policy. Both branches bring strong constitutional claims and strong policy preferences to foreign policy making. On some occasions their struggles have led to cooperation, while on others they have yielded only conflict. For a brief period of time from the mid-1950s to the mid-1960s, members of Congress largely removed themselves from foreign affairs in the belief that the national interest would be best served if the president had free reign. When that deference culminated in a bitter and divisive war, executive-legislative affairs returned to their historical norm.

What of the future? Congressional activism shows every sign of persisting, if only because the factors that prompted and facilitated the resurgence of congressional activism after Vietnam continue to operate. The demise of the Soviet Union further lowered the perception of external threat and with it the political costs to members of Congress who choose to challenge the president. So long as no state replaces the Soviet Union as a threat to U.S. interests, the public will tolerate extensive legislative dissent on foreign affairs. At the same time, interest group activity on foreign policy remains substantial, and political power on Capitol Hill continues to be widely dispersed. As a result, members of Congress have no incentive to squelch debate on foreign policy and no means of doing so if they did.

The nature of executive-legislative relations in foreign policy will change, of course, if the preferences of the two branches of government become more similar. Should the 1992 elections prove to have marked a return to unified government rather than having been an aberration, cooperation between Congress and the White House will increase. After all, members of Congress have much less reason to challenge a president from their own party who is carrying out policies with which they agree. Yet congressional cooperation should not be mistaken for acquiescence. Where the president departs from policies acceptable to a sizable portion of Congress, as Bill Clinton discovered in the fall of 1993 with Haiti, Somalia, and the North American Free-Trade Agreement (NAFTA), disputes between the two branches will be inevitable.

2   LEGISLATIVE MOTIVATION
AND FOREIGN POLICY

IN THE FALL OF 1977, Jimmy Carter asked the Senate to approve the Panama Canal treaties. For Sen. Edward Zorinsky (D-Neb.) the request created a political headache. While he was personally inclined to vote for the treaties, polls showed that most Nebraskans opposed returning the canal to Panama. Caught between his own policy preferences and those of the voters, Zorinsky announced he would poll Nebraskans and vote whichever way the majority preferred. To help build support back home for the treaties, he arranged for the president to brief influential Nebraskans on why returning the canal to Panama served U.S. security interests. But when polls continued to show that most Nebraskans favored keeping the canal, Zorinsky voted no.[1]

Senator Zorinsky's behavior supports the widely held belief that the foreign policy views of members of Congress extend no further than the next election. When voter interest is low, which is true on most foreign policy issues, members are presumed to have no incentive to address substantive matters. When voter interest is high, as was the case with the Panama Canal, constituent passion almost always outruns constituent knowledge, thereby forcing members such as Senator Zorinsky to sacrifice their judgments about wise policy to the whims of the voters. The normative conclusion that follows is straightforward: Congress is too tied to constituency opinion to be counted on to provide sustained and reasoned attention to foreign policy.

The intuitive appeal of the electoral explanation is undeniable. Members of Congress listen to voters. But the electoral explanation falters on two accounts. First, it exaggerates the electoral incentives that discourage members from addressing substantive issues while it ignores their nonelectoral incentives to undertake detailed legislative work. Second, the electoral explanation miscasts the nature of the relationship between voters and members. When listening to constituents, members are far less interested in learning which positions to adopt than they are in learning which positions to avoid.

Rather than slavishly following constituent opinion, members of Congress try to accomplish their personal, policy, and political goals subject to a constraint laid down by constituent opinion. So long as members prefer (for whatever reason) policies acceptable to their constituents, they are free to act as they please. They encounter trouble only when their policy preferences conflict with constituency preferences. Here members must calculate the benefits to be had in pursuing their own agenda against the costs of alienating their constituents. But because most voters do not care about foreign policy most of the time, such conflicts are infrequent and members have considerable freedom to chart their own course on foreign policy.

To suggest that members of Congress try to enact their policy visions subject to a constituency constraint is not to say that Congress makes decisions in the dispassionate, rational fashion of the textbook bureaucracy or that policy considerations always dominate congressional debate. Because all members need to win reelection, congressional decision making is inherently political. At times, constituent opinion so narrows the range of politically acceptable positions that members do act as if they are single-minded seekers of reelection. Likewise, members continually look for political gain in their legislative endeavors, and they ardently try to avoid blame. But as irksome as these behaviors may be, they should not obscure the considerable incentives members of Congress have to attend to the substance of foreign policy.

A SIMPLE ELECTORAL EXPLANATION

Most explanations of congressional behavior on foreign policy point to constituency opinion. Media accounts of foreign policy debates invariably emphasize the electoral motives members have to vote as they do.[2] News accounts on the eve of the vote to authorize the Gulf War, for example, portrayed members of Congress calculating the likely political consequences of their votes.[3] Even when foreign policy issues elicit considerably less public interest, the news media focus on the electoral connection. Stories of the Senate's failure in 1992 to muster enough votes to override a threatened presidential veto of legislation ending China's most-favored-nation trade status, for instance, highlighted the support President Bush received from farm state Democrats. These senators feared China would retaliate by buying fewer American farm products.[4]

Electoral explanations are equally popular with political scientists. In his 1974 book, *Congress: The Electoral Connection,* David Mayhew presented a theory of congressional decision making based on the simple assumption that members of Congress are single-minded seekers of reelection.[5] Although he recognized that any complete theory of Congress would have to recognize that members had goals besides reelection, Mayhew argued that the electoral assumption alone was sufficient to explain the great bulk of congressional behavior. His argument proved persuasive. Since the publication of *Congress: The Electoral Connection,* political scientists have turned out a slew of books and articles based on the assumption that reelection drives congressional decision making.

What does a theory based on the assumption that members of Congress are single-minded seekers of reelection, or for the sake of convenience what I will call the simple electoral explanation, predict about congressional behavior on foreign policy? The question lacks an easy answer because most research on Congress examines how the institution handles domestic policy. Relatively few studies of congressional decision making on foreign policy have been published, and the ones that do exist do not develop explicit theories of congressional behavior. Nonetheless, the basic logic of the simple electoral explanation generates three expectations about congressional behavior on foreign policy:

1. *Extensive deference to the administration on the substance of foreign policy.* Electoral explanations hold that members of Congress pay attention to issues that matter to voters. But survey research corroborates what the newspaper publisher Horace Greeley knew over a century ago: "The subject of deepest interest to an average [American] is himself. Next to that he is most concerned with his neighbors. Asia and the Tongo Islands stand a long way after these in his regard."[6] Because voter interest in and knowledge about foreign policy is low, it presents members with few opportunities to gain an electoral payoff through detailed legislative work.

The flip side of the coin is that challenging the administration on foreign policy poses significant electoral risks to members of Congress. Future electoral opponents may use the challenge as evidence that a member is unpatriotic. As one anonymous House Democrat explained Congress's initial reluctance to force President Bush to seek congressional authorization for the Gulf War: "The time is not right yet to oppose the President, and there's nothing more politically suicidal than opposing a war too early."[7] At the same time, members may fear that the administration will punish its critics. The Defense Department, for instance, is frequently accused of manipulating defense spending to punish members it considers unfriendly. In light of the slim potential for electoral profit, the potential for significant electoral loss discourages members from detailed legislative work on foreign policy.

The simple electoral explanation recognizes, of course, that members of Congress will undertake some work on foreign policy. The defense and foreign policy committees, after all, are charged with shepherding various money bills through Congress. But even within the committees, work will be biased toward fiscal and management oversight rather than policy oversight. Fiscal oversight is necessary to bring the president's budget into accord with what Congress is willing to spend; if no bill passes, constituents will be harmed. Management oversight is politically attractive because voters applaud efforts to ferret out government waste, fraud, and abuse. Relatively little policy oversight occurs, however, because few constituents demand it.[8]

2. *A Penchant for Position Taking and Grandstanding.* Although the electoral incentive discourages attention to the substance of policy, members of Congress do have incentives to speak out on foreign policy. As Mayhew argues, position taking—publicly enunciating and reaffirming values and positions held by constituents—is a valuable electoral tool.[9] The positions that members stake out vary with the attitudes of their constituents. For members from hawkish constituencies, the electoral payoff comes from acting as superpatriots who support high levels of defense spending and an interventionist foreign policy. For members from dovish constituencies, the electoral payoff comes from acting as superdoves who support lower defense spending and a noninterventionist foreign policy.

Most position taking consists simply of affirming values that constituents hold dear. A hawkish representative from Texas tells voters at a town meeting that the United States needs to remain strong, while a dovish senator from Iowa tells marchers at a local peace rally that America needs to turn its swords into plowshares. But some position taking efforts, what critics often term "grandstanding," involve members actively trying to attract media coverage of their public statements and behavior. Members often ask pointed questions at committee hearings and give impassioned speeches on the floor with an eye toward the evening news. Sometimes members try to draw attention to themselves by leaking information on an issue of public interest. And occasionally members participate in obvious publicity stunts, as when five representatives took a sledgehammer to a Toshiba radio on the grounds of the Capitol to protest the Japanese company's violation of the strategic embargo on the Soviet Union.[10] With grandstanding, then, position taking becomes a tool for advertising the member to voters.[11]

Position taking, and grandstanding in particular, may affect the substance of foreign policy. A well-timed leak or theatrical questioning at a congressional hearing may embarrass the administration or derail diplomatic negotiations. But while changes in policy may result from position taking, that is not its purpose. The payoff for the position-taking member of Congress lies in affirming values and positions important to constituents and not in translating those preferences into policy outcomes. Because the payoff lies in speaking rather than doing, member interest fades once an issue ceases to attract headlines.

3. *Attention to Parochial Matters.* The one instance in which the simple electoral explanation predicts sustained congressional interest in foreign policy occurs when an issue involves sizable constituency interests. Again, voters care about foreign policy to the extent that what happens overseas affects them directly. Textile workers in South Carolina follow the twists and turns in trade policy, and aerospace workers in southern California worry about the future of defense spending. Voter interest in such issues gives members of Congress good reason to be interested as well.

Whether the parochial imperative leads members of Congress to challenge or support the administration depends on which policies emerge from the White House. If administration policy works to the advantage of constituents, as was true for the defense industry during the Reagan years, the parochial imperative drives members to support the administration. But where administration policy deviates from constituency interest, as happened with the textile industry during the Reagan years, members who represent affected constituencies can be counted on to oppose the administration.

Of course, when government policy affects parochial interests, members of Congress may have no say over policy outcomes. In defense policy, for example, "the prime contract award process is structured to preclude routine political meddling by members who want to channel contracts to their constituents."[12] But even when members are constrained in their ability to advance parochial interests, they still seek to cultivate the impression that they can shape policy to benefit constituents. As Mayhew argues, credit claiming is a valuable electoral tool.[13] Members stand to reap electoral gain whenever they can convince voters they are fighting for the economic interests of the constituency. Such claims become convincing because most voters lack detailed knowledge of how government decisions are made.

The simple electoral explanation, then, paints a pessimistic portrait of the role Congress plays in foreign policy making. To keep their seats in Congress, members generally avoid foreign policy. When they do turn to foreign policy, they take positions designed to win favor with voters or attend to narrow parochial concerns. Lost in the pursuit of electoral gain is detailed attention to the substance of foreign policy. The normative conclusion that follows is clear: An institution whose members put their self-interest before the national interest should not be making policy.

PROBLEMS WITH THE SIMPLE
ELECTORAL EXPLANATION

The popularity of the electoral explanation in political science is due partly to the fact that it produces parsimonious and testable models. But on a deeper level the popularity of the electoral explanation lies in its intuitive appeal: it fits our inherent understanding of how Congress works. In modern Washington, a congressional seat is a career, and to remain in office members must maintain the support of the voters. Moreover, as Senator Zorinsky's decision rule for the Panama Canal treaties attests, members of Congress give ample evidence that they act as weather vanes for constituent opinion.

But are members of Congress little more than single-minded seekers of reelection? Given the intuitive appeal of the simple electoral explanation, one would expect that the available evidence would weigh heavily in its favor. On closer inspection, though, it leaves many of Congress's actions on foreign policy unexplained.

To start with, the simple electoral explanation fails to account for the tremendous growth in congressional activism in the 1970s and 1980s. As Chapter 1 discussed, a partial explanation for the rise in congressional activism lies in increased public interest in foreign policy at the start of both decades. In the early 1970s, Vietnam shook the national consciousness and challenged basic conceptions of the proper allocation of authority between the executive and legislative branches of government. In the early 1980s, U.S.-Soviet relations and the threat of a nuclear war emerged in public opinion polls as the most important problem facing the country.[14] But a surge in public opposition to the Vietnam War and growing concerns about nuclear war fail to explain why congressional activism strayed far beyond the topics of U.S.-Vietnamese and U.S.-Soviet relations or why congressional activism persisted in the late 1970s and again in the late 1980s even as the public's interest in foreign affairs plummeted.

The simple electoral explanation also fails to explain why congressional activism on foreign policy often diverges from public sentiment. "Congress could have ended American participation in the Southeast Asia war at any time . . . simply by refusing to appropriate money to fight it. However, in the House this was never done, even during the dying days of the war when public sentiment against it was overwhelming."[15] The Senate approved the Panama Canal treaties by the required two-thirds majority even though polls showed that as much as 60 percent of the public wanted to retain U.S. ownership of the canal.[16] In 1983, Congress passed by comfortable margins legislation authorizing U.S. Marines to remain in Lebanon, even though Americans were divided over their presence in Beirut and though a majority opposed any increased involvement.[17] And Congress gave varying amounts of aid to the contras despite the fact that public opinion surveys consistently showed that opponents of the Reagan administration's policy toward Nicaragua outnumbered supporters by roughly two to one.[18]

The simple electoral explanation fares no better when it comes to the scholarly research on Congress and foreign policy. In studying congressional decision making on foreign policy, political scientists have pursued three broad lines of inquiry. The first seeks to compare member behavior with constituent opinion. A 1963 study by Warren Miller and Donald Stokes found a moderate correlation between members' perceptions of constituency opinion and their roll-call votes on foreign policy.[19] More recent studies reported similar results. L. Marvin Overby found that the results of state referendums on the nuclear freeze helped to predict subsequent voting in the House on the freeze.[20] Larry Bartels analyzed voting in the House during the first year of the Reagan defense buildup and found a strong relationship between constituency demand for increased defense spending and how members voted.[21]

Although the studies by Miller and Stokes, Overby, and Bartels all found a link between constituency opinion and congressional behavior, they should not be taken as proof of the simple electoral explanation. To begin with, all three studies concluded that other factors, especially ideology, also influenced member behavior. At the same time, a finding that constituency opinion correlates with member behavior does not establish that members of Congress voted as they did *because* of constituent opinion. One problem is that members are exposed to the same objective events that their constituents are, raising the possibility that members and constituents are simply responding in similar fashion to the world around them. Indeed, such a possibility is likely since the entire recruitment process for members means that they will share many of the same assumptions, values, and policy attitudes as their constituents.[22]

The studies by Miller and Stokes, Overby, and Bartels are valuable because they examine constituent opinion in individual states and congressional districts. Such data are rare, however, which has forced researchers interested in the determinants of roll-call voting to use proxies for constituent opinion.

In following this second line of inquiry, some researchers have used the region of the country members of Congress come from or the president's share of the vote in the last election to capture the effects of constituent opinion.[23] An even more common proxy has been a constituency's economic interest in defense and foreign policy programs.[24] Whichever proxies have been used, the studies have produced at best weak support for the simple electoral explanation. For example, despite the popular belief that members of Congress are pork barrelers, many studies have found that parochialism often fails to drive voting. Rather than parochialism or any other proxy for constituent opinion, study after study has found that ideology and party affiliation provide better predictors of voting behavior.

In addition to studies that use direct or indirect measures of constituent opinion, a third line of inquiry has used interviews with members of Congress and their staff to analyze the link between voters and members. Using data derived from interviews with staffers and representatives during the 98th Congress (1983–84), Eileen Burgin analyzed the decisions that seventy representatives made about their participation in congressional debates on foreign policy.[25] She found that when it came to deciding whether to participate (beyond the mere act of voting), representatives were more likely to join a legislative debate over issues important to their supporters and less likely to join in on issues they believed their supporters did not care about. With respect to the question of how actively to participate, however, she found that members' perceptions of constituent opinion mattered far less than did their personal policy interests, committee and leadership assignments, and desire for influence. In a subsequent article, Burgin used interview data to examine the influences on how members voted in January 1991 on the question of whether to use force against Iraq. She found that while the views of supporters mattered, members' own policy views were the most significant influence in determining how they voted.[26]

In reviewing the efforts to assess the links between constituent opinion and member behavior, it should be said that the research is open to criticism. Some studies commit statistical errors; the proxies for constituent opinion and interest are often crude; and, even when taken together, the studies do not exhaust the subject. What remains striking despite these failings is that analysts using a diverse set of research strategies repeatedly find that the simple electoral explanation misses much of congressional behavior and that in some cases its predictions run contrary to how members actually behave. Given the immense intuitive appeal of the electoral explanation, the abundant evidence to the contrary is disturbing.

Why is the simple electoral explanation at odds with the available anecdotal and statistical evidence? Part of the answer lies in the assumptions it makes about the constituency. The simple electoral explanation focuses on the geographic constituency rather than on the various groups that constitute it.[27] While the average voter may ignore foreign policy, those belonging to the attentive public may care passionately. One source of interest in foreign policy is ethnic ties. Jewish Americans, Greek Americans, Armenian Americans, and a host of other ethnic groups take great interest in their ancestral homelands. Other parts of the attentive public may focus their concern on specific foreign policy issues, such as human rights, the environment, or world peace. When a sizable portion of the constituency, in terms either of number or of campaign contributions, takes an interest in foreign policy, members have an incentive to work foreign policy issues.

Besides the incentives to address foreign policy created by members of the attentive public, there are incentives created by interest groups (many of whose members come from the ranks of the attentive public). As Chapter 1 mentioned, the 1970s and 1980s saw a tremendous growth in interest group activity on all aspects of foreign policy. Interest groups have the incentive and the means to distinguish between position taking and credit claiming, on the one hand, and serious legislative endeavors, on the other, and they can reward or punish members accordingly. As a result, members of Congress who attend to the substance of policy can expect to be rewarded for their efforts.

It is easy to comprehend the rewards a member of Congress can reap by working a foreign policy issue that matters to a major defense contractor or a powerful trade lobby. But there are also rewards to be gained by working issues that matter to smaller and less powerful groups. Perhaps the most visible example is the career of Rep. Stephen Solarz (D-N.Y.). When Solarz first assumed the chair of the Foreign Affairs Subcommittee on Asian and Pacific Affairs in 1981, the panel was lightly regarded in Congress. But Solarz's work on Asian issues, particularly his early and persistent criticism of Ferdinand Marcos, brought him increased public attention. Increased campaign contributions soon followed. By 1989, he had amassed the second largest campaign treasury in the House. Most of the campaign contributions came from Americans of Asian descent living outside of his Brooklyn district.[28] And while Representative Solarz represents the extreme, other members of Congress benefit from interest group support as well. For example, Rep. Helen Delich Bentley's (R-Md.) efforts on behalf of Serbia following the collapse of Yugoslavia won her more than $80,000 in campaign contributions from Serbian Americans.[29]

If the simple electoral explanation overlooks the diversity within constituencies, it also takes too narrow a view of electoral incentives facing members of Congress. While some members see legislative work as a cost to be avoided, others see it as an investment that will produce electoral benefits in the future. As the careers of Sam Nunn (D-Ga.), William Cohen (R-Maine), and Richard Lugar (R-Ind.) in the Senate and Les Aspin (D-Wis.), Lee Hamilton (D-Ind.), and David Obey (D-Wis.) in the House all show, members can become influential in Congress by working on defense and foreign policy. And greater influence in Congress translates into more media attention (thus, more visibility back home) and more say over the flow of government benefits, two advantages in any reelection campaign.

Members of Congress may also believe legislative work promotes their aspirations for higher office. Establishing a reputation as a foreign policy expert can serve the ambitions of members both by attracting more media attention and by fostering their images as serious legislators. Senators with an eye on the White House seem particularly eager to establish their credentials on foreign policy. In the 1970s and 1980s several of the Democratic presidential contenders, including Frank Church (D-Idaho), John Glenn (D-Ohio), Al Gore (D-Tenn.), Gary Hart (D-Colo.), Henry Jackson (D-Wash.), and Paul Tsongas (D-Mass.), made a name for themselves in the Senate with their work on foreign policy.

Of course, recognizing that some constituents care deeply about foreign policy and that members may take a broad view of the electoral imperative does not invalidate the claim that reelection drives congressional behavior. The simple electoral explanation can be recast to recognize the electoral incentives encouraging members of Congress to address foreign policy. But incorporating more sophisticated assumptions changes both the empirical predictions and normative conclusions that flow from the simple electoral explanation. A sophisticated electoral explanation would predict significantly more detailed legislative work on foreign policy, which in turn weakens the normative argument against congressional involvement in foreign policy.

At the same time, however, adding more sophisticated assumptions about constituents and electoral incentives leaves other problems with the simple electoral explanation unaddressed. The studies by Miller and Stokes, Overby, Bartels, Burgin, and others all suggest that any explanation of how Congress handles foreign policy must recognize the nonelectoral incentives that motivate legislative behavior.

One nonelectoral motive ignored by the simple electoral explanation is the desire members of Congress have to advance their conceptions of good public policy. People run for Congress not simply because they want a career—many members could make more money with far less work outside Congress—but because they want to shape public policy and to further what they see as the interests of the country. The efforts by Senator Lugar to end U.S. support for Ferdinand Marcos, by Sen. David Boren (D-Okla.) and Rep. David McCurdy (D-Okla.) to revamp the structure of the intelligence community, and by Rep. Joseph Moakley (D-Mass.) to pressure El Salvador to observe human rights were motivated far more by each member's belief about good policy than by any electoral considerations.

Of course, not all members of Congress devote themselves to foreign policy issues. On any given issue, whether foreign or domestic, most members are followers and not leaders; their expertise and passions lie elsewhere. But some members do choose to lead, and their efforts set the congressional agenda. An obvious source of leadership in Congress on foreign policy is the foreign policy committees. Another source is the individual policy entrepreneurs who work within as well as outside of the committee system to champion specific policies.

Besides being motivated by their beliefs about good policy, members of Congress are also driven by their sense of duty. The major source of duty for members is committee membership. The foreign policy committees review budget requests and oversee agency decisions because that is their assignment. Of course, much of the commentary on Congress derides the ability of congressional committees to oversee the executive branch. But as Chapter 3 discusses in greater detail, the foreign policy committees are involved in far more oversight than is commonly recognized. Another source of duty for members is party affiliation. As foreign policy views have become more homogenous within both the Democratic and Republican parties, both party leaders and rank-and-file members have felt increased political pressure to vote with their party.

To recognize that some members of Congress have personal, chamber, or party reasons to tackle foreign policy issues does not mean that these members are legislative altruists who pursue their policy work with total disregard for their electoral interests. To the contrary, members have every reason to extract electoral gain from their efforts.

To make their policy work electorally profitable, members of Congress employ the same credit claiming, position taking, and advertising strategies that any self-interested legislator uses. Members give careful thought to how they can tie their policy work to issues that matter to constituents. One representative involved in the effort to increase the U.S. quota for the International Monetary Fund (IMF) knew his constituents cared little for the IMF. According to a staffer, however, the representative also knew his supporters "were very interested in how the banking system works and how rural economies fare with the banking community. So he tied the issue to their interests. . . . He thought that politically it would be a good issue for him because of these things. And boy did it play well back home."[30] Another member sponsored a bill to ban certain types of missile tests. Although the genesis for the proposal lay in arms control, the member sold the issue to deficit-conscious voters back home as part of his bid to save the federal government money.[31]

The ability of members of Congress to define the meaning of their legislative activities has been enhanced in recent years by changes in the way the media operate. The advent of low-cost satellite and fax technology, combined with the media's need to hold down the cost of political reporting, has led many local news outlets to rely more on press and video news releases provided by members of Congress.[32] Members have used this dependence to put their legislative efforts in the most favorable light. As one congressional press secretary put it: We use self-developed interviews and video news releases to "cut off bad publicity—to put our own spin on things."[33]

CONSTITUENTS AS A CONSTRAINT

One cannot deny the importance of the electoral imperative to congressional decision making. Constituent opinion clearly matters to members of Congress. What can be disputed, though, is the claim that few electoral incentives exist for members to address the substance of foreign policy and the assumption that reelection is the only motive driving congressional behavior. Members have both personal and political reasons to attend to the substance of foreign policy.

What also can be disputed is the nature of the link between voters and members of Congress. Electoral explanations, whether of a simple or a sophisticated variety, contend that constituent opinion tells members how to act. But constituent opinion probably acts more as a constraint on behavior than as a guide.[34] As Robert Dahl observed more than four decades ago:

> Constituent opinion may set broad limits within which the Congressman must operate, even when this opinion does not define specific conduct within these limits. This is another way of saying that although electoral opinion may remain passive as long as the Congressman chooses among certain broad alternatives, his selection of an alternative outside this accepted range would activate constituent opinion. Thus it seems likely that in 1948, except in a very small number of special cases, few Congressmen could safely have

adopted a position sympathetic to the foreign policies of the U.S.S.R. But *within* the broad range of anti-Soviet polices, many Congressmen probably had considerable choice among alternative ways of dealing with Soviet expansionism. Their "mandate" defined certain broad objectives but not the specific means to those objectives.[35]

Constituent opinion, then, acts primarily to tell members what *not* to do and only secondarily to tell them what *to* do.

Members of Congress clearly prefer situations in which their policy preferences fall within the range of policies acceptable to their supporters.[36] It is likely that this is what happens a good deal of the time. One reason is the apathy and ignorance of the American public. Most voters pay little or no attention to foreign affairs and, as a result, will tolerate a wide range of legislative behaviors, even when it comes to major foreign policy issues.[37] Another reason is the process of recruiting members. The need to reside in a district (usually for much of one's lifetime), to build a coalition of supporters, and to win an election makes it likely that members will share many policy attitudes with their constituents. Moreover, members have some freedom to construct a reelection constituency that reflects their own policy views.[38] This is especially true for senators. The tremendous diversity among voters at the state level makes it possible to assemble winning coalitions that support greatly divergent views on defense and foreign policy. During the 103d Congress (1993–94), for example, twenty states sent one Democratic and one Republican senator to Capitol Hill.

How do members of Congress behave when a policy they favor falls within the range of policies that constituents will tolerate? In deciding both which position to take and how actively to work the issue, members no doubt look first to their policy preferences. The more intense a member's policy preferences, the more inclined he or she will be to act on them. The advantage to members in using personal preference as a guide to behavior is not only that it minimizes cognitive dissonance—something some members handle better than others—but that it provides a consistent voting record. Members value consistency because they "find it difficult to explain inconsistency to their constituents."[39]

But personal policy preferences are not sacrosanct. Members sometimes abandon their preferred policy for electoral reasons, either because the new policy stance has greater political appeal or because the shift enables them to obtain benefits for the constituency. Likewise, the demands of party and chamber can push members to act differently than they would on the basis of their personal preferences alone. During the MX debate, for example, the

House Democratic leadership shifted from near-uniform support to uniform opposition to the missile when liberal Democrats pledged to unseat party leaders who supported the missile.[40] Members may also be swayed by the likely impact their behavior will have on the outcome of debate. Members who know that their actions will not be pivotal have a greater incentive to abandon their personal preferences.

As much as members of Congress prefer issues where their actions will (at a minimum) not antagonize constituent opinion, they sometimes find that their personal preferences or chamber and party demands push them toward policies that lie outside the range acceptable to their supporters. Since the constraints voters place on members are by no means binding, cross-pressured members can, at their own peril, take positions as they please. In deciding whether to respect constituent opinion, members have to calculate the costs and benefits of the courses of action available to them. No doubt such calculations are crude. Constituent preferences for specific policy options often are difficult to discern and may change over time. Still, members can and do estimate how their behavior will affect their electoral prospects.

An obvious influence on member calculations is the cost of violating the constituency constraint. Not all violations create significant political headaches. On some issues a member may calculate that however much constituents disapprove, the issue is not important enough to sway many votes. On other issues a member may calculate that however angry voters may be now, their anger will fade with time. And on still other issues members may calculate that they can stand by the preferred policy and deflect the electoral costs of their position by declining to take an active role on the issue. But on some issues violating the constituency constraint is electoral poison, and on issues such as these most members adopt positions acceptable to their constituents.

A second factor that influences the willingness of a member of Congress to violate the constituency constraint is the importance of the issue to the member. Members are more willing to take an unpopular stand when the issue is one they care deeply about. J. William Fulbright, the longtime chair of the Senate Foreign Relations Committee, made this point well in a speech at the University of Chicago in 1946.

> The average legislator, early in his career, discovers that there are certain interests, or prejudices, of his constituents which are dangerous to trifle with. Some of these prejudices may not be of fundamental importance to the welfare of the nation, in which case he is justified in humoring them, even though he may disapprove. The difficult case is where the prejudice concerns fundamen-

tal policy affecting the national welfare. . . . As an example of what I mean, let us take the poll-tax issue and isolationism. Regardless of how persuasive my colleagues or the national press may be about the evils of a poll tax, I do not see its fundamental importance, and I shall follow the views of the people of my State. . . . On the other hand, regardless of how strongly opposed my constituents may prove to be to the creation of, and participation in, an ever stronger United Nations Organization, I could not follow such a policy in that field unless it becomes clearly hopeless.[41]

Putting aside Fulbright's dubious assessment of the poll tax, the general lesson of his remarks holds: members of Congress will not risk their careers for issues they do not care deeply about.

The third factor that members of Congress consider when they find themselves cross-pressured can also be found in Senator Fulbright's remarks: the likelihood of winning. Although academics and journalists lionize members who hold views contrary to those of their constituents, members know that legislators who needlessly make enemies will have short careers. As a result, the incentive members have to violate the constituency constraint diminishes as their activities become less pivotal to the outcome of a vote. The historic debate in 1941 over a measure to extend the term of Selective Service, which eventually passed with one vote to spare, illustrates how the likelihood of winning influences vote calculations in Congress:

> Many, including several who had voted for Lend-Lease, appear to have believed that the bill would be passed with a reasonable margin and that therefore they could afford to shirk the responsibility for supporting an unpopular measure. A good many Congressmen were evidently willing to take a long chance to escape the odium of voting to keep their constituents and their constituents' offspring in camp. As one of them wrote to his colleagues before the roll call: "If you don't watch your step, your political hide, which is very near and dear to you, will be tanning on the barn door." On this basis a substantial number of Congressmen came close to outsmarting themselves.[42]

Thus, if cross-pressured members favor a policy that is likely to win, they can vote as constituents wish while still obtaining the outcome they prefer. By the same token, if cross-pressured members favor a policy that is likely to lose, a vote on conscience will alienate voters without advancing the policy the members prefer.

THE POLITICS OF CONGRESSIONAL
DECISION MAKING

Members of Congress try to balance both electoral considerations and policy preferences when addressing foreign policy issues. But recognizing that members act on their policy preferences is not to say that congressional decision making is apolitical or that policy concerns always override electoral ones. Because members of Congress must try to enact their policy visions subject to a constituency constraint, politics permeates congressional decision making.

Yet the extent to which electoral considerations influence Congress's handling of foreign policy varies from issue to issue. In some instances electoral calculations determine both *which* issues appear on the congressional agenda and *what* positions members take. Where constituent opinion is intense and narrow, members usually see themselves as having no choice but to follow voters. In June 1991, for example, House Democrats voted by more than three-to-one in favor of the foreign aid bill. But when a virtually identical version of the bill emerged from a House-Senate conference in October, nearly half the Democrats voted to kill it. The reversal was due not to policy concerns but to a sudden rise in public anger over the economy. Many members did not want to have to explain to voters in the midst of a recession why they supported sending taxpayer dollars abroad.

Situations in which constituent opinion forces members of Congress to sacrifice their good judgment are usually memorable—they provide the grist for many of the stories of members bowing to constituency pressures. But to repeat the point made earlier, most of the time members have considerable leeway to decide which positions to take. Yet even when voters will support a range of policies, electoral calculations influence which issues Congress addresses. Because of the need to win reelection, members interested in substantive policy issues have an incentive to work issues that will advance both their electoral prospects and their policy preferences.

The desire to seek electoral gain in legislative activity explains why much of Congress's involvement in foreign policy is reactive. When an issue becomes salient with constituents, members of Congress suddenly have an incentive to address it. Thus, when U.S. relations with China became an issue after the massacre at Tiananmen Square, members of Congress suddenly began to fall over one another in their zeal to introduce legislation or hold hearings. In much the same fashion, the furor in the mid-1980s over the Pentagon's pricing of spare parts led to a flurry of committee investigations into weapons acquisition policy.

The work of policy entrepreneurs is similarly influenced by the desire to extract electoral gain from legislative activity. Within any issue area a policy entrepreneur is free to address an array of issues. Thus, a member interested in African politics might address starvation in Eastern Africa, reports of torture and mass killings in Liberia, or communal violence in South Africa. Yet policy entrepreneurs know that time and resource constraints mean they can address at most one or two issues productively at any given time. The need to be selective, combined with the need to win reelection, encourages policy entrepreneurs to favor issues that offer the most potential for becoming politically profitable in the future. And the reverse is also true. If an entrepreneurial effort fails to pay off in terms of either electoral or policy success, all but the most committed member is likely to move on to another issue.

None of this is to argue that electoral calculations alone determine which issues appear on Congress's agenda. A substantial amount of proactive legislative activity occurs even when no immediate electoral payoff exists because members of Congress have personal policy preferences and chamber responsibilities. The foreign policy committees devote considerable time to little-noticed issues because it is part of their job. Likewise, an issue might have so much personal importance with individual policy entrepreneurs that they will continue their work even when it fails to yield anything in terms of electoral profit. But politics remains an important force shaping Congress's agenda.

If electoral calculations influence which issues Congress addresses and to a lesser extent what positions members take, they play an even greater role in influencing *how* members handle issues. Members who want to change policy know they must craft legislation that meets the political needs of their colleagues. Take, for example, the debate over the plan to send humanitarian aid to the Soviet Union following the August 1991 coup. Despite the impressive array of senior members sponsoring the bill, it foundered over rising public resentment that more was not being done to meet humanitarian needs at home. The bill moved through Congress only when its sponsors repackaged it as an effort to reduce the nuclear threat to the United States.[43] Likewise, during the Reagan and Bush years, Democratic leaders refused to allow funding for the IMF to come to a vote unless the president wrote a letter specifically requesting the money. The refusal stemmed from an incident in 1982 when Republican candidates attacked Democrats who had voted to fund the IMF of supporting an institution that lent money to Communist countries, even though "the Democratic lawmakers had voted for the money at the request of Ronald Reagan."[44]

The lesson of the Soviet aid and IMF funding debates is simple: no member of Congress wants to support legislation that is difficult to defend to constituents.[45] The need members have to avoid blame explains why the House and Senate often consider symbolic resolutions that pass on unanimous or near-unanimous votes. Whether Democrat or Republican, liberal or conservative, members know that votes on "Apple Pie" themes can complicate their voting records and thereby insulate them against political attack. Closed rules, motions to table, and other procedural maneuvers provide much the same kind of political protection.[46]

Of course, critics of Congress usually point to symbolic resolutions and procedural votes as evidence of legislative cowardice. And on occasion the charge has merit. Martyrs are in short supply on Capitol Hill. Yet rather than enabling members to hide from substantive issues, symbolic resolutions and procedural votes frequently enable them to act on their policy preferences by providing them with the requisite political cover. During the bitter battles over defense spending during the Reagan years, for example, the Democratic leadership in the House made frequent use of the so-called king-of-the-hill rule. Under this procedure only the last in a series of successful amendments is actually adopted. Thus, when Republicans offered amendments that were more politically attractive than those offered by Democrats, moderate and dovish members "could vote for both the Republican and Democratic alternatives . . . confident the latter would prevail because it held the cleanup position in the sequence of votes."[47]

Procedural maneuvers played a similarly important role in securing the passage of the Panama Canal treaties. During the debate it became clear that the treaties would not pass unless certain ambiguities in the text of the agreements were clarified. Senate leaders responded by crafting amendments intended to clarify the disputed passages. The leadership deliberately chose to introduce the amendments on the floor rather than in the Foreign Relations Committee so that "a majority of Senators could co-sponsor them and receive credit with their constituencies for 'toughening up' the treaties."[48] Without the fig leaf offered by the leadership amendments, several senators would have voted against the treaties, thereby killing them and imperiling U.S. relations with Panama and the rest of Latin America.

It also is worth emphasizing that both sides in any congressional debate are usually being driven by a mix of electoral calculations and policy concerns. The reason is that the values and attitudes of constituents vary across states and congressional districts; hence, members differ in the amount of leeway they enjoy on any issue. When it comes to the subject of automobile import quotas, for example, the range of trade policies acceptable to voters in southeastern Michigan is probably much smaller than that which is acceptable to the voters of Maine. Thus, an issue that leaves one member with no choice but to follow the wishes of the voters offers another member the opportunity to pursue a favored policy initiative.

Recognition that a mix of policy and electoral motivations generally drives both sides in congressional debate should dispel the notion, implicit in many discussions of Congress and foreign policy, that electoral and policy considerations are inherently at odds. Policy-motivated members have every reason to portray their favored policy as serving the electoral interests of their colleagues. After all, the votes of electorally motivated members count just as much as the votes of their policy-minded colleagues. By the same token, electorally motivated members have good reason to focus attention on the merits of their favored policy. Emphasizing the substantive advantages of their policy proposal can help them build a winning coalition by attracting the support of members who have no significant electoral stake in the debate.

To push this point a bit further, electoral self-interest actually helps stimulate congressional scrutiny of the merits of policy proposals. This is particularly true where parochial economic interests are at stake. The battle over the V-22 Osprey offers a case in point. The leaders of the fight to save the tilt-rotor plane, Reps. Curt Weldon (R-Pa.) and Peter Geren (D-Texas), represented constituencies that benefited heavily from the V-22. Conversely, the plane's most vocal opponents represented constituencies that built the helicopters the V-22 was designed to replace. Although the V-22 seems to be a straightforward story of parochialism, far more members of Congress supported the plane than can be accounted for by explicit, parochial incentives. Most members had no stake in the program. Moreover, neither Weldon (a Republican in a Democratic Congress) nor Geren (a first-term member) were well-positioned to reward or punish members for their votes on the V-22. Instead, the success of the pro-Osprey forces was the result of other factors, in particular, the arguments made behind the scenes by Marine Corps officers that the plane was essential for maintaining highly mobile forces.[49]

Policy concerns figured prominently in the V-22 debate, as they do in many other supposedly parochial disputes, because constituency interests usually are not sufficiently widespread to make a program invincible on Capitol Hill.[50] To build a winning coalition, supporters can engage in logrolls and other quid pro quos or threaten to punish opponents. But most members of Congress are poorly placed to build a winning coalition through rewards and threats alone. They also need to marshal a body of evidence that will win over members with no parochial interest at stake. Because the opposing coalition will respond with facts and figures of its own, what results is a substantive debate aimed at persuading undecided members.[51]

The fact that congressional debates reflect a mix of policy and electoral motivations also has important implications for understanding congressional behavior. Anyone who wants evidence that self-interest is driving a congressional debate on foreign policy usually can find at least a few members who view the issue through the prism of the next election. Yet the fact that electoral self-interest drives the behavior of *some* members on a given issue does not warrant the conclusion that it drives the behavior of *most*.

CONCLUSION

Most accounts of congressional decision making on foreign policy emphasize the electoral connection between voters and members of Congress. Senators and representatives are portrayed as vote-maximizers currying to the whims and prejudices of their constituents. Stories of members such as Senator Zorinsky who abandon their policy preferences to please constituents are widely cited. The overall thrust of the conventional wisdom is to fuel skepticism that Congress can contribute to U.S. foreign policy.

Despite the intuitive appeal of electoral explanations, they distort the nature of congressional decision making. Members of Congress do have incentives to address the substance of foreign policy. The average voter may care little about foreign affairs, but attentive publics and interest groups do follow and reward members who advance their cause. Personal policy preferences, committee responsibilities, and party duties all provide members of Congress with nonelectoral incentives to undertake detailed legislative work. And the very passivity of the average voter gives members considerable freedom in the positions they take on foreign policy. In short, constituents constrain but do not dictate legislative behavior.

Recognition that powerful incentives exist for members of Congress to address foreign policy issues does not mean that congressional decision making is a rational, apolitical process. Politics permeates congressional decision making. Where the political climate is hostile, or constituents are ardently opposed, or significant parochial interests are threatened, members of Congress can be expected to act as the simple electoral explanation would suggest. Likewise, the time and resource constraints facing members, combined with the need to win reelection, means that policy-driven members must pursue their legislative efforts with an eye toward actual or potential political profit. But the politics inherent in congressional decision making should not obscure the very real incentives that exist for members of Congress to undertake detailed legislative work on foreign policy.

DECISION MAKING IN CONGRESS

WHO IN CONGRESS makes decisions on foreign policy? To judge by the comments of scholars and practitioners alike, the answer is nearly everyone. Critics complain that almost every congressional committee has a say in foreign policy. Mackubin Thomas Owens protests that "some thirty committees and seventy-seven subcommittees claim some degree of oversight over defense."[1] Former secretary of the navy John Lehman objects that "there are now more than eighty chairmen whose staffs are micromanaging all parts of the national security policy of the executive."[2] Some critics even worry that Capitol Hill has become home to 535 secretaries of state. Then-Rep. Dick Cheney (R-Wyo.) complained in 1985: The president has "to put up with every member of Congress with a Xerox machine and a credit card running around the world cutting deals with heads of state."[3]

Claims that congressional decision making on foreign policy is a free-for-all, while popular, misrepresent the allocation of authority and interest on Capitol Hill. Although more than half the standing committees in Congress claim some foreign policy jurisdiction, and while floor debates on foreign policy sometimes become intense, the bulk of Congress's work on foreign policy occurs in eight committees: Senate Foreign Relations, House Foreign Affairs, and the armed services, appropriations, and intelligence committees in each chamber. Each of the big eight committees delves more deeply into the details of foreign policy, and each is more willing to challenge the executive than was true in the 1950s and 1960s. At the same time, the relative influence of the committees has changed. In particular, Foreign Relations, once a titan on foreign policy, now finds itself pushed to the margins of policy by the armed services and appropriations committees.

COMMITTEES IN CONGRESS

Committees are central to congressional decision making on foreign policy. Very few bills make it to the floor of the House or Senate without first having been the subject of committee hearings and deliberations. In turn, the overwhelming press of business means that members on the floor can seldom challenge more than a few items in any piece of legislation. The central role played by committees raises a key question: Which committees in Congress have jurisdiction over foreign policy?

In terms of the sheer number of committees involved, jurisdiction over foreign policy is widely distributed. Many committees besides the big eight have a formal claim to some aspect of foreign policy. The agriculture committees, for instance, supervise commodity export programs. The banking committees oversee both the Export-Import Bank and U.S. contributions to the International Monetary Fund. The budget committees usher the concurrent budget resolutions, which include spending limits for defense and foreign policy programs, through Congress. The House Merchant Marine Committee and the Senate Commerce Committee have jurisdiction over the Panama Canal. And because tariffs were once the primary source of federal revenues, the House Ways and Means Committee and the Senate Finance Committee both handle trade policy.

The list of committees involved in foreign policy goes beyond those who have formal jurisdiction. When a foreign policy issue becomes attractive, whether for political or personal reasons, almost every committee and subcommittee chair can define the issue to be within his or her mandate. At the initiative of then-Rep. Al Gore (D-Tenn.), for example, the House Science and Technology Committee used the nuclear winter controversy as a wedge with which to join the debate over arms control. In the mid-1980s, the Senate Judiciary Committee became a participant in the controversy over waste, fraud, and abuse in the Defense Department when Sen. Charles Grassley (R-Iowa) used the Judiciary Subcommittee on Administrative Practice and Procedure to highlight how defense contractors had inflated the prices they charged for spare parts.

The dispersion of committee jurisdictions makes congressional decision making look at first glance like a free-for-all. On closer inspection, however, most of Congress's work on foreign policy takes place in one of the big eight committees. The formal stake other committees have in foreign affairs is limited. The Merchant Marine Committee, for example, carries no weight on foreign policy matters aside from maritime matters and the Panama Canal, and the foreign policy influence of the agriculture committees stops with agricultural export programs. At the same time, committees that try to poach on politically attractive foreign policy issues face a formidable obstacle: on Capitol Hill, dollars are power. Unless a committee authorizes or appropriates funds for individual programs, its ability to influence policy is severely constrained. Thus, the budget committees occasionally hold hearings on defense and foreign policy, but their inability to affect the funding for individual programs renders them a marginal player in policy making.

THE FOREIGN RELATIONS AND FOREIGN AFFAIRS COMMITTEES

On paper, both the Foreign Relations Committee and the Foreign Affairs Committee occupy a central role in congressional decision making on foreign policy. Their formal jurisdictions give them a say in almost every foreign policy issue. In practice, however, the two committees find themselves remarkably ineffective in shaping U.S. foreign policy. As one official in the Reagan administration described Foreign Relations and Foreign Affairs: "One has died on the vine; the other has fragmented into little empires."[4]

Foreign Relations historically is one of the most prestigious committees in Congress.[5] For much of the twentieth century the committee stood at the forefront of U.S. foreign policy with its chairs regarded as giants on Capitol Hill. After Vietnam, however, "the era of giants came to a close."[6] Not even members of Foreign Relations consider the committee to be the power it once was. In the words of one former chair, Sen. Richard Lugar (R-Ind.): "The committee as a whole is not really a major player in this business."[7]

The truth of Lugar's lament can be seen in the committee's woeful legislative record. Each year from 1985 until 1991 the committee failed in its main legislative task: drafting a foreign aid authorization bill acceptable to the Senate. When the Iran-contra affair broke in 1987, the Senate leadership bypassed Foreign Relations and set up a special panel to investigate the matter. And when the Senate faced the decision of whether to authorize the use of force against Iraq, the committee had no role in drafting either of the resolutions considered on the floor, and Sen. Claiborne Pell (D-R.I.), the chair of Foreign Relations, was virtually invisible during the debate. In light of these problems it is not surprising that some senators have abandoned Foreign Relations for seats on other committees.[8]

Foreign Relations has lost influence on Capitol Hill in part because the foreign policy agenda has changed. Treaties play a much smaller role in foreign policy than they did during the committee's glory years, and the amount of foreign aid declined substantially in the 1980s. At the same time, the issues that have come to dominate the agenda—aid to Nicaragua, modernization of the armed forces, and trade, to mention only a few—lie within the jurisdiction of other committees. And those committees have fought vigorously to keep Foreign Relations off their turf.

The biggest reasons for the declining importance of Foreign Relations, however, are internal. During the 1970s and 1980s the committee became polarized between dovish Democrats and hawkish Republicans, thereby making agreement hard to come by.[9] The problems created by the partisan division were in turn exacerbated first by a rapid turnover in chairs and then by a lack of strong leadership. In the decade after Sen. J. William Fulbright (D-Ark.) retired in 1974, Foreign Relations went through four chairs, none of whom served longer than four years. In 1986, Senator Pell became chair, and while he broke the four-year jinx, most observers dismissed him as "weak," "detached," and "more of a 'packman' than a 'pointman.'"[10] Pell made little use of the subcommittees, and he rarely tried to lead the committee on legislative issues. Moreover, he failed to stop Sen. Jesse Helms (R-N.C.), the ranking minority member, from using the committee's partisan divisions to create a legislative stalemate.

The declining prestige of Foreign Relations has not been lost on members of the committee. In 1991 the Democrats on the committee pushed through reforms designed to rejuvenate the moribund subcommittees. The changes gave two subcommittees authority to mark up legislation, and all of the subcommittees won the right to hire their own staff. The reforms apparently had some effect. Later in 1991 the committee ushered the foreign aid bill through the Senate for the first time since 1985, and the number of subcommittee hearings rose sharply. Yet, in the end, structural reforms by themselves cannot solve the problems created by the combination of partisan division and weak leadership.

While Foreign Relations has long been seen as a prestigious committee, Foreign Affairs traditionally has not—in the 1940s, one member called it "a dump heap, where service was a chore rather than a privilege."[11] Part of the problem is that Foreign Affairs lacks the jurisdiction over treaties and cabinet nominations that gives Foreign Relations much of its visibility. At the same time, the committee has often lacked dynamic leadership. It was said of Rep. Sol Bloom (D-N.Y.), chair of Foreign Affairs in the 1940s, that he approved everything the president did in foreign policy "so long as he was telephoned fifteen minutes before the executive action was announced. His primary concern seemed to be less the substance of policy and more that he not be embarrassed when the press called to ask his opinion about the Administration's foreign policy decisions."[12] In the first several decades after World War II, the committee was chaired by men such as Rep. Thomas E. "Doc" Morgan (D-Pa.) who were "not aggressive advocate[s] of congressional involvement in foreign policy and [who] generally supported the administration position on the principle of 'bipartisanship.'"[13]

In the mid-1970s, however, Foreign Affairs stirred from its slumber.[14] Oversight of the executive branch became a priority. The number of committee and subcommittee hearings more than doubled during the 1970s, and the number remained high throughout the 1980s. The amount of legislation emerging from the committee also increased. The spurt in activity stemmed in part from the fact that Morgan's successors as chair, Reps. Clement Zablocki (D-Wis.) and Dante Fascell (D-Fla.), were both less reluctant to challenge the administration. At the same time, the House delegated substantial powers to its subcommittees in the 1970s, enabling them to operate independently of the full committee. And when the Republicans took control of both the White House and the Senate in 1981, Democrats lost the two most visible platforms for advocating their visions for foreign policy. Foreign Affairs suddenly became the only game in town.

The increased activism of the committee, however, has not translated into a commensurate increase in influence or respect within the House. Fascell himself acknowledged the low regard with which his colleagues hold the committee when he complained in 1990 that the work of Foreign Affairs had become "almost irrelevant."[15] On the eve of the vote to authorize the use of force against Iraq, Speaker of the House Thomas Foley (D-Wash.) made it clear just how low Foreign Affairs stood in the eyes of the House. The House leadership had authorized debate on two resolutions, but some committee members wanted to introduce their own resolution. In a blunt tongue lashing delivered behind closed doors, Foley told members of Foreign Affairs that the leadership "was allowing the committee to meet for purposes of holding hearings, but had not formally constituted it for reporting out legislation in the new Congress."[16] A third resolution never reached the floor.

As with Foreign Relations, Foreign Affairs now finds it difficult to retain and attract members.[17] In 1991, Rep. Howard Wolpe (D-Mich.) gave up the chair of the Africa subcommittee to chair a subcommittee of the Science, Space and Technology Committee. At the same time, in a move rare in a seniority-conscious Congress, Reps. Gerry Studds (D-Mass.) and Peter Kostmayer (D-Pa.) quit to take seats on other committees despite having fifteen and eight years service respectively on Foreign Affairs. Studds explained his decision in blunt terms: "There was not really much happening" on the committee. New members were no more eager to join Foreign Affairs. Even though the committee had eight vacancies when the 102d Congress met in January 1991, not one of the twenty-five first-term Democrats requested a seat on Foreign Affairs. [18]

Foreign Affairs has failed to turn its legislative activism into legislative influence for several reasons. Like Foreign Relations, Foreign Affairs suffers from the fact that many of the major issues now on the foreign policy agenda lie within the jurisdiction of other committees. As a result, the committee's legislation frequently turns out to be more symbolic than substantive. During the nuclear freeze debate in 1983, for instance, Chairman Zablocki admitted that despite all the histrionics over the committee's bill, nothing in the legislation would "preclude the development, modernization, and production of U.S. nuclear systems." [19]

Foreign Affairs also has suffered because neither Zablocki nor Fascell had a well-defined legislative agenda. Fascell, in particular, took a hands-off approach to running the committee. As a House Democrat complained on the eve of the Gulf War: "Whether it's War Powers or other congressional prerogatives, [Fascell] says he wants to protect those prerogatives. On the other hand, he's too quiescent. He won't fight for turf against other committees, he won't scream at the leadership." [20] Fascell was equally reluctant to impose discipline on the subcommittee chairs. Although many of the subcommittees chairs were effective legislators in their own right, with no leadership from the chair they often fell into squabbling amongst themselves.

Another problem for Foreign Affairs is that its primary legislative chore has become an exercise in futility. The repeated inability of the Foreign Relations Committee to shepherd a foreign aid bill through the Senate means that Foreign Affairs usually finds itself having to rely on the good will of the House Appropriations Committee to get its preferences on aid policy translated into law. And on the occasions when the Foreign Relations Committee has been able to act, luck has not been with Foreign Affairs. When the Senate finally passed a foreign aid bill in 1991, partisan politics derailed the bill in the House.

The legislative impotence of Foreign Relations and Foreign Affairs does not make the committees entirely irrelevant. A seat on either committee gives members of Congress instant legitimacy as foreign policy experts as well as a platform from which to articulate their policy preferences. Because House rules give subcommittee chairs significant authority to call their own hearings, the value of the committees as platforms is greatest to subcommittee chairs on Foreign Affairs. To the extent that foreign policy is influenced by public debate as well as by funding decisions, members of Foreign Relations and Foreign Affairs have the means to affect policy.

THE ARMED SERVICES COMMITTEES

During the first years of the cold war, the armed services committees played a remarkably small role in defense and foreign policy. They were widely derided as "real estate committees."[21] Their members focused overwhelmingly on the military construction account, which they examined in detail. The committees reviewed and authorized the remaining 97 percent of the defense budget through lump-sum authorizations. These authorizations generally were no more specific than, for example, "the Secretary of the Air Force may procure guided missiles and 24,000 serviceable aircraft."[22] The failure of the armed services committees to oversee most defense programs meant that major spending decisions were made during the appropriations process. As a result, officials in the executive branch regarded the armed services committees "with a kind of gracious toleration that borders on contempt."[23]

Over the past two decades, however, the armed services committees have become Congress's leading actors on defense policy. The disarray afflicting Foreign Relations and Foreign Affairs has even enabled the armed services committees to carve out a leading role for themselves on many foreign policy issues. When the Reagan administration tried in the mid-1980s to redefine the ABM treaty to allow greater testing of strategic defense technology, the fight to preserve the traditional interpretation was led by Senator Nunn and not by Senator Pell. During the debate over Operation Desert Shield, the first and most visible congressional hearings were held by Senate Armed Services and not by the Foreign Relations Committee. And when the Soviet Union collapsed in late 1991, Aspin and Nunn, not Fascell and Pell, spearheaded the effort to assemble an aid package for the former Soviet republics.

The shift by the armed services committees from the margins to the heart of policy making is due to four factors.[24] The first is the growth of the annual authorization process. The Russell Amendment of 1959 stipulated that all appropriations for the procurement of aircraft, missiles, and naval vessels had to be preceded by specific annual authorizations. Over the next twenty-five years, the armed services committees gradually extended the line-item requirement to include the entire defense budget. They pushed for line-item authorizations in part "to reduce the discretionary power of the Office of the Secretary of Defense . . . and to strengthen legislative control of programs."[25] Even more important was the desire to reclaim power within Congress. So long as the appropriations committees alone determined how much was spent on military programs, they, not the armed services committees, would determine defense policy.

The transformation of the armed services committees is also due to the subcommittee reforms of the 1970s. Before Watergate, the chairs of the armed services committees ran the committees as their personal baronies. The subcommittee reforms turned the system on its head. Powers traditionally concentrated in the hands of the committee chair were dispersed to subcommittees. The decentralizing trend went further in House Armed Services because of the more comprehensive nature of the House reforms. The ability of subcommittees to oversee the Defense Department was further enhanced by the vast expansion of committee staff.

The growth of line-item authorizations and the rise of subcommittees gave the armed services committees the opportunity to influence defense and foreign policy. The willingness of the committees to pursue a more vigorous role is the result of a third development: the dissolution of the congressional consensus on foreign policy after Vietnam. Throughout the 1970s and 1980s, members of the armed services committees were significantly more hawkish than the House and Senate as a whole.[26] The ideological gap between the committees and their parent chambers prompted rank-and-file legislators to use floor amendments to try to wrest control over defense policy away from the committees.[27] At the same time, the emergence of defense policy as a salient political issue created incentives for dovish members to join the committees. Whereas few doves sat on the armed services committees in the early 1970s, two decades later the House committee was chaired by Ron Dellums (D-Calif.), one of the most dovish members of Congress, and doves such as Rep. Patricia Schroeder (D-Colo.), Sen. Edward Kennedy (D-Mass.) and Sen. Carl Levin (D-Mich.) held subcommittee chairs in both chambers. The combination of attacks from outside and changing attitudes within pushed the committees toward a more activist role on defense and foreign policy.

The final factor that transformed the armed services committees into major actors on defense and foreign policy was the emergence of strong chairs on both committees. During the 1970s and early 1980s, neither committee enjoyed dynamic leadership. Either the chairs lacked a clear policy agenda of their own, as was true of Rep. Melvin Price (D-Ill.) and Sen. John Stennis (D-Miss.), or their tenures were too brief to have much impact, as was true of Sens. John Tower (R-Tex.) and Barry Goldwater (R-Ariz.). That changed when Representative Aspin and Senator Nunn became chairs in the mid-1980s. Unlike their predecessors, both Aspin and Nunn came to the chairmanship with detailed preferences about U.S. defense policy.

Nunn and Aspin took very different routes to their chairmanships. Nunn slowly worked his way up the ladder of seniority. He built his reputation as *the* defense expert in the Senate by painstakingly working behind the scenes on a wide range of defense issues. When Senator Goldwater chaired Armed Services, Nunn acted almost as a shadow chair. On becoming chair in his own right in 1987, he centralized the staff structure, thereby concentrating authority in his own hands. Nunn's control of Senate Armed Services became so great that observers took to calling the committee "Sam Nunn Inc."[28]

Representative Aspin, on the other hand, began his career in Congress as a defense gadfly who tried to legislate by press release. In 1985, he engineered a legislative coup that catapulted him past five more senior Democrats to replace Price as chair. Aspin's first term as chair was rocky, and in 1987 the Democratic Caucus briefly deposed him. He eventually consolidated his control over the committee, in part because the subcommittee chairs who resented his ascent to the chair died or retired and in part because he reclaimed control over the committee staff from the subcommittee chairs. Nonetheless, the extensiveness of the subcommittee reforms and the more sizable liberal contingent in the House made Aspin more responsive to his subcommittee chairs and to floor pressure than his Senate counterpart.

Although the style of their chairs might differ, both armed services committees use inside and outside strategies to influence policy. The inside strategy is the authorization process. The ability to determine spending levels enables the committees to define and revise defense programs. The outside strategy seeks to influence policy by shaping the terms of the public debate. As already mentioned, Senator Nunn used committee hearings and floor speeches to shape policy on issues such as the interpretation of the ABM treaty, the restructuring of the defense budget, and aid to the Soviet republics. Under Aspin's leadership, House Armed Services was even more fond of the outside strategy. In the first six months of 1992, for example, the committee issued eleven major white papers, an eighty-nine page analysis of the lessons of the Gulf War, and a blizzard of press releases.[29]

THE APPROPRIATIONS COMMITTEES

Any program that requires funding ultimately comes within the jurisdiction of the appropriations committees.[30] Unlike other congressional committees, the appropriations committees rely almost totally on their subcommittees, which are essentially autonomous actors. Five appropriations subcommittees in each chamber lay claim to some aspect of foreign policy. The energy and water development subcommittees handle appropriations for nuclear warheads; the commerce, justice, state, and judiciary subcommittees handle funding for the Department of State and United Nations peacekeeping activities; and the military construction subcommittees handle appropriations for military facilities. But the most important subcommittees by far are the defense subcommittees, which oversee the Pentagon, and the foreign operations subcommittees, which oversee foreign aid programs.

The defense and foreign operations subcommittees are usually thought of as "budgeteers" that comb through the administration's budget requests looking for places to save money. They are seldom thought of as major contributors to the substantive debate on foreign policy. When foreign policy issues become controversial, the debates in Congress are usually led by members of the various authorizing committees and not by members of the appropriations committees. Appropriators often go to great lengths to acknowledge the greater policy expertise of the authorizers. For instance, Rep. David Obey (D-Wis.), chair of the House Foreign Operations Subcommittee, readily grants that when it comes to foreign policy, the members of the Foreign Affairs Committee "most of the time know more about these issues than we do."[31]

The tilt toward budgetary matters and away from policy matters stems partly from the nature of legislators who seek seats on the appropriations committees. Unlike Foreign Relations and Foreign Affairs, which historically attract legislators with strong personal interests in foreign policy, or the armed services committees, which began to attract policy-motivated legislators in the 1980s, few members join the appropriations committees primarily to advance their policy preferences. House Appropriations typically attracts legislators interested in wielding power within Congress. As committee member Norman Dicks once put it: House Appropriations is "where the money is. And money is where the clout is."[32] For its part, the Senate Appropriations Committee typically attracts senators who want to advance the economic interests of their constituents.[33]

The tilt away from policy issues also stems from a simple reality in Congress: "There are many more authorizers than appropriators."[34] Every member of an authorizing committee has an interest in limiting the domain of the appropriators. Thus, if the appropriations subcommittees regularly poach on the turf of the authorizing committees, reprisals by the parent chamber are inevitable. Of course, the appropriations subcommittees at times find it difficult to keep their work distinct from that of the authorizing committees. This is especially true of the defense subcommittees. With the advent of line-item authorizations, the authorizers increasingly have come to duplicate the work of the appropriators, and conflict between the committees has risen.

Despite the tendency of the appropriations subcommittees to avoid taking the lead on substantive matters, in the 1980s they began to move beyond budgeteering into the broader domain of policy making. In 1985 the House Appropriations Defense Subcommittee played a key role in imposing a moratorium on the testing of antisatellite weapons.[35] When the Bush administration sought to forgive Egypt's $6.7 billion debt to the United States in an effort to reward Egyptian support for Operation Desert Shield, Secretary of State James Baker entered into detailed negotiations with Representative Obey and Sen. Patrick Leahy (D-Vt.), the chair of the Senate Foreign Operations Subcommittee.[36] And when the Bush administration in 1991 postponed consideration of $10 billion in loan guarantees for Israel, Senator Leahy emerged as the primary broker between the White House and Congress.[37]

What explains the increased prominence of the appropriations subcommittees? The answer has less to do with the subcommittees than with the authorizing committees. Where the authorizing committee is strong, the appropriations subcommittee takes a back seat on policy issues. The Senate Appropriations Defense Subcommittee, for instance, remains closest to the traditional role of budgeteer. The reason is the strength of Senate Armed Services. When the two committees divide over policy issues, "neutral senators tend to side with Nunn, out of trust in his moderation and expertise, [and as a result] the appropriators do not want to fight him on the floor on *his* bill."[38]

In the 1980s, the House Appropriations Defense Subcommittee found itself in a different position. For much of the decade, the conservative majority on the House Armed Services Committee insisted on reporting authorization bills that ignored both budgetary constraints and the policy views of the House. With authorizations far exceeding what was likely to be appropriated and with the floor at odds with the Armed Services Committee, members of the Appropriations Defense Subcommittee found themselves caught in the middle of defense policy debates. The subcommittee responded by adopting whatever position commanded the support of a majority of the House. When Chairman Aspin finally consolidated his control over Armed Services, the authorization and appropriations figures came into closer alignment and House Armed Services reclaimed its role as the House's leading voice on defense policy.

Unlike the defense subcommittees, the foreign operations subcommittees effectively had no authorizing committee to respond to during the 1980s. With a foreign aid authorization bill passing Congress only in 1981 and 1985, the foreign operations subcommittees became responsible both for legislating and for funding foreign assistance programs. The growing length and complexity of the foreign aid appropriations bill attests to the result. In 1978, for example, the foreign operations appropriations bill spanned 12 pages with 27 general headings and 26 general provisions. By 1992, however, it ran 70 pages with 168 headings and 107 general provisions.

By all accounts, the foreign operations subcommittees draft their legislation in consultation with Foreign Relations and Foreign Affairs. But consultation, however extensive, cannot obscure the fact that the authorizers are the supplicants in the exchange. Because the subcommittees are free to strike out on their own path, one senior senator on Foreign Operations could say, with some hyperbole, that "it's the little old Foreign Ops [sub]committee, which is never on TV, that sets the foreign policy of the United States."[39]

THE INTELLIGENCE COMMITTEES

The House and Senate Permanent Select Committees on Intelligence are the newest entrants into the congressional fray on foreign policy. During the first three decades of the cold war, Congress avoided overseeing the intelligence community.[40] In the words of Sen. Leverett Saltonstall (R-Mass.), the lack of oversight resulted from Congress's "reluctance, if you will, to seek information and knowledge on subjects which I personally, as a Member of Congress and as a citizen would rather not have."[41] Efforts to overcome this reluctance made no headway. In 1955, Sen. Mike Mansfield (D-Mont.) submitted legislation creating a Joint Committee on Central Intelligence. The bill encountered stiff resistance; President Eisenhower pledged that "this kind of a bill would be passed over his dead body."[42] The Senate rejected Mansfield's bill by a two-to-one margin, "with half a dozen cosponsors voting against it."[43]

Congress's reluctance to oversee the intelligence community evaporated in the mid-1970s after the Church and Pike committees discovered that the CIA had repeatedly violated its charter and U.S. law. To rectify the situation, the Senate created an intelligence committee in 1976. The House followed suit a year later. Although both committees are designated select committees, meaning their charters are not written into the standing rules of the House or the Senate and their members are chosen by congressional party leaders rather than by the party caucuses, in practical terms they have the same rights and privileges as standing committees. Unlike other committees, though, tenure on the intelligence committees is limited to six consecutive years in the House and eight in the Senate. The term limits are intended both to involve more legislators in intelligence oversight—the committees, especially the House committee, are relatively small by congressional standards—and to make it less likely that the intelligence community will coopt its overseers. To foster bipartisanship in an extremely sensitive policy arena, Senate rules designate the ranking minority member as the vice-chair of the committee with the authority to run the committee in the absence of the chair.

The impact of the intelligence committees is difficult to assess.[44] The obvious problem is secrecy; the committees are designed to labor in obscurity. They seldom resort to public hearings: in the 1980s, neither committee held public hearings featuring CIA witnesses more than four times in a year. At the same time, most of the decisions the committees make, especially those having to do with funding decisions, are classified.

From what is known, the impact of the intelligence committees is mixed. In one well-known instance, the committees clearly failed. If a Beirut newspaper had not reported the arms-for-hostages deal, it is unlikely that the intelligence committees would have uncovered the Iran-contra affair. Yet Iran-contra also attests to the importance of the intelligence committees. Notification that the United States was aiding the contras led the House Intelligence Committee to try to bar U.S. aid from being used to overthrow the Sandinista government in Nicaragua. The ban evolved into the Boland amendments, which in turn fueled William Casey's desire for an off-the-books covert operations capability. If the intelligence committees had been ineffectual in their oversight efforts, Casey would not have felt compelled to bypass normal CIA channels.

The instances in which the intelligence committees succeed in changing policy attract nowhere near the attention given to failures such as Iran-contra. The asymmetry stems largely from the fact that while covert operations sell newspapers and books, most of the work of the intelligence committees involves issues that have a very limited appeal, even among the cognoscenti who follow foreign policy. Yet the committees have provided valuable critiques of CIA assessments, pushed the intelligence community to improve its human intelligence assets, and forced useful changes in budgets.[45] The committees have had a particular effect on nuclear verification issues. The Senate Intelligence Committee raised concerns about the verification procedures in the Intermediate Nuclear Forces Treaty that forced the secretary of state to return to Geneva to renegotiate parts of the treaty.[46]

The intelligence committees at times also influence plans for covert operations. In the vast majority of cases, the committees agree with the administration on the need for an operation, though individual members and staffers may object to potential risks. In a few instances in which the committees and the administration are known to have disagreed, the committees wanted to expand the scope of the operation. In the early 1980s, for instance, the committees demanded more spending on covert operations inside Afghanistan.[47] More often, though, when the committees disagree with the administration, they want the operation halted.

The precise number of covert operations the intelligence committees have killed or modified is not known publicly. But on at least four occasions the committees have stopped a covert operation. In 1978, the Senate Intelligence Committee deleted funds for one covert operation, thereby killing it.[48] In 1983, the intelligence committees persuaded President Reagan to rescind approval for a plan to fund the overthrow of the government of Suriname.[49] In 1988, the Senate Intelligence Committee reportedly derailed a plan to fund the overthrow of Panama's general Manuel Noriega.[50] And, in the late 1980s, the Senate Intelligence Committee forced the CIA to stop a covert program that funneled money to political candidates in Haiti who opposed Jean-Bertrand Aristide.[51] Because the administration does not need the approval of the intelligence committees to proceed with an operation, the burden rests with committee members to derail operations they think unwise. Besides voting to deny funding for an operation, the committees can try to block a covert action by voting on the wisdom of the operation (though no vote is required), holding private talks with administration officials, and threatening to expose classified information.

If Iran-contra does not mean that the intelligence committees are irrelevant, it does highlight their Achilles heel: they can oversee the intelligence community only if the executive branch shares information. Unlike the other committees concerned with foreign policy, the intelligence committees cannot count on the news media and interest groups to provide alternative sources of information (though the media and interest groups sometimes do provide leads that the committees follow). And while "virtually all CIA assessments go to the two congressional intelligence committees," access to CIA analyses does not guarantee that the committees will receive timely notification about policy decisions.[52] The committees have little recourse when administration officials withhold information or, worse yet, lie, as National Security Adviser Robert McFarlane did in 1985 when he responded to a letter from Rep. Lee Hamilton (D-Ind.), the chair of the House Intelligence Committee, raising questions about the activities of Oliver North by claiming "with deep personal conviction that at no time did I or any member of the National Security Council staff violate the letter or spirit" of the Boland restrictions.[53]

A second weakness of the intelligence committees stems from the compartmentalization of information. The two committees generally do not share information. Sometimes this causes great embarrassment. In 1984, for instance, Senator Goldwater, then chair of the Senate Intelligence Committee, lambasted Casey for failing to make it clear to the committee that the United States had begun to place mines in Nicaraguan harbors. It turned out that the House Intelligence Committee knew about the plan. By the same token, compartmentalization inhibits the sharing of information among staff members, which impedes oversight.[54]

The dependence on the executive branch for information and the compartmentalization of information mean that members of the intelligence committees face greater oversight costs than do their counterparts on other committees. As a result, successful intelligence oversight depends even more than usual on the presence of highly motivated members.[55] Unless some members of the intelligence committees are willing to invest time and effort in overseeing the CIA and related agencies, the committees are not likely to uncover instances of agency ineptitude or misjudgment.

The high level of member interest in the intelligence committees suggests that the supply of dedicated overseers is substantial. In 1983, nearly thirty members applied for three Democratic openings on the House Intelligence Committee.[56] In 1987, sixty representatives signed up for four openings on the House Intelligence Committee.[57] No doubt some members seek the assignment because of the prestige that comes with knowing the country's deepest secrets. But given the limited electoral utility of a seat on the intelligence committee, most members probably seek the assignment for policy reasons.[58]

To provide further stimulus to oversight, the House and Senate actively seek to balance the committees along ideological lines. For instance, when the House leadership appointed Rep. David McCurdy (D-Okla.), a conservative pro-defense Democrat, chair of the House Intelligence Committee in 1991, it balanced his appointment by appointing three die-hard liberals to the committee as well.[59] Congressional leaders try to promote a mix of political views in the belief that ideologically heterogeneous committees are less likely to be coopted by the intelligence community and more likely to command respect on the floor of the House and Senate.

THE FLOOR

Although committees carry most of the burden of decision making in Congress, their decisions still must win the approval of their parent chambers.

And since the end of the Vietnam War the foreign policy committees have found it more difficult to secure that approval. The rising number of challenges from the floor reflects the tremendous decentralization that swept Congress in the 1970s. The members that came to Capitol Hill in the wake of Vietnam and Watergate were far more inclined than their predecessors to dismiss committee decisions and to follow their own political and policy interests.

The change in norms about challenging committee decisions has fueled a sharp rise in the number of informal congressional caucuses seeking to influence foreign policy. Whereas there were only three ad hoc foreign policy caucuses when Dwight Eisenhower stepped down as president, during Ronald Reagan's presidency there were nearly one hundred.[60] Many caucuses deal with matters pertaining to constituency economic interests (the Steel Caucus and the Textile Caucus). Others address ethnic and regional interests (the Ad Hoc Congressional Committee on Irish Affairs and Friends of Ireland). Still others address the policy interests of members of Congress (the Congressional Working Group on China and the Military Reform Caucus).

Whether acting on their own or through ad hoc caucuses, committee outsiders frequently try to influence which issues appear on committee agendas and how legislation is drafted. But the bulk of the activity by outsiders comes once legislation hits the floor. At the extreme, outsiders can push for the rejection of a committee bill, as the House did in 1991 when it voted down the foreign aid authorization bill. Far more commonly, though, outsiders try to amend committee legislation rather than to defeat it outright.

As was true of Congress more generally, the number of floor amendments on foreign policy exploded in the 1980s. Because appropriations bills in recent years have almost always come in the last days of the legislative session (often in the form of mammoth omnibus continuing resolutions) when little time is available for debate, the authorization bills are the most popular targets of amendments. In the case of the defense authorization bill, during the 1970s the House and Senate considered on average twenty-four amendments each year; in the 1980s they each averaged more than three times that number.[61] While the foreign aid and State Department bills are reported biannually or not at all, they too trigger extensive amending activity when they come to the floor. The 1987 State Department authorization act, for instance, attracted eighty-six amendments on the Senate floor.[62]

The increased number of floor amendments is due to a host of different factors. The new, more aggressive legislators who arrived in the 1970s were more inclined to buck the committee system and to offer their own amendments. The legislative agenda also became more complex as the domestic impact of foreign policy, the number of interest groups, and the size of congressional staff all grew. But the biggest reason for the surge in amending activity was the politicization of defense and foreign policy during the Reagan years. Deep policy differences often separated the floor from its own committees, and members on the floor turned to amendments to shape legislation to their liking. At the same time, the tremendous publicity that attended many foreign policy debates increased the electoral value of floor amendments. As Senator Nunn once complained, "There is much greater public relations value in a floor amendment—irrespective of its value—than there is in proceeding with responsible suggestions through the committee process."[63]

The parent chambers are not, however, as influential as the raw number of amendments might suggest. To begin with, the procedural machinations that attend controversial issues inflate the number of amendments. For example, when it became clear in 1983 that the nuclear freeze resolution had enough votes to pass in the House, freeze opponents launched a "filibuster by amendment" rather than admit defeat.[64] Over the course of six days of debate they offered a slew of amendments, each time hoping to find some politically appealing language that would gut the resolution. At one point, opponents "were writing amendments faster than the leadership could close debate and vote on them."[65] In the end, the freeze debate generated roughly one hundred floor amendments, even though the outcome of the vote was known from the start.

Whatever the motive for offering amendments, most are rejected on the floor or dropped in conference. And of those that succeed in running the legislative gauntlet, most make trivial changes in the committee bill. During the freeze debate, for example, supporters employed an "'embrace or deflate' strategy whereby they accepted harmless amendments."[66] Likewise, in 1992 the House Armed Services Committee disposed of sixty-six of the more than one hundred amendments pending on the defense authorization bill by approving them en bloc.[67] The vast majority of the sixty-six amendments simply requested reports or expressed the nonbinding sentiment of Congress.

Although the floor seldom overrules the committees on major issues, amending activity has considerable indirect impact. Committees are powerful to the extent to which they can usher their legislation through Congress. As a staff member on House Armed Services puts it: "Whatever else the committee and its staff accomplish, they must draw up legislation that will be approved. Defeats on the floor for whatever reason must be avoided like the plague."[68] When hawks on the House Armed Services Committee forgot this lesson in the early 1980s, they found their influence on Capitol Hill diminished. As a result, pressure from the floor gives committees incentives both to review administration policy aggressively and to incorporate strongly held floor views into the legislation they report.

The controversy in the mid-1980s over the Defense Department's policy on the pricing of spare parts illustrates the indirect influence the floor has on committees. Once rank-and-file legislators began to garner national head-lines with stories about how the Air Force was paying $1,000 for a plastic stool cap and $7,000 for a coffee maker, the defense committees suddenly made investigations of Pentagon procurement practices a top priority. In the same vein, the explosion of floor activity on arms control issues in the early 1980s pushed the defense committees into giving nuclear weapons programs a much closer political scrub.[69]

PARTY LEADERS

For the first quarter century after the end of World War II, congressional party leaders shied away from foreign policy issues. In the golden era of bipartisanship, party leaders saw their duty as supporting the president in foreign affairs.[70] The support cut across party lines. As late as 1970, Demo-cratic leaders in the House manipulated procedures to prevent amendments seeking to reverse the foreign policies of a Republican president from coming to a vote on the floor.[71] And while party leaders often insisted that Congress had a responsibility to advise the president, they seldom insisted on true consultation. Senate Majority Leader Mansfield's admonition to his col-leagues in 1962 captured the traditional view held by congressional party leaders: Congress should not "look over the President's shoulder 24 hours a day . . . telling him how to conduct the foreign policy of the United States. That is the President's responsibility. . . . It will be a disservice to the Nation . . . to impede him, for whatever reason, in exercising it."[72]

Tradition was turned on its head in the 1980s. Although Republican party leaders remained stalwart supporters of presidential prerogative—no doubt reflecting which party held the White House—Democratic party leaders increasingly challenged the president. Rather than encouraging legislators to defer to the president, Democratic leaders began to mobilize rank-and-file Democrats on foreign policy issues where there were clear party splits. With the Senate in Republican hands from 1981 to 1986, House Democratic leaders were far more active than their Senate counterparts. During the nuclear freeze debate, the House Democratic leadership developed a sophisticated vote mobilization operation built around issue-specific task forces. "From the mid-1980s on, such leadership task forces worked on selected arms control amendments with an impressive record of success."[73] When conservative members of the House Armed Services Committee undercut the work of the task forces by conceding floor amendments in conference, Speakers Thomas P. "Tip" O'Neill (D-Mass.) and Jim Wright (D-Tex.) responded by appointing special conferees who could be counted on to defend House positions.[74]

Democratic congressional leaders also assumed a more prominent role as party spokesmen in the 1980s. To counteract the media success of Ronald Reagan, the House Democratic leadership devoted considerable effort to improving its media operation. Top leaders appeared on more weekend interview shows, scheduled additional meetings with key reporters, and set aside time to plan their daily media message.[75] For much of the 1980s Senate Democratic leaders lagged behind their House counterparts in prominence, partly because the chamber was controlled by Republicans for six years and partly because Democratic leader Robert Byrd (D-W. Va.) came across badly on television.[76] The presumed effectiveness of George Mitchell (D-Maine) as a spokesperson aided his election as majority leader in 1989. Mitchell fulfilled the expectations, taking the lead in criticizing the Bush administration's policy toward China after the Tiananmen Square massacre as well as on other issues.

The sudden activism of Democratic party leaders flows from the demands of their job: to meet the needs of the party rank and file. Members have come to "expect their leadership to help them pass legislation that further their legislative goals. Increasingly they also expect their leaders to act as spokesmen, explaining party positions to the media, and thus to the public, thereby advancing their policy goals and often providing political protection."[77] As foreign policy issues came to the forefront of the congressional agenda in the 1980s, Democratic leaders faced intense pressure to lead, pressure they could ignore only at their own peril.

The pressure on Democratic congressional leaders to take a more active role in foreign policy was most visible during the House debate over the MX missile. Speaker O'Neill was the only member of the Democratic leadership to oppose the House decision in May 1983 to release funds for flight testing the MX. Angered by the support that party leaders gave the Reagan administration, House Democrats opposed to the MX began to speak privately of unseating members of the leadership who supported the missile in the future. The threat worked. In another MX vote in July, only Majority Whip Thomas S. Foley (D-Wash.) voted to build the missile. In May 1984, however, he joined the rest of the House Democratic leadership in active opposition to the MX.[78]

This is not to say that the foreign policy activism of Democratic congressional leaders comes solely in response to pressures from the rank and file. Speaker Wright's forceful (if questionable) initiative in November 1987 to mediate among the parties to the Nicaraguan civil war probably surpassed what House Democrats expected of him, and Majority Leader Mitchell's impassioned criticisms of U.S. policy toward China no doubt reflected genuine disagreement with the White House. Yet in the final analysis, congressional party leaders operate primarily as agents of their members rather than as independent actors. If foreign policy issues cease to animate Democrats or come to divide rather than unite them—developments likely to happen with Bill Clinton in the Oval Office—the activism of Democratic party leaders will decline. By the same token, however, Republican congressional leaders undoubtedly will abandon their "My president right or wrong" stance with the White House in Democratic hands.

CONGRESSIONAL STAFF

Members of Congress occupy the spotlight when the House and Senate address foreign policy issues. But members do not labor alone. The immensity of the congressional workload forces them to delegate considerable responsibility. Today much of the work of analyzing policy proposals, drafting legislation, and writing speeches is done by congressional staff.

The staff members with the greatest influence on foreign policy are those who work for the foreign policy committees. Table 1 shows the growth in committee staff in the 1970s and 1980s. The size of most committee staffs at least doubled in the two decades after 1970, with the staff of Foreign Affairs increasing nearly fivefold. What also stands out in table 1 is that the staff assigned to the appropriations subcommittees remains small. "The subcommittees can live with these numbers because their job is basically reactive and critical."[79]

The organization of staff varies from committee to committee. Some, such as the House Armed Services Committee and the House Appropriations Defense Subcommittee, work through a unified staff. Others, such as Senate Armed Services and Senate Foreign Relations, have separate majority and minority staff. However staff are allocated between Democrats and Republicans, most committee staff work in a bipartisan fashion. The one exception is Foreign Relations. The partisanship among its staff reflects the deep ideologi-

Table 1

Staffs of the House and Senate Foreign Policy Committees, Various Years

Committee	1970	1975	1981	1985	1989
House					
Foreign Affairs	21	54	84	97	98
Armed Services	37	38	49	64	66
Appropriations	71	98	127	182	196
(Defense)	n.a.	(3)	(11)	(12)	(12)
(Foreign Operations)	n.a.	(1)	(2)	(3)	(4)
Intelligence	—	—	15	15	12
Senate					
Foreign Relations	31	62	59	61	58
Armed Services	19	30	36	48	51
Appropriations	42	72	79	85	80
(Defense)	(4)	n.a.	(5)	(7)	(10)
(Foreign Operations)	(2)	n.a.	(2)	(3)	(4)
Intelligence	—	—	2	30	40

Sources: Staff figures for Foreign Affairs, Foreign Relations, Armed Services, and the full appropriations committees are taken from Norman J. Ornstein, Thomas E. Mann, and Michael J. Malbin, *Vital Statistics on Congress, 1991–1992* (Washington, D.C.: CQ Press, 1992), pp. 131–34. Figures on the defense appropriations subcommittees, the foreign operations subcommittees, and the intelligence committees are derived from *Congressional Staff Directory* (Mount Vernon, Va.: Congressional Staff Directory, various years). *Congressional Staff Directory* did not provide a separate list of staff assigned directly to the House Appropriations Defense Subcommittee and the House Appropriations Foreign Operations Subcommittee in 1970. *Congressional Staff Directory* did not provide a separate list of staff assigned directly to the Senate Appropriations Defense Subcommittee and the Senate Appropriations Foreign Operations Subcommittee in 1975.

cal differences among committee members and the lack of leadership from the chair.

If the staffs of the foreign policy committees generally operate in a spirit of bipartisanship, they, like the committees they work for, differ in how they define their jobs. Some committee staff focus on big picture questions. The staffs of the armed services committees, for instance, are sometimes likened to think tanks. The staffs of Foreign Affairs and Foreign Relations similarly emphasize policy questions. In contrast, the staffs of the appropriations subcommittees shy away from policy issues and focus on budgetary details. As one appropriations staff member explains: "Whenever we get a new guy here . . . most want to do policy, to generate a think piece. . . . I say 'No,

No, we're a creature of the Appropriations Committee, it's about money! How'd you use it last year, why do you need $150 million this year?'"[80] Likewise, the staffs of the intelligence committees primarily address technically complex intelligence matters.

Second in importance to the committee staff in shaping congressional action on foreign policy are personal staff members. In 1989 the House employed 7,569 personal staff, and the Senate employed 3,387.[81] Although the House employs twice the number of personal staff, the staff members must be distributed across four times as many legislators. The result is that while most senators employ at least one foreign policy specialist, most representatives do not. The training of the personal staff who work foreign policy issues varies greatly, with level of expertise generally being greater in the Senate.

The ability of members of Congress to address foreign policy issues is further strengthened by the four congressional support agencies. The two most important are the General Accounting Office (GAO), which in 1989 had 1,519 staff members working directly for Congress, and the Congressional Research Service (CRS), which had 860 staff members. GAO operates as Congress's watchdog agency, investigating the efficiency and performance of federal agencies and programs. CRS functions as an information resource for the entire Congress, providing historical research, summaries of legislation, and legal and policy analysis on the request of any member. Less central on foreign policy matters is the work of the Congressional Budget Office (226 staff members) and the Office of Technology Assessment (143).[82]

The activism of congressional staff frequently provokes complaints that they are independent policy makers elected by no one.[83] Yet while some staff members at times do pursue their own agendas, on the whole, most operate as subordinate agents. No one doubts, for instance, that the staff of the Senate Armed Services Committee carry out the wishes of Senator Nunn or that the staff of the appropriations subcommittees do the bidding of Representative Obey and Senator Leahy. As former Rep. Charles Whalen (R-Ohio) remarks: "It must be remembered that [staff] do not exercise a Svengali-like influence over their 'bosses.' Rarely, if ever, is a representative moved to sponsor a proposition with which he disagrees. What staff expansion has done, however, is broaden a congressman's participation both in his field of specialization . . . and in those areas where he has little personal knowledge, expertise, or committee involvement."[84]

CONCLUSION

It sometimes seems as if everyone in Congress has a say in foreign policy. But primary authority over foreign policy in Congress rests where one would expect it, in the eight committees most directly concerned with foreign affairs. The big eight committees, however, are not equal in stature. In the 1980s the Senate Foreign Relations Committee and the House Foreign Affairs Committee increasingly found themselves pushed toward the margins of policy making. Their loss of influence came about partly because the foreign policy issues that spawned the most impassioned debate fell in the jurisdiction of the armed services, appropriations, and intelligence committees.

But jurisdiction is not destiny. The declining importance of Foreign Relations and Foreign Affairs also derives from the fact the neither committee enjoys dynamic leadership. Committees such as Senate Armed Services and House Armed Services grew in stature in the 1980s because their chairs established control over the staff and pursued well-defined legislative agendas. Whether the armed services committees maintain their influence or Foreign Relations and Foreign Affairs regain theirs ultimately depends on the ability of their chairs to assemble a working legislative majority.

4 SUBSTANTIVE LEGISLATION

ON THE MORNING OF 4 JUNE 1989, Chinese troops poured into Beijing's Tiananmen Square, killing hundreds of prodemocracy demonstrators. The reaction in Congress to the massacre was swift. Members rushed to condemn the killings, and congressional staffers began to draft legislation that would punish the Chinese government for the massacre and the subsequent crackdown on protestors. By the end of June, dozens of pieces of retaliatory legislation had been introduced in both the House and the Senate. Most of the legislation sought to penalize the Chinese government by revoking the country's most-favored-nation trade status.

Nineteen months later in January 1991 the House and Senate responded to another foreign policy crisis: the Iraqi occupation of Kuwait. Despite initially denying that congressional authorization was needed to send troops into combat, President Bush asked Congress to approve his decision to liberate Kuwait by force. After months of informal discussions on Capitol Hill on the merits of Operation Desert Shield, members of Congress suddenly found themselves asked to choose between economic sanctions and war.

The congressional reaction to Tiananmen Square and the congressional debate over the Gulf War illustrate the most well-known policy-making tool available to members of Congress: the authority to write laws that specify the substance of U.S. relations with other countries. But the struggles over China policy and the Gulf War also highlight the limits inherent in substantive legislation: members of Congress find it difficult to pass laws the president opposes or to withhold their approval for laws he wants. Despite overwhelming congressional support, none of the bills introduced in the immediate aftermath of the Tiananmen Square massacre became law. And despite widespread misgivings about the wisdom of a war with Iraq, members of Congress gave President Bush the authority he requested.

The difficulties faced by members of Congress in trying to write their foreign policy preferences into law are usually attributed to the inherent advantages of the presidency, the pro-executive branch bias of the Supreme Court, the institutional and partisan divisions on Capitol Hill, and the electoral calculations of members. But equally important in explaining why members of Congress seldom defeat the president on foreign policy is that they often have sound *policy* reasons for not wanting to win. The rejection of a presidential request may jeopardize U.S. relations with other countries. Legislation almost by necessity is rigid, but diplomacy usually requires flexibility. Congress acts slowly, but issues can change rapidly. In some cases, resorting to legislation may mean taking a sledgehammer to a problem that requires a scalpel. Legislation may even create perverse incentives: presidents may drag their feet implementing congressional directives because they believe any policy failure will be blamed on Congress. In short, members often do not want to win because they believe that legislated solutions will prove unwise or unworkable in practice.

The disadvantages of substantive legislation push members of Congress to view the threat of legislation as a lever with which to extract policy concessions from the administration. Members calculate that presidents and their advisers will prefer to concede some points to satisfy congressional sentiment rather than risk either being denied necessary legislative authority or being saddled with more restrictive legislation. The use of legislation as a lever highlights the danger of judging the importance of Congress in the making of foreign policy by counting how many bills it passes. Members may be willing to suffer a legislative defeat if the administration tailors its policies to incorporate congressional reservations.

TREATIES AND
EXECUTIVE AGREEMENTS

The most visible legislative tool that Congress, or more accurately, the Senate, has to influence foreign policy is the treaty power. In international law, treaties are binding contracts between nations. But in constitutional law no treaty commitment becomes binding unless the Senate gives the required two-thirds consent. Thus, by granting or withholding its consent the Senate can greatly shape U.S. relations with the rest of the world and has sometimes done so.

In making treaties subject to the approval of the Senate, the framers deliberately excluded the House of Representatives. The reason for the exclusion lay in the concern that representatives elected every two years would lack the political maturity needed to handle foreign policy matters of supreme significance. As John Jay put it in "Federalist No. 64": "They who wish to commit the [treaty] power . . . to a popular assembly, composed of members constantly coming and going in quick succession, seem not to recollect that such a body must necessarily be inadequate to the attainment of those great objects, which require to be steadily contemplated in all their relations and circumstances." In contrast, Jay and others believed that six-year terms would allow senators to "continue in place a sufficient time to become perfectly acquainted with our national concerns, and to form and introduce a system for the management of them."[1]

In assigning the treaty power to the Senate, the framers expected that senators would consult closely with the president throughout the negotiating process. In one of his earliest acts as president, George Washington sought to breathe life into this vision. Four months after his inauguration, Washington went to the Senate to solicit advice on the terms of a treaty with the Creek Indians. Worried that Washington's presence would inhibit frank discussion, opponents of the proposed treaty successfully pushed for a two-day delay so the Senate could consider the issue. Insulted by the Senate's reluctance to discuss the treaty with him, Washington reportedly vowed "he would be damned if he ever went there again."[2]

Although Washington continued on occasion to solicit senatorial advice on treaty negotiations—though never again in person—the Senate's rebuff of his overture on the treaty with the Creek Indians marked a death blow to the advice function of the Senate.[3] Future presidents might include members of Congress on international delegations out of political pragmatism, or they might consult with trusted friends on Capitol Hill about the acceptability of negotiating proposals. But no president after Washington would feel obliged as a matter of tradition or constitutional principle to solicit the advice of the Senate before signing a treaty. Indeed, with the growth of the imperial presidency after World War II, presidents made it clear that they looked to the Senate, as Sen. J. William Fulbright (D-Ark.) once put it, not for advice and consent but for "consent without advice."[4]

Unable to compel the president to solicit its advice, the Senate today does not participate in treaty making in most instances until after the agreement is signed and its consent is needed. When faced with a finished treaty the Senate has three choices. First, it can consent to the treaty as proposed. As table 2 shows, the Senate approved 90 percent of the treaties submitted in the first two hundred years of the republic. The vast majority passed without change.

Second, the Senate may withhold its consent. It can do so simply by

Table 2
Fate of Treaties Submitted to the Senate, 1789–1992

	Number	Percent of All Treaties
Treaties approved by the Senate which entered into force	1,627[a]	90.1
Treaties that did not enter into force because of Senate action	178	9.9
a. Not acted on by the Senate	(118)[b]	(6.5)
b. Rejected because of changes made by the Senate	(43)	(2.4)
c. Rejected by Senate vote	(17)	(1.0)

Sources: Ellen C. Collier, "U.S. Senate Rejection of Treaties: A Brief Survey of Past Instances," Congressional Research Service, Report no. 87-305F, 30 March 1987, pp. 2–3, and U.S. Congress, Senate Committee on Foreign Relations, Legislative Calendar (various years).

Notes: [a] The total number of treaties listed here differs from that reported in table 3 because of differences in counting procedures.
[b] Treaties that were withdrawn because the Senate never took action on them or which had been pending more than five years as of 1 January 1993.

refusing to consider an agreement. As table 2 shows, the Senate blocked 118 treaties between 1789 and 1992 by declining to act on them. On occasion a treaty may escape senatorial purgatory if political winds change. For instance, the Senate consented to the Geneva Protocol on chemical and bacteriological warfare in 1975, almost fifty years after it was first submitted for consideration.[5] Similarly, the Convention on the Prevention and Punishment of the Crime of Genocide languished in the Senate for more than thirty-five years before it was approved in 1986. But most treaties never emerge from purgatory. Of the 118 treaties the Senate refused to consider, 88 were subsequently withdrawn.[6]

Senators may also withhold consent by rejecting a treaty. As table 2 shows, outright defeats are rare. The Senate voted down only seventeen treaties between 1789 and 1992. Most of the defeated treaties dealt with minor matters. Only three—the treaty annexing Texas, the Treaty of Versailles, and the treaty creating the World Court—involved matters of great historical import. Moreover, once the United States claimed the role of global superpower, the Senate became particularly reluctant to reject treaties. Only two of the more than five hundred treaties signed in the four decades after the end of World War II went down to defeat on the Senate floor.[7]

In between the extremes of accepting or rejecting a treaty, the Senate has the third option of modifying it. Senators can do so in several ways. First, in a practice that dates back to the Jay Treaty of 1794, the Senate can amend a treaty. In the early years of the Republic a treaty could be amended only with the approval of two-thirds of the Senate, but in 1868 senators rewrote the standing rules of the chamber to give themselves the right to amend treaties by majority vote. When the Senate attaches amendments to a treaty, the new language changes the formal text of the agreement, and, if it is accepted by the signatories, it becomes binding law. Thus, during the debate over the Panama Canal treaties the Senate attached the so-called leadership amendments, which reaffirmed the right of the United States to intervene if the security of the canal was threatened as well as the right of U.S. warships to expeditious passage through the canal.

The Senate also can modify a treaty through less far-reaching changes such as reservations and understandings. Unlike treaty amendments, reservations and understandings are not binding. Many simply state the Senate's interpretation of the treaty. Others address agreements that technically are not part of the treaty but that senators believe merit a formal statement. For example, in the negotiations that led to the signing in 1991 of the treaty on conventional forces in Europe (CFE), the Soviet Union pledged to neutralize an additional 60,000 weapons not covered by the agreement. When the treaty was submitted to the Senate, the Foreign Relations Committee added a reservation stating that the Soviet pledge was "so important to U.S. vital interests that, if it were violated, the United States would consider exercising its rights to withdraw from the pact or to deviate from compliance in some way that was proportionate to the Soviet action."[8]

Reservations and understandings sometimes state the Senate's view of the obligations of the executive branch. For instance, in 1985 the Reagan administration proclaimed a new interpretation of the ABM treaty. Administration officials based the reinterpretation on the claim that the testimony given by executive branch officials in the 1972 hearings on the treaty had been inaccurate. Many senators objected to the administration's stand, arguing that if presidents were free to reinterpret treaties as they saw fit, the Senate's role in the treaty-making process would be reduced, as Sen. Sam Nunn (D-Ga.) put it, to that of "potted plants."[9] To discourage future presidents from unilaterally reinterpreting U.S. treaty obligations, the Foreign Relations Committee attached declarations to both the Intermediate Nuclear Forces (INF) Treaty and the CFE treaty stipulating that Senate approval hinged on the "assumption that administration witnesses testifying to Senate committees had provided 'authoritative' testimony."[10]

So long as amendments and reservations are acceptable to all the signatories (including the president)—as they were in the case of the CFE, INF, and Panama Canal treaties—a treaty will go into effect. But senatorial changes are not always acceptable. As table 2 shows, the Senate killed more than forty treaties between 1789 and 1992 by adding unacceptable stipulations. Killing treaties with amendments and reservations is not a new tactic. The first such rejection came in 1803 when changes made by the Senate prompted Great Britain to disavow the King-Hawkesbury Convention.[11] Because so-called killer amendments can enable opponents to scuttle a treaty under the guise of improving it, treaty opponents find them politically attractive. Perhaps the best-known use of killer amendments came during the debate over the Treaty of Versailles, where Sen. Henry Cabot Lodge (R-Mass.), President Wilson's archfoe, decided early on that the best strategy for defeating the treaty was to "proceed . . . by way of amendment and reservation."[12] More recently, conservative senators resorted to killer amendments in their (unsuccessful) bids to derail the Panama Canal and INF treaties.

The ability of the Senate to kill a treaty either directly or indirectly means that the law of anticipated reactions is likely to govern executive branch behavior.[13] Presidents facing strong opposition in the Senate have an incentive to negotiate a treaty that reflects senatorial views. Thus, when the Carter administration was negotiating the Panama Canal and SALT II treaties, it devoted considerable time and effort trying to draft agreements that would satisfy critics in the Senate. In the case of the Panama Canal treaties, the effort to anticipate senatorial reactions worked. In the case of SALT II, it failed.

But presidents need not always heed their critics. Presidents can skirt a truculent Senate through the use of executive agreements. As table 3 shows, executive agreements became the method of choice for concluding international agreements after the end of World War II. Executive agreements constitute a binding commitment by the United States, and they enjoy the same constitutional status as treaties.[14] And, like treaties, executive agreements may involve commitments of the greatest significance. The destroyers-for-bases deal of 1940, the Yalta and Potsdam agreements, and SALT I were all handled by executive agreement.

Where executive agreements differ from treaties is in not requiring the approval of two-thirds of the Senate. Indeed, most executive agreements require no congressional approval at all, either because they are based on the inherent powers of the presidency (especially the commander-in-chief clause)

Table 3

Number of Treaties and Executive Agreements, 1789–1990

Years	Number of Treaties	Number of Agreements	Percent of Total as Executive Agreements
1789–1839	60	27	31
1840–1889	215	238	57
1890–1939	524	907	63
1940–1949	116	919	89
1950–1959	138	2,229	94
1960–1969	114	2,324	95
1970–1979	173	3,040	95
1980–1990	170	3,851	96
Total	1,510	13,535	90

Sources: Michael Nelson, ed., *Congressional Quarterly's Guide to the Presidency* (Washington, D.C.: Congressional Quarterly, 1989), p. 1104, and Harold W. Stanley and Richard G. Niemi, *Vital Statistics on American Politics,* 4th ed. (Washington, D.C.: CQ Press, 1994), p. 280.

Note: The total number of treaties listed here differs from that reported in table 2 because of differences in counting procedures.

or because they are made pursuant to previous legislation (although the meaning of the legislation is often stretched to justify the agreement). For reasons having to do with statute, tradition, and political pragmatism, other executive agreements require the approval of a majority of both the House and Senate. Under U.S. law, for instance, all trade agreements are handled as executive agreements and must be submitted to Congress for simple majority approval. The Nixon administration submitted SALT I for congressional review because the legislation creating the Arms Control and Disarmament Agency stipulates that all executive agreements limiting U.S. weaponry must be approved by Congress.[15] Even when an executive agreement requires congressional approval, presidents prefer it to a treaty because they usually find it far easier to round up majority support in both chambers than a supermajority in the Senate.

If presidents can use executive agreements to nullify the treaty power of the Senate, what distinguishes an executive agreement from a treaty? Despite two hundred years of practice, no objective distinction exists. "When Senator Gillette of Iowa asked the State Department in 1954 to make everything perfectly clear, the Department (or so Gillette informed the Senate) replied 'that a treaty was something they had to send to the Senate to get approval by two-thirds vote. An executive agreement was something they did not have to send to the Senate.'"[16] In 1974, the State Department published Circular 175, which listed the criteria to be used for designating an agreement as either a treaty or an executive agreement.[17] But the criteria are open to interpretation. As a result, only the president decides whether an agreement with other nations will be handled as an executive agreement or as a treaty.

Senators can, of course, try to influence the president's decision. Their main leverage is the threat to make the administration pay a political cost if it fails to submit an agreement as a treaty. Such threats usually fail. In 1972, for example, the Senate twice approved resolutions urging President Nixon to submit agreements governing U.S. military bases abroad as treaties. Nixon ignored both resolutions. Presidents hold the upper hand in the battle at least in part because they can exploit institutional rivalries on Capitol Hill to defeat any Senate effort at retaliation. Because the House has no role in treaty making, representatives usually support administration decisions to proceed with executive agreements that require the majority approval of both chambers. In 1990, for instance, the Bush administration decided to treat a chemical weapons pact with the Soviet Union as an executive agreement rather than as a treaty, despite a formal protest by eighteen of the nineteen members of the Foreign Relations Committee. When Secretary of State James Baker subsequently appeared before the House Foreign Affairs Committee, Chairman Dante Fascell (D-Fla.) actually congratulated the administration for treating the pact as an executive agreement and not as a treaty.[18] (Consideration of the pact was subsequently held up by the disintegration of the Soviet Union.)

The extensive use of executive agreements periodically prompts concern on Capitol Hill. In the 1950s, proponents of the Bricker Amendment sought unsuccessfully to curtail their use. As criticism of the imperial presidency mounted in the 1960s, proposals to limit executive agreements reappeared on the congressional agenda. In 1969, the Senate passed the National Commitments Resolution, which stated that both the executive and the legislative branches should be involved in decisions to enter into agreements with other countries. Supporters of the resolution argued that presidents were using executive agreements to handle major foreign policy issues while relatively minor matters were being submitted as treaties. In one instance that critics found especially galling, President Johnson declined to tell the Senate he had committed the United States to defend Thailand against communist aggression but at the same time asked senators to approve a treaty with Thailand on the subject of double taxation.[19]

The National Commitments Resolution was, however, only symbolic legislation. It did not legally bind the executive branch, and the Nixon administration ignored it. Congress responded in 1972 by passing the Case-Zablocki Act. Amended in 1977, the act stipulates that the executive branch must inform Congress of all executive agreements within sixty days of their entering into force. Classified agreements are sent to the Senate Foreign Relations Committee and the House Foreign Affairs Committee with the understanding that the agreements are to remain secret.

The Case-Zablocki Act has had, at best, a modest impact. Its primary virtue is that it enables members of Congress to keep abreast of agreements made by the president. Even here, though, executive branch compliance is sometimes sluggish. In the first fifteen years the act was in place, one-fifth to one-third of all agreements were reported late.[20] And in the end, Case-Zablocki is no more than a notification requirement. Presidents remain free to conclude executive agreements as they see fit, and while in some circumstances a delay in notifying Congress might pose political costs for an administration, it has no effect on the legal status of an agreement. Although some members claim that all international agreements should be subject to congressional review, bills to give Congress the power to annul executive agreements remain unpopular.

THE WAR, TRADE, AND APPROPRIATIONS POWERS

The ability of Congress to specify the substance of foreign policy goes far beyond the treaty power of the Senate and instances in which the House and Senate are asked to approve executive agreements. Every year members of Congress consider a host of different bills and amendments that seek to translate substantive policy preferences into policy outcomes. This legislation generally falls pursuant to one of three powers of Congress: to declare war, regulate foreign commerce, and appropriate money. Unlike the case with treaties, Congress exercises the war, trade, and appropriations powers through simple majority approval (provided, of course, the president declines to veto the bill in question).

The most far-reaching step Congress can take in foreign affairs is to declare war. In all, Congress has declared war four times—the War of 1812, the Spanish-American War, World War I, and World War II—and recognized the existence of a state of war once in the case of the Mexican-American War.[21] (The Civil War was undeclared because a declaration of war would have recognized the legitimacy of the Confederate government.) Congress may also pass legislation which, while falling short of a formal declaration of war, authorizes the president to use military force. By one count, the president used military force pursuant to congressional authorization eighty times between 1798 and 1972, most notably in Vietnam in 1964 following the passage of the Gulf of Tonkin Resolution.[22] The most recent congressional authorization of force came, of course, in January 1991 at the start of the Gulf War.

Although Congress enjoys the power to declare war and to authorize the use of force, events have rendered the practical import of such authority questionable. As is well known, since the end of World War II Congress has been reluctant to exercise its war powers and presidents increasingly have come to claim far-reaching war powers of their own.[23] The debate over the Gulf War might be read to suggest that members of Congress have reclaimed at least part of their say over decisions to use force. But the point should not be pushed too far. Both the House and Senate refused to invoke the War Powers Resolution—despite a lack of executive-legislative consultation on the decision to use force to evict Iraq from Kuwait—and they both declined to vote on Bush's policy until one week before the U.N. deadline, when their freedom to exercise discretion was narrow. Likewise, in 1993, Congress refused to invoke the War Powers Resolution when U.S. peacekeeping troops in Somalia came under attack, and the Senate overwhelmingly defeated an amendment, initially sponsored by Senate Majority Leader Robert Dole (D-Kans.), that would have required President Clinton to obtain congressional authorization before he could send U.S. peacekeeping troops to Haiti.[24]

For all the attention given to declarations of war and authorizations of force, they are the least common type of substantive legislation. Much more common is substantive legislation that dictates U.S. trade relations with other countries. Most trade legislation deals with economic objectives. In any given year, members of Congress are likely to find themselves considering legislation to protect textile workers in South Carolina, auto workers in Michigan, and sugar farmers in Louisiana.

Congress may also use trade legislation to achieve political goals abroad. The underlying assumption here is that rewards or (more commonly) punishments will force other countries to alter their behavior. The neutrality acts of the 1930s were based on Congress's power to regulate foreign commerce. Although Pearl Harbor left neutrality legislation with a permanent stigma, economic sanctions remain a popular foreign policy tool on Capitol Hill. In 1978, Congress imposed trade sanctions on Uganda in an effort to destabilize the government of Idi Amin.[25] In a more famous case in 1986, Congress overrode President Reagan's veto and imposed trade sanctions on South Africa in an effort to pressure Pretoria into dismantling apartheid. And as noted at the beginning of the chapter, members of Congress responded to the Tiananmen Square massacre by trying to revoke China's most-favored-nation status.

Congress occupies solid constitutional ground when it flexes its muscles on trade policy. The Constitution, after all, specifically assigns it the power "to regulate commerce with foreign nations." As a result, debates over Congress's use of the trade power revolve around the prudence of congressional actions rather than their constitutionality. Thus, the debate over revoking China's most-favored-nation status turned on judgments about whether a carrot or a stick approach would work best in modifying the behavior of the Chinese government and not on whether Congress had the authority to withdraw most-favored-nation status.

Although members of Congress at times use trade legislation to achieve political and economic goals abroad, the most popular congressional instrument for influencing the substance of foreign policy is the appropriations power. Much of the effort in Congress to shape the substance of foreign policy is aimed at the various bills that authorize and appropriate funds for foreign and defense programs. The popularity of authorization and appropriations bills is due in part to the fact that dollars often are policy. Talk of a "Peace Shield" is just that if Congress refuses to fund ballistic missile defenses, and denunciations of Iraqi human rights abuses carry little weight if agricultural credits continue to flow to Baghdad.

Members of Congress use the power of the purse to accomplish a variety of ends. One of the most common is to stipulate how foreign aid can be spent. The practice of earmarking grew dramatically in the 1980s, to the point where the executive branch was left with relatively little discretion in how to spend foreign aid. The 1988 foreign aid bill, for example, earmarked specific spending levels for 92 percent of all military aid, 98 percent of all economic aid, and 49 percent of all development aid.[26] Members also use the appropriations power to dictate the content of defense policy. Throughout the 1980s and into the 1990s they fought amongst themselves and with the administration first over which weapons would be procured as part of the Reagan defense buildup and then over which ones would be terminated as part of the post–cold war build-down.

Congress also uses the appropriations power to give teeth to its other constitutional powers on foreign policy. On several occasions in the 1970s and 1980s, Congress used its control of the purse strings to limit U.S. military involvement abroad. The passage of the so-called Eagleton Amendment in 1973 compelled the Nixon administration to halt all U.S. military activities aimed at Cambodia and Laos. The Clark Amendment of 1975 barred the United States from aiding any military or paramilitary operations in Angola for nearly a decade. The Boland amendments placed constraints of varying intensity on the operation of the Nicaraguan contras.

In the same vein, Congress has used its power of the purse to protect the Senate's treaty power as well as to ensure that the United States complies with its treaty obligations. When the Reagan administration reinterpreted the ABM treaty to allow virtually unlimited testing of ABM technologies, supporters of the traditional interpretation turned to the defense authorization bill. In 1987, the armed services committees added provisions to the bill limiting the air force to only those tests of the Strategic Defense Initiative that would conform to the traditional interpretation of the ABM treaty.[27] Likewise, in 1986 Reagan announced that the United States would no longer comply with the limits on the number of submarines set forth in the (unratified) SALT II treaty. Opponents responded by inserting provisions in the 1987 and 1988 defense authorization bills that, without mentioning the treaty by name, directed the president to retire submarines in a fashion that kept the United States near SALT II's limits on warheads.

Besides giving Congress a means of enforcing treaty compliance by a reluctant president, appropriations give the House an opportunity to block implementation of a newly ratified treaty. The issue is an old one in U.S. history. When the Senate approved the Jay Treaty of 1794, opponents in the House sought to block the agreement by refusing to appropriate the funds needed to implement it. President Washington and the Chief Justice of the Supreme Court insisted that the House was constitutionally obligated to appropriate the funds because, once ratified, a treaty is the supreme law of the land. In the House, however, James Madison argued that representatives had a "clear constitutional right and duty . . . to deliberate on the expediency or inexpediency of carrying such Treaty into effect, and to determine and act thereon, as, in their judgment, may be most conducive to the public good."[28] The two sides eventually compromised. The House approved legislation appropriating the funds but added language affirming the right of Congress to withhold funding for treaties. Washington, in turn, agreed to sign the legislation.

The precedent set by Madison and his colleagues returned to haunt Jimmy Carter. When he asked Congress to appropriate the funds needed to implement the Panama Canal treaties, the House balked. Some representatives opposed the implementing legislation out of conviction, others because of electoral fright. Still other representatives saw the legislation as an opportunity to vent their spleen at continually being slighted on foreign policy matters. Rep. John Dingell (D-Mich.) castigated a group of administration officials sent to defend the request for funds: "We in the House are tired of you people in the State Department going to your tea-sipping friends in the Senate. Now you good folks come up here and say you need legislation [to implement the treaties] after you ignored the House. If you expect me to vote for this travesty, you're sorely in error."[29] When the conference committee issued its first report on the bill, the House rejected it. The House reversed itself only after the administration launched an intensive lobbying effort involving former secretary of state Henry Kissinger and other Republican notables.[30]

As the case of the Panama Canal treaties attests, the authority of Congress to use appropriations to shape policy is extensive.[31] The Supreme Court has never struck down any use of the appropriations power as an unconstitutional infringement on executive authority.[32] Some limits on the appropriations power do exist. In *United States v. Lovett*, the Court ruled that Congress cannot punish specific employees of the executive branch by refusing to fund their salaries. Although the issue is not settled, the appropriations power probably also cannot be used to nullify an enumerated power of the president. Thus, the Court in all likelihood would strike down any congressional effort to deny the president the funds needed to receive foreign ambassadors or to negotiate treaties. But aside from these two narrow exceptions, debate over Congress's use of the power of the purse, as with its use of the trade power, revolves around the prudence of its actions rather than their constitutionality. To take the disputes over defense procurement during the Reagan years, even as staunch an Irreconcilable as Secretary of Defense Dick Cheney acknowledged that "no one can dispute Congress's constitutional power to decide what weapons should be funded."[33]

THE LIMITS OF
SUBSTANTIVE LEGISLATION

The power to legislate gives members of Congress the ability to dictate the content of foreign policy. Several times during the 1980s, members did just that. In defense policy, Congress canceled plans by both the army and navy to develop a new generation of tactical nuclear missiles, blocked efforts to deploy an antisatellite weapon, limited deployment of the MX missile, and compelled the air force to develop the Midgetman missile.[34] In foreign policy, members blocked an attempt to reinterpret the ABM treaty, imposed sanctions on South Africa, and placed so many constraints on relations with El Salvador and Nicaragua that by the end of the Reagan presidency "U.S. policy toward Central America was effectively being set by Congress."[35]

Although substantive legislation is an indisputably powerful instrument of policy making, it has three distinct disadvantages. The first is that some aspects of foreign policy lie beyond the reach of legislation. It is well established in constitutional law and practice, for example, that the authority to negotiate lies with the president and not Congress. In the oft-quoted words of John Marshall: "The President is the sole organ of the nation in its external relations, and its sole representative with foreign nations."[36] Thus, while senators can refuse to consent to treaties and both senators and representatives can refuse to approve some executive agreements, they cannot compel the president to negotiate an agreement. As Ronald Reagan demonstrated when he refused to concede the Strategic Defense Initiative at the Strategic Arms Reduction Talks (START), so long as presidents are willing to take the political heat, they and they alone decide which proposals will be put on the negotiating table, when concessions will be made, or whether to negotiate at all.

Congress can, of course, pass legislation that has the indirect effect of limiting the president's negotiating leverage. A case in point arose during negotiation of the 1990 London Protocol on ozone depletion. The Bush administration initially resisted proposals by the Soviet Union and West Germany for a quick halt to the production of methyl chloroform, an industrial solvent that destroys stratospheric ozone. The administration abandoned its position, however, when Congress amended the Clean Air Act to require a rapid phase-out of methyl chloroform.[37] Yet the success Congress enjoyed on ozone depletion is an exception. Most efforts to constrain the president's negotiating flexibility through substantive legislation involve issues where presidential preferences are far more intense and where presidents are likely to spend more time trying to defeat legislation. Thus, President Reagan devoted considerable time and effort to defeating congressional efforts to kill weapons systems that he argued were essential to concluding an arms control agreement with the Soviet Union.

The second disadvantage of substantive legislation is that it is far easier to call for new laws than it is to pass them. One reason why Congress spends more time debating than doing is because presidents can veto legislation they dislike. If the president opposes a bill, it typically takes a supermajority of *both* houses before legislative preferences become law. When a bill seeking to condition China's most-favored-nation status on improvements in human rights came to the floor of the House and Senate in 1991, for example, it garnered the votes of 313 representatives and 55 senators—nearly 85 percent of the members of Congress. Yet the bill never became law; supporters lacked the votes needed to overturn President Bush's veto in the Senate. The battle over China's most-favored-nation status is typical. Congress overrode only two foreign policy vetoes between 1972 and 1993. The proven success of the veto means that members often drop efforts to write their policy preferences into law when confronted with solid presidential opposition.

Presidents generally see their vetoes sustained in part because they need to convince so few members of Congress to win. Thirty-four senators can frustrate the will of the other 501 members. Presidents also win because they have tremendous resources with which to sway undecided members. During the 1981 debate over the sale of AWACS aircraft to Saudi Arabia, for example, the Reagan administration doled out favors to several wavering senators. "These included: 1.) acceleration of a U.S. attorney appointment for a candidate favored by Charles Grassley (R-IA); 2.) money for a Public Health Service Hospital for Slade Gorton (R-WA); 3.) agreement not to campaign against Dennis DeConcini (D-AZ); and 4.) approval of a coal fired power plant for John Melcher (D-MT)."[38] When it comes to matching the rewards offered by the White House, congressional opponents are, in the words of then-House Majority Whip Thomas S. Foley (D-Wash.), "in a rowboat looking down 16-inch [battleship] guns."[39] The result of the imbalance in the abilities of the two branches to offer rewards means, as Sen. Lawton Chiles (D-Fla.) once noted, that "it's hard to beat the president. . . . You'd have to have 10 or 15 votes to spare because he can always get one or two [turned around]."[40]

The difficulties members face in navigating legislation through Congress cannot be attributed entirely to the presidential veto. Congress itself is also to blame. Institutional and partisan divisions mean that lacking consensus— and consensus is often absent on foreign policy—Congress will not act. Further exacerbating the tendency toward inertia is the sheer press of business on Capitol Hill. The legislative docket in Congress is overloaded. Foreign policy issues vie with domestic policy issues for attention. Many bills get lost in the shuffle.

Congressional inertia is hard to overcome even when the administration supports the bill. Take the effort in 1987 by Rep. William Broomfield (R-Mich.) to punish New Zealand for its decision to adopt a nuclear-free weapons policy by revoking its right to buy U.S. military goods at preferential rates. The Reagan administration welcomed the bill. Officials at Defense and State even suggested how to introduce the bill for maximum effect, and they asked that language in the bill giving the president discretion in revoking the preferences be deleted.[41] The amendment took nearly a year to wind its way through the House. Yet despite Broomfield's efforts and the support of the Reagan administration, the Senate never acted on it. The Broomfield Amendment finally died when the 100th Congress came to a close in January 1989.

Beyond the problems inherent in institutional design and partisan division, the ability of Congress to pass substantive legislation is complicated by the willingness of many members to defer to presidential leadership. Congressional deference derives partly from electoral calculations. Members want to avoid stands that might leave them open to blame and, thus, to punishment at the polls. Because much of the public believes in the need for strong presidential leadership, many members find that the politically safest course lies in following the president's lead. But to attribute congressional deference only to electoral calculations shortchanges members of Congress. Deference also stems from the belief, widely held on Capitol Hill, that the president *should* be allowed to lead on foreign policy. Contrary to the complaints of Irreconcilables and Skeptics alike, members recognize that they are ill-equipped to manage foreign policy and that a successful foreign policy requires strong presidential leadership.

Even if an issue lies within the reach of legislation and presidential opposition and congressional inertia can be overcome, substantive legislation faces a third disadvantage: law is inherently limited as a foreign policy instrument. One problem is that world events may make legislation obsolete overnight. In 1979, for instance, the House Foreign Operations Subcommittee responded to reports of human rights abuses by Emperor Jean-Bedel Bokassa by adding language to the foreign aid bill that barred all assistance to the Central African Empire. The emperor was overthrown, however, before the bill finished its legislative journey through Congress.[42]

The standard antidote for legislative rigidity is to give the president the right to waive provisions of a law if the circumstances warrant. But discretion also gives the president the opportunity to thwart congressional intent.[43] When Congress appropriated military aid for El Salvador in the early 1980s, it provided that the president "certify every six months that the Salvadoran government was 'achieving substantial control' of its armed forces . . . that it was 'implementing essential economic and political reforms,' . . . and that it was holding free elections and demonstrating a willingness to negotiate a political settlement."[44] President Reagan repeatedly provided the required certification, even though many observers doubted whether El Salvador had met any of the conditions.[45]

Presidents can find discretion even in legislation that appears to be quite specific. At the extreme they can ignore the law—as happened during the

Iran-contra affair. Far more often, though, presidents and their advisers simply read discretion into the law. The Reagan administration responded to legislation directing that aid to the contras be spent on humanitarian items by issuing "an executive order in March 1986 [that] defined surface-to-air missiles and training by U.S. Special Forces as 'humanitarian aid.'"[46] White House officials have demonstrated similar ingenuity on issues of less renown. For instance, the so-called Pressler Amendment, which states that "no assistance shall be furnished to Pakistan and no military equipment or technology shall be sold or transferred to Pakistan" if it developed a nuclear weapons capability, turned out to mean less in practice than its sponsors thought. In 1992 the Bush administration approved commercial military sales to Pakistan, even though Pakistani officials admitted their country had the ability to make nuclear weapons. A State Department legal adviser defended the arms sales on the grounds that the Pressler Amendment was attached to the foreign aid bill and did not specifically ban commercial sales.[47] As Chapter 7 discusses at greater length, members of Congress have received little help from federal courts in their efforts to limit the ability of the executive branch to read discretion into laws.

If the value of substantive legislation is undercut by the need to give the president discretion and the president's ability and willingness to find discretion in the law, it is also diminished by the public nature of the legislative process. Diplomatic success often hinges on secrecy. The same promises and threats that work in private may fail miserably in public. This is especially true when the aim is to compel another country to change its behavior. Members of Congress learned the lesson the hard way with the passage of the Jackson-Vanik Amendment in 1974. While poking a finger in the eye of the Soviet Union proved emotionally and politically satisfying to many members, it resulted in a dramatic drop in the rate of Jewish emigration, the very opposite of what the law was designed to accomplish.

The value of legislation may also be diminished by the need to compromise. To navigate a bill through Congress, its sponsors must be willing to modify the language of the proposed law until it satisfies a majority of Congress as well as the White House. When the issue at stake is one of distributive politics, a willingness to split the difference works quite well. But many foreign policy issues do not involve distributive politics. In these instances, what results from the process of give and take can be legislation that disappoints both its supporters and its critics.

Efforts to stop U.S. bombing in Indochina provide a case in point. In early 1973, the Nixon administration resumed saturation bombing of Cambodia to stave off a Khmer Rouge advance on Phnom Penh. Opponents in Congress responded by trying to cut off all funding for air operations over Cambodia. After months of wrangling and one presidential veto, President Nixon and Congress settled on compromise legislation that put a forty-five day deadline on the bombing. Thomas Franck and Edward Weisband point out the sense-lessness of the compromise law:

> If the object was to spare further Cambodian suffering and prevent possible loss of pilots, then the instrumentally correct answer should have been to stop at once rather than to go on bombing pointlessly for more than another month. If the intention was to inflict costs on the Khmer Rouge in order to induce them to negotiate, only a policy of bombing for the indefinite future could hope to advance that purpose. As soon as the Communists knew that bombing would end at a legislative deadline, the aerial war lost whatever psychological capacity it once might have had to induce restraint.[48]

Because compromises may result in self-defeating legislation, members may find that half a legislative loaf proves to be more damaging than none at all.

Legislation may also have the perverse effect of advancing the president's agenda and not Congress's. When Congress legislates its preferences, the policy in question ceases to be the responsibility of the president and becomes the responsibility of Congress. Presidents may in turn drag their feet imple-menting congressional directives, calculating that any policy failure will be blamed on Congress. During the battle over the MX missile, for example, many swing voters worried that killing the missile would encourage Presi-dent Reagan to filibuster at the START talks. Swing voters argued that if the MX were canceled, Reagan would blame Congress for robbing him of the leverage he needed to conclude an arms control agreement.[49]

The administration may even see legislation as a convenient scapegoat for policies that have begun to go bad. For example, when Congress debated motions in 1975 to cut off all U.S. aid to the Angolan rebels, a bipartisan group of senior senators approached Secretary of State Henry Kissinger with a proposal: Congress would continue some funding for the rebels while the administration quietly phased out the Angolan operation. Even though a motion to terminate the aid clearly had the votes needed to pass, the secretary of state declined the offer. "The Senators concluded that Kissinger knew that the operation was a fiasco and simply wanted to shift the blame to Con-gress."[50]

SUBSTANTIVE LEGISLATION
AS A LEVER

Members of Congress know firsthand that substantive legislation is a flawed policy-making tool. But rather than abandoning efforts to legislate policy preferences into law, many members view debate over substantive legislation as a lever with which to shape policy. Administration critics often can extract major policy concessions from the White House if there is strong opposition to executive branch policy on Capitol Hill.

It should be noted from the start that not all members of Congress will look at a given bill as leverage. Attitudes toward any piece of legislation are as varied as its supporters. While some supporters may be willing to trade their votes for policy concessions, others may not. During the MX debate, for example, about one-third of the anti-MX coalition was composed of members who opposed procuring the missile under any condition. These die-hard opponents tended to dismiss swing voters, in the words of Rep. James Shannon (D-Mass.), as politicians "who will take any position they need to take to become players on a big issue."[51] Thus, in a very real sense the threat to legislate is ultimately the tool of the moderates in the congressional debate.

In using substantive legislation as a lever, members of Congress count on the power of anticipated reactions. Just as the possibility that the Senate will reject a treaty encourages the administration to anticipate senatorial views, members hope that officials in the executive branch will conclude that it is better to concede on some issues and thereby defeat a legislative initiative than it is to stand firm and run the risk Congress will pass even more restrictive legislation. The utility of legislation as a lever presumes, of course, that grounds for compromise exist. This need not be the case. Issues such as whether or not to use force to evict Iraq from Kuwait have no middle ground. Yet most foreign policy issues do offer the possibility of compromise; hence, the threat of legislating congressional preferences becomes useful leverage in executive-legislative negotiations.

Examples abound of presidents changing the substance of their policy proposals in order to defeat even more restrictive legislation. In the case of defense policy, for example, Congress seldom kills weapon systems outright. But many legislative battles force the administration to make significant changes to procurement plans. In 1969, for example, President Nixon replaced the Sentinel ABM program with the Safeguard system when it became unlikely that the Senate would approve further funding for Sentinel. President Carter advanced several variants of the multiple protective shelter basing mode to contain opposition to the MX missile. Finally, President Reagan abandoned his October 1981 interim silo basing plan for the MX as well as several successor basing options because of opposition on Capitol Hill.[52]

Many members find the threat of legislation useful in shaping trade policy. When members become dissatisfied with the administration's handling of trade issues, they turn quickly to protectionist legislation. A flurry of trade bills usually prompts proponents of free trade to cry that the protectionist wolf is at the door. Robert Pastor observes: "As the debate proceeds, and restrictive pressures become more threatening, several new developments occur. . . . the Executive shows, in various ways, that it is listening to the Congress. . . . In short, the signals from Congress are received, and upon recognizing this, the congressional frustration quotient drops, and a liberal trade law is passed, or at the least, a restrictive bill fails."[53]

The Reagan administration's behavior in the mid-1980s illustrates the dynamic on trade policy. The administration initially neglected trade policy, preferring to rely on market forces. The attitude of neglect changed in a hurry when a spate of protectionist bills appeared on the congressional calendar. Then-Vice President George Bush explained the administration's sudden interest in trade issues in blunt terms: "Frankly, we are trying as hard as we can to derail the protectionist juggernaut now sweeping through the United States Congress. . . . That's one more reason why our recent actions have been necessary. If we don't demonstrate good faith in enforcing our existing trade laws, we risk inviting sterner medicine from Congress."[54]

The threat of legislation sometimes provides members of Congress with a lever with which to push the administration to change policies that themselves are not subject to legislation. The route is through what can be called hostage taking, using legislation aimed at one issue to pressure the president to change his foreign policy. The MX debate provides a classic example. Many of the swing voters in the MX debate were concerned less with the missile itself than with what they saw as the Reagan administration's lack of interest in pursuing arms control talks. Led by the so-called Gang of Six— Reps. Les Aspin (D-Wis.), Norman Dicks (D-Wash.), and Albert Gore (D-Tenn.), and Sens. William Cohen (D-Maine), Sam Nunn (D-Ga.), and Charles Percy (R-Ill.)—they used their votes on MX funding to elicit changes in the administration's negotiating posture at START.[55]

The threat of legislation at times even influences the behavior of other countries. Foreign governments often try to deflate efforts to pass punitive legislation with conciliatory gestures. For example, when China was threatened with termination of its most-favored-nation status in 1990, it released hundreds of pro-democracy activists from prison. When Congress revisited the issue of Beijing's most-favored-nation status in 1991, "China agreed to join the Nuclear Non-Proliferation Treaty, and, for the first time in its history, allowed an international human rights commission to visit China."[56]

As is the case with actually making law, a threat to legislate by no means gives Congress a foolproof instrument with which to influence policy. One of the first problems is mounting a credible challenge to executive branch policy. An administration is not likely to make policy concessions if legislation it opposes has no chance of passing or legislation it supports is certain to pass. The importance of credibility makes it crucial that a legislative challenge enjoy strong support in both the House and Senate. The Reagan administration was able to dismiss many of the foreign policy challenges it faced on Capitol Hill because ideologically sympathetic Republicans controlled the Senate until 1986. At the same time, the president may be able to build an unassailable coalition with only minor concessions. In the case of efforts to end China's most-favored-nation trade status, President Bush blocked the legislation by making largely cosmetic changes in his initial policy.

Equally important in determining whether the threat of legislation provides leverage is the intensity of administration preferences. On some issues presidents may see defeat as no better, or even worse, than compromise. Ronald Reagan made it amply clear that he regarded the Strategic Defense Initiative as nonnegotiable. And the willingness to compromise on a particular issue may well change from president to president. Reagan largely resisted congressional attempts to rewrite his Central America policy. In contrast, George Bush made negotiation of an executive-legislative detente over Central America one of the first priorities of his administration.

The use of legislation as leverage poses two problems as well. One is that members of Congress may miscalculate and the threat may become reality. Take the Reagan administration's request in 1985 to have Congress consider the results of the U.S.-Canada free trade negotiations under fast-track status, a procedure under which members give up their right to amend legislation. By law, either the House Ways and Means Committee or the Senate Finance Committee could deny the request by passing a motion to disapprove. Although most of the members of the Senate Finance Committee believed that the trade talks were necessary and that denying fast-track status would damage relations with Canada as well as future trade negotiations, they were angered by what they saw as an incoherent American trade policy. To bring pressure on the White House to take trade issues more seriously, several committee members decided to support the disapproval motion. In doing so, they were "expecting to lose; theirs was to be a protest vote."[57] On the day of the vote, however, it became clear that the disapproval motion had enough support to pass. Only after quick parliamentary maneuvers and intense behind-the-scenes pressure did the administration muster enough votes to kill the disapproval motion. Thus, in attempting to send a signal to the administration, opponents came within a hairsbreadth of derailing the process entirely.

The more common danger with using legislation as a lever is that the White House may not carry out its end of the bargain. The problem of enforcing agreements is especially keen when the quid pro quo is an administration pledge to negotiate more enthusiastically or to take a harder line in dealing with other countries. When swing voters traded support for the MX for changes in the U.S. negotiating posture at the START talks, die-hard MX opponents complained that the Reagan administration had sold the Gang of Six a bill of goods. In the months that followed, many swing voters came to the same conclusion. Members do have some tools with which to enforce executive-legislative bargains: a program may need appropriations in the future, and an executive agreement or treaty may need congressional consent. But such checks lose their value once a program has been approved or if the administration has no interest in reaching an agreement.

CONCLUSION

Discussions of Congress's role in foreign policy typically focus on the ability of members of Congress to generate and pass their own substantive policy proposals. After decades of declining to write their own foreign policy preferences into law, members shed their reluctance in the 1980s. But the amount of substantive legislation emerging from Congress nowhere matches the amount of legislative activity. Efforts to pass substantive legislation continue to founder on the inherent advantages of the presidency, the pro-executive branch bias of the Supreme Court, and the institutional and partisan divisions of Congress. On top of these three obstacles, many members recognize that substantive legislation may not always be the best tool for influencing foreign policy.

The problems with using substantive legislation encourage members of Congress to use proposed legislation to extract policy concessions from the executive branch. When members can mount credible challenges to administration policy, executive branch officials may choose to incorporate congressional views into their own proposals. But using legislation as a lever carries with it considerable irony. The traditional standard for judging whether

Congress matters on foreign policy is its ability to pass legislation. Yet, as Stanley Heginbotham observes, when members use legislation as leverage, "congressional victory is achieved when restrictive legislation loses, but Congress extracts some policy compromises reflecting congressional concerns."[58] As a result, executive-legislative relations on foreign policy are far more complicated than can be captured simply by examining which bills pass. Rather than acting overtly, members of Congress often influence foreign policy indirectly, a point the next two chapters develop at greater length.

PROCEDURAL
LEGISLATION

IN THE SUMMER OF 1988, Iraqi troops attacked several Kurdish villages with chemical weapons. The Senate Foreign Relations Committee responded to the attacks by proposing legislation that would have imposed sanctions on Iraq, but the 100th Congress concluded before action could be completed on the bill. When Congress reconvened in January 1989, Foreign Relations abandoned its effort to single out Iraq for punishment in favor of broader legislation imposing sanctions on any country that used chemical or biological weapons. For the next two years the White House and the committee fought over the details of the sanctions legislation, with President Bush demanding that he be given discretion to decide if sanctions should be imposed and members of the committee insisting that the sanctions be mandatory. Compromise language was finally agreed upon in 1991, and the legislation became law. [1]

The bill imposing sanctions on countries found to be using chemical weapons illustrates one of the major instruments available to members of Congress for shaping foreign policy: procedural legislation. Unlike substantive policy legislation, which specifies what the content of policy will be, procedural legislation targets the structures and procedures by which foreign policy is made. The underlying premise is that if Congress changes the decision-making process it will change the policy. As then-Rep. Les Aspin (D-Wis.) once wrote, "Often by establishing new procedures, which are, of course, ostensibly neutral, Congress is able to effect substantive policy changes."[2] Political scientist Morris Fiorina puts the same point even more forcefully: "The Congress controls the bureaucracy, and the Congress gives us the kind of bureaucracy it wants."[3]

Congress uses a variety of procedural changes to influence foreign policy. It creates new executive branch agencies, adds or removes participants from the

decision-making process, makes administration decisions subject to legislative vetoes, writes rules that foreign policy programs must adhere to, and
imposes an assortment of reporting requirements on the foreign policy bureaucracy. As the Bush administration's efforts to water down the legislation
on chemical weapons suggests, the executive branch chafes at the new restrictions. Because of the opposition of the executive branch, procedural legislation has a mixed record of success. While some procedural changes succeed in
injecting congressional preferences into policy, others fail to achieve the aims
of their legislative sponsors.

THE APPEAL OF
PROCEDURAL LEGISLATION

The Constitution gives Congress considerable power to set the procedures
and structures by which the executive branch makes foreign policy. To the
extent that the content of policy reflects the process by which it is made,
Congress's ability to determine the procedures and structures of government
gives it potentially great say in what policy will be. Changes in how policy is
made can "change the expected policy outcomes of administrative agencies
by affecting the relative influence of people who are affected by the policy.
Moreover, because policy is controlled by participants in administrative
processes, political officials can use procedures to control policy without
bearing costs themselves, or even having to know what policy is likely to
emerge."[4]

Even though procedural legislation is very useful for shaping policy outcomes, not every congressional effort to change the decision-making process
is necessarily designed to influence policy. Members at times may derive a
psychological benefit from seeing that the decision-making process is structured in ways they perceive to be fair and consistent.[5] Members may also
tinker with the decision-making process as part of a blame avoidance strategy
designed to shield themselves from constituent wrath.[6] Yet, procedural
legislation probably isn't used very often simply to pass the buck for decisions
to the bureaucracy. If constituents are intelligent and forward looking, they
will see through the ruse and the incentive to use procedural legislation will
evaporate. Conversely, if constituents are ignorant about what Congress
does, then members do not need the protection the legislation affords.[7]

Procedural legislation has a wide appeal on Capitol Hill as an instrument
for shaping policy. For members who want to advance their own visions of
good public policy, procedural legislation often has the virtue of being seen as

politically neutral. As a result, members often find it easier to build a winning coalition around procedural legislation than around substantive legislation.

Policy-oriented members of Congress also find merit in the labor-saving character of procedural legislation. Members know all too well the wisdom of the adage that "an ounce of prevention is worth a pound of cure." A procedural change that succeeds in incorporating congressional preferences into executive branch decisions early on relieves members of the need to push for substantive legislation. Procedural changes can also shift the burden of monitoring agency behavior onto the executive branch (e.g., offices of the inspector general) or onto interested private groups (e.g., private sector advisory groups). And when procedural legislation targets a class of issues—say, for example, the rules used for allocating foreign aid—they save policy-oriented members from having to fight the executive branch each and every time the issue arises. In each case, policy-oriented members can use the time and effort saved by the procedural legislation to address other policy issues or to devote more attention to the tasks needed to win reelection.

The appeal of procedural legislation is not lost on members whose commitment to public policy trails their commitment to reelection. For electorally oriented members, procedural legislation can offer opportunities for political profit. Changes in the decision-making process are often designed to enable affected groups to seek remedies from the agency, the courts, or even Congress itself. These procedural changes in turn create a system of fire alarms that alerts members to issues that concern their constituents.[8] Procedural fire alarms enable members to allocate their oversight activities in a much more electorally efficient manner than would be the case if they themselves had to ferret out instances in which their constituents were hurt by executive branch actions.

PROCEDURAL LEGISLATION IN FOREIGN POLICY

The procedural changes Congress makes in foreign policy fall into five major categories: new agencies and positions in the executive branch, new participants in policy making, legislative vetoes, new procedural requirements, and reporting requirements.

New Agencies and Positions

One way Congress influences the policies that emerge from the bureaucracy is by creating new agencies and positions inside the executive branch. Using new agencies and positions to remedy perceived shortcomings in the executive branch did not originate with the post-Vietnam Congress. In 1961, for instance, Congress created the Arms Control and Disarmament Agency (ACDA) because members believed the administration was neglecting arms control.[9] More recently, Congress has created the Special Operations Command and the post of undersecretary of defense for acquisition to remedy perceived deficiencies in the Defense Department, established an independent inspector general's office at the Central Intelligence Agency (CIA) to help prevent a repeat of the Iran-contra affair, and directed the State Department to open a new bureau for South Asia to ensure that the United States gives greater emphasis to the Indian subcontinent.

Congressional efforts to create new agencies and positions proceed from a simple assumption about bureaucratic life: policies that don't have champions in the bureaucracy are doomed. By the early 1970s, for example, many on Capitol Hill had become convinced that the State Department, which at that time was the lead executive branch agency on trade policy, "was unsympathetic and unresponsive to domestic interests and that responsibility should be assigned elsewhere."[10] By creating the Office of the U.S. Trade Representative (USTR) in 1974 and assigning it primary responsibility for trade policy, members hoped to create an executive branch agency that would defend American economic interests. Likewise, in the mid-1970s many in Congress concluded that human rights issues often got no more than lip service in U.S. foreign policy because no agency had a stake in promoting human rights. To remedy the situation, Congress passed legislation in 1977 creating the Bureau of Human Rights and Humanitarian Affairs in the State Department.[11]

To help new agencies and positions succeed, Congress often specifies in great detail their relations with existing agencies. Take the case of the independent Office of the Director of Operational Test and Evaluation (DOT&E), an office created in 1983 to ensure that the Defense Department conducts realistic operational tests of new weapons systems. To give DOT&E clout in its inevitable battles with the military services, Congress stipulated that the Pentagon could not proceed beyond low-rate initial production of a weapons system until DOT&E had reported to both Congress and the secretary of defense. Congress also sought to enhance the clout of DOT&E by stipulating that its director would report directly to the secretary of defense rather than to other Pentagon officials. And leery that career military officials would be vulnerable to pressure from their parent services, Congress directed that the director of DOT&E be a civilian appointee. [12]

New Decision-making Participants

Efforts to create new agencies and positions require major changes in the structure of government. A less drastic tool members of Congress can use to shape the policies that emerge from the executive branch is to change the participants in policy making. Underlying this procedural change is the belief that restructuring the decision-making process will produce policy proposals more in accord with congressional preferences.

One way members of Congress can restructure the decision-making process is by rearranging responsibility among existing decision makers. The Omnibus Trade and Competitiveness Act of 1988, for example, transferred responsibility for deciding whether the United States should retaliate against unfair trading practices abroad from the president to the USTR. Although the USTR is an executive branch agency and though the omnibus trade act permits the president to waive retaliation for economic or national security reasons, sponsors of the provision judged that giving the USTR the power to order retaliatory action would "make it harder for the president to refuse retaliation; to do so would give the appearance of blocking the lead trade agency in the conduct of its newly mandated duties." [13]

Congress also restructures the decision-making process by adding new participants. Sometimes the newly enfranchised groups are existing government agencies that share the preferences of Congress. In the 1980s, Congress grew increasingly concerned that the Defense Department was failing to take into account U.S. economic interests when negotiating agreements with foreign governments to co-produce weapons systems. To reverse the trend, Congress in 1988 required the Pentagon to solicit recommendations from the Commerce Department when negotiating agreements on the co-production of defense equipment. [14] When the storm broke in 1989 over co-production of the FSX fighter with Japan, Congress passed legislation that included a provision requiring the secretary of commerce to review any future agreements relating to the FSX. The authors of both provisions believed that the Commerce Department would be more sensitive to American commercial interests and more vigorous than the Pentagon in considering the potential impact of co-production agreements on the American industrial base. [15]

At other times, Congress incorporates private groups into decision making. The Trade Act of 1974, for example, created private sector advisory committees to advise the executive branch during trade talks. The committees, which draw their members from a wide range of consumer, industry, and labor organizations, advise the president about policy objectives and bargaining positions during negotiations as well as about the operation and implementation of agreements. The executive branch is required to keep the advisory committees informed about the progress of negotiations, and committee members may even be included in the negotiating delegation. This elaborate advisory system enables members of Congress to follow the actions of the executive branch. It also enables both the White House and Capitol Hill to know which constituents would be hurt by, hence likely to oppose, a proposed trade agreement.[16]

Members also legislate themselves into decision making. Congress, for instance, created a role for itself in monitoring the Helsinki Accord.[17] The eighteen members of Congress, along with three officials from the executive branch, who composed the United States Commission on Security and Cooperation in Europe—known less formally as the Helsinki Commission—were charged with seeing that communist countries of Eastern Europe complied with their pledges to respect human rights. The commission members participated in talks related to the Helsinki Accord, including meetings of the Conference on Security and Cooperation in Europe (CSCE) at which agreements were negotiated.[18]

An even more notable instance in which Congress has thrust itself into decision making comes in trade policy.[19] The Trade Act of 1974 stipulates that five members of the Senate Finance Committee and five members of the House Ways and Means Committee be designated official advisers to trade negotiations. The congressional advisers are entitled to consult regularly with U.S. negotiators and to participate directly in trade talks. Select congressional staff also are entitled to monitor the talks and to attend negotiating sessions. To remedy potential informational imbalances between the executive and Congress, the act further directs the executive branch to keep the House and Senate currently informed on the status of trade talks.

Some dispute surrounds the ability of Congress to mandate changes in executive branch decision making. President Bush vetoed the legislation dealing with the FSX, arguing among other things that the provision requiring the secretary of commerce to review future agreements involving the plane interfered with "executive branch management and infringe[d] on the president's authority with respect to deliberations incident to the exercise of executive power."[20] Secretary of Commerce Robert Mosbacher, however, had previously persuaded President Bush to include the Commerce Department and the USTR in any new negotiations involving the exchange of military technology.[21] In 1990, Congress passed legislation that barred the executive branch from making financial contributions to any meeting held under the auspices of the CSCE if congressional members of the Helsinki Commission were not included in the official U.S. delegation to talks on conventional military forces in Europe. President Bush signed the legislation but stated that he would not be bound by what he judged to be an unconstitutional intrusion into his right, as president, to conduct foreign policy.[22] Whether Bush had the authority to ignore the congressional directive became moot when the talks resumed in a CSCE forum where the Helsinki Commission was represented.[23]

The Legislative Veto

A third type of procedural change that members of Congress use to influence foreign policy is the legislative veto. All legislative vetoes share the same basic quid pro quo: Congress delegates authority to the president but reserves the right to veto the president's actions by passing a simple (one-house) or concurrent (two-house) resolution, neither of which is subject to a presidential veto.[24]

First devised in 1932, the legislative veto made one of its initial appearances in foreign policy legislation in the Lend-Lease Act of 1941. Over the next three decades, Congress occasionally inserted legislative vetoes into foreign policy legislation. As differences between the White House and Capitol Hill on the U.S. role in the world widened in the 1970s, however, the legislative veto became the tool of choice for imposing congressional preferences on foreign policy. Congress inserted vetoes into legislation dealing with a range of foreign policy issues, including arms sales, foreign aid, and trade. The most famous legislative veto, though, was inserted into the War Powers Resolution, which among other things empowered Congress to order the withdrawal of U.S. troops through a concurrent resolution if they had been sent into combat without the benefit of a declaration of war or a specific congressional authorization.

In the 1983 case *I.N.S. v. Chadha,* the Supreme Court sharply limited the use of legislative vetoes.[25] The Court ruled that under most conditions legislative vetoes violate the constitutional principles of bicameralism and presentment of bills to the president. Congress has modified statutes containing legislative vetoes on a case-by-case basis. Many statutes remain untouched despite *Chadha.* Indeed, Congress continued to insert vetoes into legislation even after the Court declared them unconstitutional. The persistence of legislative vetoes reflects the simple reality that both Congress and the executive branch often prefer them, whatever the status of their constitutionality, to the alternative of having to pass a bill.

In other instances, Congress responded to *Chadha* by shortening authorization periods and by inserting reporting and consultation requirements into the law. Congress has also added so-called report-and-wait requirements to some laws, as it did to the legislation governing arms sales abroad.[26] These requirements stipulate that a policy may not go into effect for some specified period of time (usually thirty or forty-five days) after Congress is informed of the decision. In the interim, Congress may block the policy by passing a joint resolution. Of course, the president benefited from the *Chadha* ruling, since joint resolutions are subject to a presidential veto.

The *Chadha* ruling, however, did not entirely forbid the use of simple and concurrent resolutions as legislative vetoes. So long as they affect congressional procedure rather than policy, legislative vetoes pass constitutional muster.[27] The Omnibus Trade and Competitiveness Act of 1988, for instance, allows the president to extend the fast-track procedure for considering trade agreements unless both the House and Senate adopt a resolution of disapproval within sixty days of the request for an extension. (Fast-track procedures bar members of Congress from trying to amend a bill, thereby speeding up the legislative process by forcing members to vote either for or against the president's proposal.) President Bush invoked the provision in March 1991 when he asked Congress to extend for two years the fast-track procedure for considering any agreement that emerged from the Uruguay Round of the General Agreement on Tariffs and Trade.[28] The threat here, of course, is that the bill the executive branch prefers will die on Capitol Hill if it is handled under the normal decision-making procedures in Congress.

New Procedural Requirements

The fourth type of procedural change Congress uses to shape policy involves writing new procedural requirements for executive branch decision making. The premise here is that the new procedures will produce decisions more to Congress's liking. The Super 301 provision in the 1988 omnibus trade act, for example, required the president to impose sanctions on "countries that maintain a consistent pattern of import barriers and market-distorting practices" if they failed to agree to end the practices.[29] The act also broadened the definition of unfair trade practices and terminated the International Trade Commission's discretion to investigate claims of dumping. Both changes were designed to make it easier for injured groups to claim relief.[30]

In writing new procedural requirements, Congress often makes use of conditional authorizations. Here Congress allows the executive branch to proceed as it sees fit so long as certain conditions are met. The rationale for and the appeal of conditional authorizations lie in providing presidents with the discretion they need to manage foreign policy on a day-to-day basis while placing clear limits on what they can do. Of course, the restrictiveness of the limits varies greatly. In some cases, presidents enjoy tremendous discretion in deciding whether a condition has been met. In other cases, it is objectively or politically difficult for the administration to claim that the conditions laid down by Congress have been met.

Like efforts to create new executive branch agencies, conditional authorizations enjoy a long lineage. In 1940, for instance, a Congress distrustful of Franklin Roosevelt's policies toward Europe inserted a provision in the naval appropriations bill stipulating that the United States could not give a foreign country military goods unless the army chief of staff or the chief of naval operations first certified that the goods were not necessary for the defense of the country, something neither military leader was likely to do. Roosevelt, however, believed that American aid to Britain was essential. Determined to circumvent the will of Congress, he orchestrated the famous destroyers-for-bases deal.[31]

Congress has imposed conditional authorizations on a wide variety of foreign policy issues. Congress reacted to extensive base closings during the 1960s by requiring the Defense Department to conduct (among other things) detailed fiscal, environmental, and strategic studies before proposing any base for closure or reduction.[32] The Jackson-Vanik Amendment barred the president from granting most-favored-nation status to nonmarket countries that deny their citizens the right to emigrate.[33] In 1981, Congress conditioned arms sales to Chile on presidential certification that Chile had taken steps to bring the murderers of Orlando Letelier to justice. And in 1983, Congress banned tests of the air force's satellite interceptor unless the president certified that he was endeavoring in good faith to negotiate a treaty to ban antisatellite weapons or that the tests were essential to national security.[34]

Conditional authorizations are the most popular, however, in the area of foreign aid.[35] Section 502B of the Foreign Assistance Act bars the United States from providing security assistance or exporting crime control equipment to countries whose governments engage "in a consistent pattern of gross violations of internationally recognized human rights."[36] The Anti-Drug Abuse Act of 1986 bars "assistance to any 'major illicit drug producing country,' defined objectively as any country producing more than five metric tons of opium or five hundred metric tons of marijuana and cocaine in a fiscal year."[37] Besides these (and other) general conditions on foreign assistance, Congress also imposes additional conditions on specific countries.

Reporting Requirements

The last major type of procedural change is the reporting requirement. In 1988, Congress required more than 700 routine, recurring reports from the executive branch on foreign policy, with 288 reports on foreign aid programs alone.[38] Requests for reports are also popular in defense policy. In the 1980s Congress requested on average five hundred reports and studies from the Defense Department each year.[39]

Reporting requirements come in three variants: notification provisions, periodic reports, and one-time reports.[40] Notification provisions require executive branch agencies to inform Congress whenever they undertake certain specified actions. Ever since the passage of the Hughes-Ryan Amendment, for example, the CIA has been required to report each covert operation to the appropriate congressional committees. Periodic reports require the executive branch to report the status of programs at specified time intervals (e.g., quarterly, semiannually, annually) or at certain milestones in the life of a program. For instance, since 1978 Congress has required the State Department to report every sixty days on the progress of efforts to resolve the Cyprus dispute, and since 1975 Congress has required the Defense Department to submit annual arms control impact statements for major weapons programs. One-time reports are requests for studies of specific issues. In recent years such one-time reports have covered topics as diverse as the help available for civilians left jobless by the closing of military bases, the effect of burning oil on troops in the Gulf War, and the status of any military cooperation between the U.S.-aided resistance in Cambodia and the Khmer Rouge.[41]

To be sure, not all reporting requirements are designed to influence policy. As Les Aspin observed while still a member of the House, "There are requests where Congress orders up a report, not to aid Congressional deliberations but as a substitute for deliberations."[42] Many reports are intended to give members something to show constituents on matters of local concern. The fiscal 1992 defense bill, for example, included requests for reports on policies for controlling ice on the Kankakee River in Illinois and on the Pentagon's plans for cleaning up munitions waste at a base in Indiana. Other reports are a sop to members who cannot muster the votes needed to pass substantive legislation. In 1991, for instance, Sen. Dale Bumpers (D-Ark.) settled for an amendment requiring the Pentagon to report on the security outlook for the

Korean peninsula because he lacked the votes needed to cut the number of U.S. troops in South Korea.[43]

But many reporting requirements are explicitly intended to influence policy. They do so in a variety of ways. Most notification requirements are designed to deter unpopular executive branch decisions by raising the prospect of early congressional involvement. A major impetus for the notification requirements regarding covert operations, for instance, was the belief that the need to notify Congress would persuade CIA officials to abort the kinds of harebrained schemes uncovered by the Church and Pike committees. And when a notification requirement fails to deter unpopular agency decisions, it has the virtue of giving members of Congress the opportunity to mobilize before the decision can be implemented.

Other reporting requirements are designed to give members of Congress the information they need to oversee foreign policy and to consider future legislation. Report information is particularly useful on Capitol Hill because it bears the stamp of the executive branch. Take the case of the report on U.S. aid to the Cambodian resistance. Sponsors of the provision cited news reports that the U.S.-supported resistance was cooperating with Khmer Rouge. But the sponsors were stymied in their efforts to move Congress to action so long as the administration denied any U.S. links to Pol Pot's forces. The reporting requirement became a lever with which to force the administration to admit what everyone else knew. When the report was filed on Capitol Hill, it contained the admission that the Khmer Rouge had benefited from U.S. aid. The resulting political pressure led the Bush administration to announce it would provide aid only to noncommunist civilians in Cambodia.[44]

Still other reporting requirements are designed to put an issue on the agenda in the executive branch, stimulate the exchange of information among executive agencies, force the administration to take a position on an important issue, or expose disagreements within the bureaucracy. In the 1980s, for example, Congress required several studies on the environmental aspects of foreign aid for the purpose of "elevating the issue to more senior agency staff and enhancing the access to these officials by outside environmental groups."[45] One of the purposes of the arms control impact statements is to enhance the influence of ACDA by promoting its communications with the Defense Department and by involving it further in the weapons acquisition process.[46] In 1983, conservative members of Congress passed an amendment mandating annual reports on Soviet treaty violations in order "to force the administration to take explicit positions on sensitive compliance issues, thereby ensuring a firm foundation for opposing future agreements until these matters had been settled."[47] And members frequently use intelligence reports "to set one executive agency against another."[48]

The fact that members of Congress often do not read the reports they request does not undermine the importance of reporting requirements for foreign policy. Much has been made, for instance, of the fact that Sen. Gaylord Nelson (D-Wis.) seldom read the reports on U.S. arms sales abroad even though he had sponsored the legislation mandating them.[49] But such reports are closely followed by interested groups outside of Congress. By requiring the Defense Department to make public its arms sales proposals, Nelson ensured that interested groups would receive advance notice and could mobilize to defeat proposals they opposed. To take another example, few if any members of Congress read the required reports on the Cyprus peace talks. The reports are, however, scrutinized by Greek and Turkish groups that are quick to alert friendly members when they see any signs of a shift in administration policy.[50] Because private parties are willing to bear the costs of combing through executive branch reports, reporting requirements constitute part of the fire-alarm network that Congress creates to keep it abreast of developments in foreign policy.

THE IMPACT OF
PROCEDURAL LEGISLATION

How successful are procedural and structural changes in shaping foreign policy? Some procedural legislation clearly fails. By almost any measure, the War Powers Resolution is a dead letter. Despite hopes that ACDA would integrate arms control concerns with military objectives, it "has always been either wholly or substantially excluded from the [weapons acquisition] process."[51] The post of undersecretary of defense for acquisition went through three appointees in its first four years, with none of the three making much of an impact.[52] DOT&E hardly fared much better. A series of studies by the General Accounting Office found that it had little success in improving operational testing.[53]

Other procedural legislation has had modest success in shaping foreign policy. The Reagan and Bush administrations deemphasized human rights issues, but the Helsinki Commission "influenced the direction and execution of United States policy as well as its substance."[54] Likewise, the Reagan administration ignored the provisions of Section 502 that linked security assistance to human rights practices, but it did follow the provisions that dealt with the export of crime control equipment. In fact, the Reagan administration "blocked more crime control equipment in the name of human rights than Carter's staff."[55] The legislation mandating congressional participation in trade talks also has had a modest effect. The congressional negotiators by no means make trade policy or negotiate agreements by themselves. They do, however, provide the administration with a clear idea of the political parameters that will govern any agreement, they participate directly in some negotiations, and on occasion they play a key role in moving the talks along.[56]

Still other procedural legislation has had a substantial impact on policy. The procedural hurdles Congress placed on decisions to close or realign military facilities essentially prevented the Defense Department from closing any bases for well over a decade.[57] The legislation governing arms sales has had a dramatic effect. Although Congress has never vetoed an arms sale, the threat of a veto has shaped many presidential proposals. The Ford and Carter administrations modified their proposed arms packages on several occasions to defuse opposition on Capitol Hill.[58] Three times between 1983 and 1985 the Reagan administration proposed selling arms to Jordan, and all three times it withdrew the proposal because of the mood in Congress.[59] In 1986 and 1987, proposals to sell arms to Saudi Arabia were approved only after the Reagan administration substantially reduced the dollar value of the packages and deleted the weapons that caused the most contention.[60] After Iraq invaded Kuwait, the Bush administration postponed another plan to sell weapons to Saudi Arabia because of congressional opposition.[61] Without the report-and-wait requirement and the threat (however remote) of a legislative veto, many of these arms deals would have been completed.

The procedural changes embedded in the omnibus trade bill of 1988 also had a substantial effect. To avoid becoming a target of the retaliatory provisions of the bill, several U.S. trading partners altered their behavior, which was precisely the point of the legislation. South Korea, for example, worked to increase its import of American-made goods.[62] Concerned that Super 301 would accelerate the move toward bilateral trade, the European Community Commission approved a proposal to strengthen the dispute settlement procedures in GATT.[63] The 1988 trade act also affected policy indirectly by changing the behavior of the White House, which underscores the link between procedural change and anticipated reactions. With the passage of the trade bill, the Bush White House made improving American access to foreign markets a high priority. The most dramatic example of the administration's interest in trade policy was the push to begin the so-called Structural Impediments Initiative talks with Japan. The talks led to agreements in which Japan pledged to open its markets to satellites, supercomputers, and wood products.[64]

The success of procedural legislation on military bases, arms sales, and trade policy might seem unremarkable given the strong constituent interest in all three issues. But procedural changes also work in areas where constituency interests are less prominent. In 1986, Congress passed the Goldwater-Nichols Bill, which sought to curtail the problem of interservice squabbling over combat missions in wartime by streamlining the chain of command and enhancing the authority of theater commanders. Many observers credit this act with helping to dampen interservice disagreements during the Gulf War. Secretary of Defense Dick Cheney, normally a passionate critic of congressional activism on defense policy, went so far as to describe Goldwater-Nichols as "the most far-reaching piece of legislation affecting the [Defense] Department since the original National Security Act of 1947. . . . Clearly, it made a major contribution to our recent military successes."[65]

Another example of a procedural change that has had great success despite minimal constituency interest is the reporting requirement for covert operations. Although it is impossible to know how many covert operations die on the drawing board because officials anticipate congressional opposition, it is likely, as Loch Johnson argues, that "the very requirement of reporting on these operations serves as a deterrent against madcap proposals like those that surfaced within the intelligence bureaucracy more easily in the past."[66] Presidents occasionally attest to the deterrent effect of the reporting requirement when they complain, as President Bush did when explaining why the United States did not support a coup attempt in Panama in October 1989, that congressional oversight discourages covert operations.[67] CIA officials also lament the deterrent effect of the reporting requirement. Robert M. Gates, then deputy director of Central Intelligence, wrote in 1987 that "the CIA today finds itself in a remarkable position, involuntarily poised equidistant between the executive and legislative branches. The administration knows that the CIA is in no position to withhold much information from Congress and is extremely sensitive to congressional demands; the Congress has enormous influence and information yet remains suspicious and mistrustful."[68]

THE LIMITS OF
PROCEDURAL LEGISLATION

Why does procedural legislation have a mixed record of success in building congressional preferences into executive branch decisions? One set of explanations points to Congress itself as the culprit. As mentioned earlier, procedural legislation might fail because it is designed to shield members of Congress from blame rather than to influence policy. According to the blame avoidance argument, if members had wanted to change policy they would have adopted procedural changes that they knew *ex ante* would be effective. A second Congress-centered explanation argues that procedural legislation has a mixed record of success because members write ambiguous and weak laws. To assemble winning legislative coalitions members sometimes fudge key legislative details, and to avoid presidential vetoes they frequently build escape hatches into legislation. Administrations later exploit the ambiguity or invoke the loophole to defeat the intent of a procedural change. A third Congress-centered explanation contends that whatever the motives of the original supporters of a procedural change, the composition of Congress, hence the nature of congressional preferences, changes over time. As congressional preferences change, so does the likelihood that a procedural change will affect the behavior of the executive branch.

Explanations that blame Congress for the failure of procedural legislation have considerable merit. Blame avoidance plays an unquestionable role in congressional deliberations. In an institution with 535 members, there will always be some who value form over substance. Likewise, a good deal of legislation is ambiguous or weak. Definitional problems, for instance, plague the War Powers Resolution, and procedural legislation frequently comes with provisions that allow the president to waive the restriction when the "national interest" or "national security" so requires.[69] And congressional preferences change over time. The 1980 Senate elections, for example, saw several leading proponents of congressional activism in foreign policy replaced by senators hostile to the procedural legislation passed in the 1970s. Although the new senators usually lacked the votes needed to repeal the laws they disliked, their ability to derail efforts to punish bureaucratic noncompliance had that effect in practice.

As illuminating as Congress-centered explanations may be, there are good reasons to doubt that they fully explain the success and failure of procedural legislation. First, the logic underlying Congress-centered explanations is not entirely compelling. The blame avoidance argument, for instance, assumes that constituents are intelligent when it comes to demanding congressional action but ignorant when it comes to assessing the consequences of congressional action. Although such an assumption might fit the average voter, it hardly seems to describe interest groups, which have both the incentives and the resources to distinguish between blame avoidance and serious legislative work. Nor does precise legislative language guarantee that procedural legislation will succeed. As already mentioned, the legislation creating DOT&E

was quite specific, but the office produced at best marginal improvements in operational testing.

Second, Congress-centered explanations fail to explain why some procedural changes fall short of their stated objectives despite vigorous congressional efforts to the contrary. To return to the example of DOT&E, the armed services committees went to great lengths to make the testing office work—even going so far as to hold funding for another defense program hostage until the Pentagon saw fit to appoint a director for operational testing.[70] Likewise, the House Foreign Affairs Committee made a concerted effort throughout the 1980s to oversee executive branch compliance with Section 502B.[71] If congressional preferences alone mattered, then both DOT&E and Section 502B should have influenced policy far more than they did.

Third, Congress-centered explanations reduce the executive branch to an empty vessel that obediently follows both the letter and the spirit of congressional directives. Yet everything we know about the executive branch makes this assumption untenable. The president's foreign policy goals at times diverge sharply from those held by a majority of Congress. Foreign policy bureaucracies have a clear sense of their own mission, and they frequently use their superior information and expertise to resist legislative efforts they deem undesirable.[72] As a result, when Congress enacts procedural changes, the executive branch usually moves to counter the effort.

Any effort to explain the success and failure of procedural legislation, then, needs to look beyond Capitol Hill and to recognize the constraints that limit the ability of members of Congress to use procedural change to shape policy. Three such constraints are crucial: the intensity of executive preferences, the cost of monitoring the executive branch, and the cost of punishing noncompliance.

The Intensity of Executive Preferences

Procedural changes are least likely to succeed when the executive branch vehemently opposes them. The reporting requirements for covert operations failed to prevent the Iran-contra affair because the Reagan administration willingly flouted the law. DOT&E stumbled in its mission because senior Defense Department officials fiercely resisted Congress's conception of what constitutes good operational testing. The intensity of executive branch preferences also helps to explain why the success of a procedural change may vary over time. Section 502B, for example, had a greater effect on the Carter administration than on the Reagan administration because some (but not all) senior officials in the Carter administration sympathized with Congress's objectives.[73]

The intensity of executive branch preferences matters because presidents and their subordinates have ample opportunities to blunt the intent of a procedural change. At the extreme, the executive branch may simply refuse to obey the law, as the Reagan administration did with its end run around CIA reporting requirements during the Iran-contra affair. Far more often officials comply with the letter but not the spirit of the law. The ways in which executive branch agencies can legally circumvent the law are legion. They may tell Congress bad news in a voice so low that most members won't hear, write implementing regulations that gut the intent of a procedural change, or staff congressionally mandated offices with people who oppose the intent of Congress.

The Cost of Monitoring the Executive Branch

The ability and willingness of the executive branch to blunt the intent of procedural change mean that members of Congress must monitor the executive branch if a procedural change is to affect the substance of policy. But monitoring imposes both time and resource costs on members. As it becomes more costly to determine if the administration is complying with a procedural change, members are less inclined to engage in monitoring and the executive branch is more inclined to ignore congressional preferences.

As a general rule, it is more costly for members of Congress to detect noncompliance in foreign policy than in domestic policy because secrecy is so much more extensive in foreign policy. Yet among foreign policy issues the costs of detecting noncompliance differ greatly. Some types of executive behavior are relatively easy to track. It is difficult, for instance, to hide a shipment of F-15s; hence, members can easily see if the administration has observed the thirty-day notice on arms sales. Likewise, the fact that the administration must ultimately reveal the contents of trade agreements makes it easy for members to detect noncompliance. Other types of executive behavior, however, are costly to monitor. Covert operations, for example, are designed to be kept secret from most of the people in the executive branch, let alone Congress; hence, members face considerable time and resource costs in trying to uncover illegalities in covert operations.

If the cost of detecting noncompliance varies from issue to issue, so does the cost of proving that the executive branch has failed to comply with the provisions of procedural legislation. On some issues, assessing compliance is straightforward. The reporting requirements for arms sales and covert operations, for instance, impose clear responsibilities on the executive branch. Failures to notify Congress of an arms sale or a covert action are beyond dispute when found, and members can move directly to debating the appropriate response. The prospect of punishment in turn deters the executive from evading congressional intent.

The cost of proving noncompliance rises sharply, however, when procedural legislation hinges on subjective judgments. Where reasonable people can disagree over whether an agency is complying, congressional energies will be consumed by debates over compliance rather than over punishment. Thus, as long as the Defense Department observes the letter of the law on operational testing and the State Department does likewise in its reports on human rights, they deny their critics the ammunition needed to marshal support for sanctions against the agency or for new legislation.

The Cost of Punishing Noncompliance

The success of any effort to force the foreign policy bureaucracy to comply with a procedural change depends ultimately on a credible commitment by members of Congress to punish noncompliance. If punishment is not forthcoming, executive branch officials have little incentive to heed congressional wishes. Yet the cost of enforcing procedural legislation varies across issues. In some situations, the very nature of the issue makes it relatively easy to punish noncompliance. In the case of intelligence reporting requirements, for example, a single leak may derail a covert operation. As a result, the CIA has good reason to anticipate the mood on Capitol Hill when designing its proposals. The cost of punishment is also likely to be low when the administration needs congressional consent. In the case of trade talks, for instance, no trade agreement can go into effect without the approval of Congress. The fact that a majority of either house can block an agreement gives the executive branch a strong incentive to listen to congressional negotiators.

In other situations, the nature of what members of Congress want to accomplish may make enforcement costly. Much as compellance is harder to achieve than deterrence, enforcement costs tend to be much higher when members want agencies to adopt new policies rather than to stop existing ones. Members have been hampered, for instance, in their effort to force the Defense Department to place more emphasis on operational testing because the traditional punishment—cutting off funding for a program—is useless; the Pentagon would be happy to do without DOT&E. Members instead tried to pressure the Defense Department by holding hostage the funding for another program. As a general rule, however, such threats are difficult to make credible. They frequently stumble over policy objections (the program being to be held hostage is needed) or parochial concerns (don't take hostage a program that employs my constituents).

An objection that might be raised at this point is that members themselves set the cost of monitoring and punishing the executive branch. (It is hard to argue that members of Congress determine executive preferences.) The objection has some merit. Monitoring costs are partly a function of the kinds of reporting requirements chosen and whether legislation is precisely crafted. And whether members delegate authority to the executive branch or hold it for themselves influences the cost of punishing noncompliance. Until the Supreme Court's ruling in *Chadha,* for instance, members could vary the cost of punishing noncompliance under the legislative veto by opting for a one-house rather than a two-house veto.

Nonetheless, the cost of monitoring and punishing the executive branch is to a great extent beyond the influence of Congress. The need for secrecy in foreign policy limits the ability of members to lower the cost of detecting noncompliance by shifting the burden of oversight onto private sector groups. (While in theory members choose secrecy and the higher detection costs it entails, the nature of world politics makes the decision between secrecy and openness something of a Hobson's choice, and constitutional practice severely restricts Congress's ability to compel an administration to disclose matters pertaining to diplomacy.) Some policy goals simply are incompatible with objective measures of compliance no matter how precisely the law is written. And members will always find it harder to compel the executive branch to adopt new policies than to block existing ones.

CONCLUSION

Congress's role as arbiter of governmental procedure gives its members a powerful tool for shaping foreign policy. By creating new agencies and writing new procedures, members of Congress can dramatically alter the policies that emerge from the executive branch. But procedural legislation by no means gives members control of foreign policy. Officials in the executive branch have their own policy preferences, and they usually try to circumvent procedural legislation that rules out policies they prefer. The success of any procedural change, then, rests on the ability of members to detect and punish instances of noncompliance.

The ability of procedural changes to shape the content of foreign policy suggests two lessons at odds with the conventional wisdom about Congress. One is that members of Congress do not necessarily abdicate responsibility when they delegate authority to the executive branch. Often members succeed in structuring the decision-making process so that the proposals that emerge from the foreign policy bureaucracy reflect congressional preferences. In the case of trade policy, for instance, Congress has repeatedly authorized presidents to negotiate trade agreements on its behalf. In doing so, however, Congress has imposed a number of procedural requirements that are designed to ensure that administrations will negotiate agreements acceptable to a majority of its members.

The other important lesson about procedural changes is that they typically succeed in changing the substance of policy without leaving behind observable signs of congressional involvement. The reason is straightforward: procedural legislation is designed to build congressional preferences into policy from the start, thereby relieving members of the need to try to kill or modify executive branch proposals. Indeed, some procedural changes may actually lessen the need for members to oversee the foreign policy bureaucracy, either because congressional preferences are incorporated into executive branch proposals or because members have shifted responsibility for monitoring the executive branch onto other groups.

DIPLOMACY, CONSULTATIONS, AND FRAMING

ON 11 FEBRUARY 1986, President Ronald Reagan told a press conference that supporters of both Ferdinand Marcos and Corazon Aquino had committed fraud in the presidential election held in the Philippines four days earlier. Reagan's comments stunned Sen. Richard Lugar (R-Ind.), the chair of the Senate Foreign Relations Committee and the head of the U.S. delegation that had overseen the voting. Only hours earlier Lugar had told the president that only Marcos's supporters had tried to steal the election. Determined to persuade Reagan to drop his support for the Philippine dictator, Lugar launched a two-week media blitz that culminated in appearances on all three of the Sunday morning network television interview shows. In each appearance Lugar called on Reagan to ask Marcos to resign. Lugar's efforts—complemented by those of other members of Congress—worked; within days Reagan withdrew his support for Marcos.[1]

Senator Lugar's media campaign provides a powerful reminder that members of Congress are not limited to passing legislation, be it substantive or procedural, in their bids to shape foreign policy. Members can also influence policy through three distinct nonlegislative means: congressional diplomacy, executive-legislative consultations, and the framing of public and elite opinion. Each approach presents members with a different set of costs and opportunities. Most members refrain from launching their own personal diplomatic initiatives because such efforts are seen by most observers as violating the president's prerogative to negotiate on behalf of the United States. In contrast, instances of executive-legislative consultations usually elicit bipartisan praise. Nonetheless, members find it difficult to convince presidents to engage in meaningful consultations when significant policy differences divide Capitol Hill and the White House. As for framing, while observers often criticize members for playing to the galleries, using the media to shape the terms of debate remains one of the most powerful tools members have to influence foreign policy.

CONGRESSIONAL DIPLOMACY

In 1793, Edmond Genet submitted his credentials as the emissary of the first French Republic to Congress rather than to President Washington. The decision earned the French ambassador a stern rebuke from Secretary of State Thomas Jefferson: "The transaction of business with foreign nations is Executive altogether. . . . Exceptions are to be strictly construed."[2] Over the next two hundred years, Jefferson's view that the president alone has the power to negotiate with other countries and to speak for the United States in foreign affairs came to be widely accepted in constitutional theory. As Justice George Sutherland wrote in the decision for *United States v. Curtiss-Wright Export Corporation:* The president "alone negotiates. Into the field of negotiation, the Senate cannot intrude; and Congress itself is powerless to invade it."[3]

The practice of American diplomacy, however, is more complicated than Justice Sutherland's words might suggest. On many occasions members of Congress find themselves involved, properly or improperly, in diplomatic negotiations. Congressional forays into the realm of diplomacy fall into three general categories: Lone Ranger diplomacy, invited participation, and routine contacts with foreign governments.

Lone Ranger diplomacy involves efforts by individual members of Congress to conduct their own foreign policy, and as such it attracts considerable criticism. The most publicized (and vilified) recent example of Lone Ranger diplomacy was Speaker of the House Jim Wright's (D-Tex.) foray into the Nicaraguan peace process.[4] In November 1987, the Reagan administration offered for the first time to meet with Nicaraguan officials to discuss security issues in Central America. Speaker Wright thereupon launched his own diplomatic effort, meeting secretly over three days with Nicaraguan president Daniel Ortega, three members of the contra leadership, and Nicaragua's cardinal Miguel Obando y Bravo. When the talks concluded, a Sandinista spokesperson bragged that Wright's initiative would "leave the Administration totally isolated."[5] Some officials in the executive branch urged that Wright be prosecuted under the provisions of the Logan Act, which forbids American citizens from conducting negotiations with a foreign power without the permission of the U.S. government.[6] Nothing came of this, largely because enforcing the Logan Act would have raised a host of legal and political difficulties.

Speaker Wright is not the only member of Congress to have indulged in Lone Ranger diplomacy over the past two decades. When a U.S. envoy went to Nicaragua in June 1979 to urge Gen. Anastasio Somoza Debayle to resign, Rep. John M. Murphy (D-N.Y.) stood at the general's side throughout the meeting.[7] In November 1979, Rep. George Hansen (R-Idaho) went to Teheran on his own to negotiate the release of American hostages.[8] In the 1980s, Sen. Jesse Helms (R-N.C.) was accused of dispatching private emissaries to negotiate with Nicaragua and Rhodesia-Zimbabwe and of leaking intelligence information to Chile.[9] In December 1990, Senate Majority Leader Robert Dole (R-Kans.), irate at the inability of Baghdad and Washington to agree on a date to hold meetings to discuss possible resolutions to the Persian Gulf crisis, "phoned the Iraqi ambassador in Washington to find out whether there was flexibility; there might be, he was told. Two days later . . . he declared that the 'American people aren't quite there yet . . . not yet committed to war.'"[10] During the Gulf War, Reps. David Martin (R-N.Y.) and Patricia Schroeder (D-Colo.) went to Korea and Japan to press those allies to contribute more money to the war effort.[11]

As these examples make clear, when it comes to Lone Ranger diplomacy neither political party can claim virtue. Both Democratic and Republican members have launched their own private diplomatic initiatives. Nor did Lone Ranger diplomacy originate with the post-Vietnam Congress. At the turn of the century, Sen. John T. Morgan (D-Ala.), the chair of the Senate Committee on Interoceanic Canals, sought to open his own negotiations with the government of Colombia on building a canal connecting the Atlantic and the Pacific. During the Paris Peace Conference that followed World War I, Sen. Henry Cabot Lodge (R-Mass.), chair of the Senate Foreign Relations Committee, corresponded with European leaders without informing President Woodrow Wilson. Lodge's successor as chair of the Foreign Relations Committee, Sen. William E. Borah (R-Idaho), initiated talks on oil exploration with the president of Mexico that directly contradicted the policy of the State Department. And in the 1950s and 1960s, members belonging to the so-called China lobby often advised Chiang Kai-Shek in his disputes with the United States.[12]

Although Lone Ranger diplomacy has a long lineage, it has never been a terribly successful strategy. As Speaker Wright discovered, the prohibition against private diplomacy is deeply ingrained in American politics, and the resulting public and elite criticism usually derails alternative diplomacy. That is why, the efforts of Speaker Wright and others notwithstanding, instances of Lone Ranger diplomacy remain fairly rare. Even if members believed they bore a responsibility for diplomacy or thought they had the clout needed to matter on the world stage—and most do not—they recognize that private diplomacy generally succeeds only in attracting criticism.

When pursuing Lone Ranger diplomacy, members of Congress operate independently of the White House. But members sometimes participate in diplomatic negotiations at the express invitation of the president. The practice of appointing representatives and, especially, senators as observers, advisers, or delegates to international conferences dates back to the War of 1812. To minimize the political fallout from negotiating a peace treaty with Great Britain, James Madison asked Sen. James A. Bayard and Speaker of the House Henry Clay to serve as members of the delegation to the conference at Ghent. Contrary to later custom, both men immediately resigned their seats in Congress, citing Article I, Section 6, paragraph 2 of the Constitution, which bars anyone from being a member of either house while "holding any office under the United States."[13]

The willingness of presidents to appoint members of Congress to international conferences has varied over the years. William McKinley frequently asked members to serve on negotiating delegations.[14] Two decades later, however, Woodrow Wilson refused to appoint any member of Congress to the U.S. delegation to the Paris Peace Conference and thereby helped to scuttle the Treaty of Versailles.[15] All too aware of Wilson's mistake, Franklin Roosevelt, Harry Truman, and (for a time) Dwight Eisenhower followed McKinley's lead. "Senators participated in the UN Conference on International Organization in 1945, the Paris Peace Conference in 1946, the Conference on the Peace Treaty with Japan in 1951, the Mutual Defense Treaty with the Philippines in 1951, the Anzus Pact, and the SEATO Treaty. For the last four of these treaties, senators were delegates and actually signed the treaties."[16] By the 1960s, presidents had again come to look with disdain on the practice of asking members to attend major negotiations. During the SALT I negotiations, for example, Sen. John Sherman Cooper (R-Ky.) failed to convince President Nixon to include senators in the U.S. delegation.[17] When Sen. Hugh Scott (R-Pa.), the Senate minority leader, announced he would visit Helsinki, U.S. negotiators met with him but declined to tell him anything of substance.[18]

Since the resurgence of congressional activism in the 1970s, members of Congress, especially senators, have demanded a greater role for themselves in diplomatic negotiations. As Chapter 5 noted, Congress has used its authority over foreign commerce to stipulate that five representatives and five senators be designated as official advisers to all U.S. delegations to trade negotiations. Elsewhere, however, members can do no more than prod the administration to include them in diplomatic delegations. To some extent, presidents have complied. Between 1980 and 1992, members, and on many occasions their staff, were accredited as representatives, advisers, and observers to more than sixty international conferences.[19]

The most notable instance in which members of Congress have been invited to participate in international negotiations has been arms control talks. In 1977, President Carter agreed to allow both senators and representatives to serve as advisers to the U.S. delegation. "Members were permitted to attend plenary sessions of the negotiations as observers, to sit in on delegation meetings in Geneva, and even to read the joint draft text of the treaty."[20] In at least one instance, the congressional advisers influenced the course of the talks: Soviet negotiators provided an official inventory of the Soviet nuclear arsenal—something they had previously refused to do—only after several members insisted that the Senate would never consent to SALT II in the absence of such an "agreed data base."[21]

The Reagan administration initially tried to reverse the precedent set by Carter of including members of Congress in arms control talks, arguing that negotiations were a presidential and not a congressional responsibility. Confronted with intense congressional pressure, however, the administration eventually relented. In 1985, a Senate Arms Control Observer Group was established. "In addition to the functions carried out by their predecessors, the new Senate observers were permitted to meet separately with Soviet negotiators, both to learn firsthand of Soviet positions and to express their own concerns."[22] During negotiations of the INF treaty, the twelve-member Arms Control Observer Group "was an important conduit of information between the administration and Senate moderates."[23]

Congressional participation in diplomatic negotiations in recent years would make it appear that members of Congress have eroded the president's prerogative to negotiate on behalf of the United States. But for the most part, the White House has ceded little to Capitol Hill. Members have been appointed mostly to minor conferences where little of note was expected to take place. In the few instances where members have been asked to participate in major negotiations, presidents extended the invitation in order to co-opt members and not to solicit their wisdom. Presidents calculate, no doubt correctly, that members are less likely to criticize agreements in which their colleagues have had a hand, however small it may be. As the Reagan administration discovered with the INF and START talks, making a handful of representatives or senators diplomatic advisers can help quiet critics on Capitol Hill.

Lone Ranger diplomacy and invited congressional participation in international negotiations have attracted considerable attention. Yet far more common than either of these two types of congressional diplomacy are routine, direct contacts between foreign governments and members of Congress. Until the 1970s, heads of foreign governments seldom communicated directly with members. Formal communications with the United States were directed to the president, the State Department, or U.S. embassy personnel. A major break in the norm of communicating through executive branch officials came in 1975 when King Hussein wrote letters to every senator and fifty key representatives asking them to support a proposed arms sale to Jordan. Since then, many foreign leaders have followed the Jordanian king's example and have communicated directly with members of Congress.[24]

The rise in direct communications between members of Congress and foreign leaders has been accompanied by an increase in the number of meetings between members and visiting foreign dignitaries. As Rep. Lee Hamilton (D-Ind.) noted while chair of the House Foreign Affairs Subcommittee on Europe and the Middle East, "Visiting heads of government used to come to Washington and visit the President; the Chairman of the World Bank; the Secretary of Defense; the Secretary of State, and go home. Now they insist on coming to Capitol Hill to meet with members of Congress."[25] During the 101st Congress (1989–90), for instance, Foreign Affairs received 132 foreign dignitaries and 34 foreign delegations, while Foreign Relations received foreign dignitaries on eighty occasions.[26]

The flip side of congressional meetings with visiting foreign dignitaries is congressional visits abroad. Of course, congressional junkets are a regular target of criticism. But for all the complaints about members travelling to Bali or Cancun, congressional trips abroad usually involve legitimate business. The collapse of the Soviet empire, for instance, triggered a rush of direct meetings between members of Congress and legislators in Eastern Europe. Senators and representatives served on international delegations overseeing parliamentary elections in Czechoslovakia, Hungary, Bulgaria, and Romania. In April 1990, the House dispatched a bipartisan task force to Eastern Europe to provide technical and procedural assistance to the newly formed legislatures. Other members acted on an individual basis to offer advice to their counterparts in Eastern Europe.[27]

Another trip abroad by a member of Congress played a key role in helping to end the civil war in El Salvador. In June 1990, Rep. Joseph Moakley (D-Mass.), chair of the House Rules Committee, met with Salvadoran rebels deep inside rebel-held territory. Moakley, who had become involved in Central American issues because of the immigration problems of his Boston constituents, was the head of a special task force investigating the November 1989 murder of six Jesuit priests by members of the Salvadoran military.

Moakley was accompanied to the meeting by William Walker, the U.S. ambassador to El Salvador. Walker, who had long wanted to meet with rebel leaders, used Moakley's trip to overcome the objections U.S. security officials had to such a meeting. Rebel leaders later told U.S. officials and journalists that Moakley's trip led to a breakthrough in the peace talks.[28]

Even more pervasive than congressional meetings with foreign dignitaries at home or abroad are meetings with foreign-embassy personnel stationed in Washington. Before the mid-1970s, most embassies conducted their business through the State Department. They rarely lobbied Congress. As members of Congress have become more active on foreign policy, however, embassies have begun to lobby on Capitol Hill. For example, New Zealand became the target of punitive legislation in 1987 after it adopted a nuclear-free weapons policy. The second secretary in the New Zealand embassy, who served as his country's day-to-day liaison with Congress, saw "the proportion of his working time usually spent on general contact work increased from forty percent to 100 percent immediately prior to the hearings, floor votes, and other legislative milestones."[29] The experience of the second secretary is typical; embassy personnel are now another group of lobbyists on Capitol Hill.[30]

Most contacts between foreign governments and members of Congress merely involve the exchange of information. Members on both sides of the aisle and officials in the executive branch generally agree that informational exchanges are a part of Congress's work. But sometimes the line separating legitimate fact finding from diplomatic negotiation is blurred. Take, for example, the extensive contacts liberal Democrats had during the 1980s with Nicaraguan officials. The members argued that the meetings were proper and that their conversations never ventured beyond urging the Sandinistas to respect human rights and to hold free elections. Officials in the Reagan administration, and even some members of the Democratic leadership, worried, however, that members were advising the Sandinistas on how to shape their diplomatic initiatives in ways that would hamper the administration's ability to win congressional approval for contra aid.[31]

The line separating legitimate fact finding from Lone Ranger diplomacy is further blurred by the fact that the White House encourages meetings with representatives of foreign governments when it thinks the discussions will persuade members of Congress to support the president's policy. In February 1975, for instance, Gerald Ford persuaded six representatives and one senator to travel to Indochina to meet with South Vietnamese and Cambodian officials. Ford hoped the meetings would help build congressional support for renewed aid to Saigon and Phnom Penh.[32] In September 1979, the Carter administration agreed to Senate Majority Leader Robert Byrd's (D-W.Va.) proposal that he meet with Soviet Ambassador Anatoly Dobrynin to discuss the troubled SALT II treaty. Administration officials hoped that Byrd could convince Soviet officials to make some positive gesture that would improve the treaty's chances in the Senate.[33] And Jim Wright's ill-fated foray into the Central American peace process came only after an emissary from the Reagan administration asked Wright to join the president in developing and sponsoring a peace plan for Central America.[34]

Whether the increase in direct contacts between members of Congress and foreign officials has helped or hindered U.S. foreign policy is hard to judge. No one knows for sure what would have happened, say, to the Salvadoran peace talks or to the Reagan administration's policy toward Nicaragua if members of Congress had followed the president's lead. What the increase in direct contacts has done is give foreign governments better intelligence about the political mood on Capitol Hill. Of course, critics worry that such information makes it possible for foreign governments to divide and conquer the American political system. But it is at least as likely that direct contacts benefit the United States by convincing foreign governments to temper their demands. During negotiation of the Panama Canal treaties, for instance, it was Senate minority leader Howard Baker's (R-Tenn.) meetings with Gen. Omar Torrijos that persuaded the Panamanian leadership to accept the reservations that made passage of the treaties possible.[35]

If increased contact between members of Congress and foreign officials gives foreign governments better information about Congress, the same holds true in reverse. This in turn means that presidents are limited in their ability to shape negotiations in their own favor. The reason is that when members do not know which negotiating proposals a foreign government considers acceptable, presidents can pick the proposal they most prefer, even if Congress and the foreign government would choose otherwise. Likewise, if presidents dislike the policies that appeal to both members and foreign governments, they can block any agreement. When Congress and the foreign government know which proposals the other will accept, they can push the president away from his ideal outcome and closer to their own. That is a lesson sure to be lamented by those who favor what the president hopes to accomplish and applauded by those who do not.

EXECUTIVE-LEGISLATIVE
CONSULTATIONS

Instances of Lone Ranger diplomacy typically trigger a flood of proposals offering to remedy the perceived crisis in U.S. foreign policy. Many of these proposals trumpet the need to rekindle the bipartisan spirit of the pre-Vietnam years when politics purportedly stopped at the water's edge. The route to bipartisanship is seen to lie in more consultation between the president and Congress.

As Chapter 1 discussed, the prevalence of executive-legislative consultations during the first post–World War II decade is often exaggerated. Although the Truman administration worked closely with senior members of Congress on the United Nations Charter, the Marshall Plan, and the Rio and NATO treaties, it made no effort to consult with members on many other foreign policy issues, including the Azerbaijan and Berlin crises, the partition of Palestine, and the Korean War. And under Eisenhower, meaningful consultations with senior members became increasingly infrequent. Eisenhower

> informed, rather than consulted with, congressional leaders about his major decisions: to accept a ceasefire in Korea without liberating North Korea, to stay out of Vietnam in 1954, to use the CIA to support coups in Iran in 1953 and Guatemala in 1954, not to go to war with China over the off-shore islands (Quemoy and Matsu), not to support the Hungarian rebels in 1956 or the British/French/Israeli cabal in 1956, to force Israel to pull out of the Sinai Peninsula in 1957, to extend aid to Tito in Yugoslavia and to hold down the cost of defense. In every case, except Vietnam in 1954, a majority of Republicans and perhaps of Congress as a whole wanted Eisenhower to adopt different policies.[36]

To the extent that Eisenhower and Secretary of State John Foster Dulles did discuss foreign policy with members, the goal "was not necessarily to receive flying instructions. Instead, Congress was consulted on the take-offs so that it could share the responsibility for the crack-ups."[37]

So long as the cold war consensus and the cult of the imperial presidency held sway on Capitol Hill, presidents did not pay a political price for failing to engage in meaningful consultations with Congress. All that changed with Vietnam and then Watergate. Suddenly members of Congress who for two decades had acquiesced in presidential domination of foreign affairs began to demand that they be consulted in policy making.

Not surprisingly, presidents resisted demands for consultations. The result was legislation designed to compel them. One of the first steps in this

direction came in 1972 with the passage of the Case-Zablocki Act, which
sought to strengthen the Senate's advice and consent role in treaty making by
requiring the president to keep Congress informed of all executive agreements. The desire for a consultative role for Congress was even more evident
with the passage of the War Powers Resolution, which explicitly stated that
"the President in every possible instance shall consult with Congress before
introducing United States Armed Forces into hostilities or into situations
where imminent involvement in hostilities is clearly indicated."[38]

Most legislative efforts to compel the executive branch to consult with
Congress have attracted far less attention than that given to the Case-Zablocki
Act or the War Powers Resolution. As Chapter 5 mentioned, Congress in 1976
created the United States Commission on Security and Cooperation in Europe
to monitor compliance with the Helsinki Accord and to serve as an independent advisory body to the president. In 1985, Congress established a formal
process for executive-legislative consultations on antidrug policy. The process
mandates discussions between representatives of the president and members of
the appropriate congressional committees, with "the substance of each consultation to be published in the *Congressional Record*."[39]

If members of Congress can occasionally legislate formal mechanisms for
executive-legislative consultations, at other times they can force ad hoc
consultations through sheer persistence. U.S. policy toward Nicaragua provides a case in point. The intensity and determination with which congressional opponents fought the Reagan administration's contra aid proposals
convinced President George Bush to search for a policy acceptable to both
ends of Pennsylvania Avenue. In March 1989, talks with congressional leaders yielded a bipartisan accord that included significant concessions by the
White House, the most notable being the decision to abandon the Reagan
administration's policy of seeking to oust the Sandinista government by
force.

The success of the bipartisan accord on Nicaragua notwithstanding, members of Congress generally find it easier to mandate and demand a consultative role for themselves than to convince presidents to engage in meaningful
consultations. The failure has been most obvious with respect to the War
Powers Resolution. Most presidents have refused to accept the resolution as
constitutional, let alone abide by its injunction to consult with Congress.
Other attempts to mandate consultations have had similarly disappointing
results. The Case-Zablocki Act has had no noticeable effect on congressional
involvement in treaty making, and the consultative process in antidrug
policy does not appear to have given members greater say in policy making.

One reason why members of Congress often fail to persuade the president to solicit their advice is that they themselves disagree over what constitutes adequate consultation. In April 1986, for example, Ronald Reagan invited a group of senior members to the White House for a briefing on plans for a U.S. air strike against Libya. The meeting started at four o'clock in the afternoon, two hours after U.S. warplanes had left their bases in Great Britain. Senator Lugar praised the White House for consulting with Congress, "as close in time to the bombing as it was."[40] Democrats, however, complained that the meeting fell far short of true consultation. As one put it, "What could we have done? . . . Told [the president] to turn the planes around?"[41] With many members happy simply to be notified of major foreign policy decisions, presidents generally do not have to pay a political price when they fail to consult with Congress.

The more fundamental problem that members of Congress face in trying to ensure meaningful executive-legislative consultations, though, is that their ability to advise depends on the willingness of the president to listen. Presidents find is easy to consult with Congress when they know that members approve of the policy they favor. (Presidents also find it easy to consult with Congress when they have no desire to act. In the spring of 1993, for instance, Bill Clinton so eagerly consulted congressional leaders on what the United States should do about the war in Bosnia that some members "began to question whether he had a policy of his own.")[42] But as the gap between executive and legislative preferences grows—and the more important consultation becomes to members of Congress—presidents become less willing to solicit congressional opinion.

The evolution of Operation Desert Shield into Operation Desert Storm illustrates the conundrum that bedevils members of Congress. Operation Desert Shield featured substantial dialogue between the White House and Congress. Before deciding to send U.S. troops to Saudi Arabia and to impose sanctions on Iraq, the president consulted with key congressional leaders. To be sure, the consultation was not perfect. For example, on August 8, President Bush tried and failed several times to reach Sen. George Mitchell (D-Maine) to inform the Senate majority leader that he had officially decided to commit U.S. troops to Saudi Arabia. Senate Armed Services chairman Sam Nunn (D-Ga.) similarly learned about the decision to send U.S. troops to Saudi Arabia after the fact.[43] But the Bush administration did go to considerable lengths to meet with members of Congress and to keep them informed about U.S. policy. In late August the president personally briefed and took questions from 170 members.[44]

As summer turned to fall, however, White House interest in congressional opinion faded. By October, congressional leaders on both sides of the aisle began to complain that they were being ignored.[45] Then in early November, after Congress had recessed for the year and the midterm congressional elections were over, President Bush announced a near doubling in the size of U.S. forces in the gulf, a decision that shifted the troops from a defensive to an offensive military posture. In reaching the decision, the president consulted with a small circle of officials in the executive branch; he pointedly avoided discussing the proposed troop increase with even ranking Republicans in Congress, and some congressional leaders learned of his decision only minutes before it was announced.[46]

The main difference between the genesis of Operation Desert Shield and that of Operation Desert Storm was the degree of consensus on the merits of the two plans. The August dialogue between Congress and the president took place amid near unanimity on the need to deter an Iraqi invasion of Saudi Arabia. This left few members of Congress inclined to complain about deficiencies in the consultative process. But no such consensus existed on using U.S. troops to free Kuwait. Faced with potentially stiff opposition on Capitol Hill should his plans to liberate Kuwait by force become known prematurely, Bush had little to gain by consulting with members in advance of announcing the change in the mission of U.S. troops.

Members of Congress have some leverage with which to overcome a president's reluctance to consult with them whenever the White House needs congressional approval. For example, Harry Truman's famed consultations with Sen. Arthur Vandenberg (R-Mich.) stemmed largely from the fact that much of what Truman wanted to accomplish overseas involved treaties and Vandenberg could deliver the Republican votes needed for Senate approval. Truman had far less use for Vandenberg or any other member in those areas of foreign policy where he was free to act on his own initiative. As Malcolm Jewell writes, Truman's "prior bipartisan consultation [was] . . . limited to certain foreign policies requiring legislative consultation. It . . . had little real applicability to diplomatic or military decisions outside the legislative sphere."[47]

The need to win the approval of two-thirds of the Senate similarly accounted for Jimmy Carter's willingness to solicit congressional views during negotiation of the Panama Canal and SALT II treaties. The Carter administration engaged in what Senator Baker hailed as an "unprecedented amount of prior consultation" on Panama as "State Department officials routinely briefed senators on the progress of the negotiations and solicited advice on the remaining military and economic issues under negotiation."[48] In the case of SALT II, Carter and his advisers actively solicited the views of Sen. Henry

"Scoop" Jackson (D-Wash.), who they believed would be a critical vote when the treaty came to the floor.

> The special attention that was paid to the Washington senator was manifested in numerous ways, including: (1) a willingness on the part of the administration to study seriously and ultimately incorporate a number of Jackson's SALT recommendations into the comprehensive U.S. proposal presented to the Soviets in March 1977; (2) an unprecedented commitment by Secretary Vance in October 1977 to meet with Jackson's Armed Services Subcommittee on Arms Control every two weeks; and (3) President Carter's agreement to reappoint General Edward Rowny, Jackson's choice, to be the representative of the Joint Chiefs of Staff on the SALT delegation.[49]

In the end, Carter's efforts came to naught; Jackson became a vehement critic of SALT II.

Because treaty making has declined in importance as an instrument of foreign policy, members of Congress are more likely to gain the leverage they need to push consultations when the success of a presidential policy initiative depends on Congress making a complementary appropriations decision. President Bush, for example, agreed to the bipartisan accord on Nicaragua to avoid a protracted battle over contra aid. Likewise, in 1991 the Bush administration angered pro-Israeli members when it decided to delay $10 billion in loan guarantees to Israel. Threatened with a major political confrontation on the eve of the Arab-Israeli peace talks in Madrid, the administration turned to Sen. Patrick Leahy (D-Vt.), chair of the Senate Foreign Operations Subcommittee, for help. Leahy played a crucial role in persuading pro-Israeli members to approve the delay in the loan guarantees. He also suggested a compromise plan, key elements of which subsequently appeared in the administration's modified proposal for the loan guarantees.[50]

Instances of executive-legislative consultation such as the bipartisan accord on Nicaragua or the compromise on Israeli loan guarantees typically draw praise from practitioners and pundits alike. Such cooperation averts the protracted debate that entangles some policies on Capitol Hill, thus enabling the United States to speak with one voice. Whether consultation actually improves the substance of U.S. policy, however, remains a subjective matter. While President Bush praised the bipartisan agreement on Nicaragua for committing "both the executive and Congress to work together," many supporters of the Reagan administration's policy of seeking to oust the Sandinistas by force saw little benefit to the United States in speaking in a unified voice if that unity meant abandoning the contras.[51]

FRAMING

In 1885, Woodrow Wilson wrote that "even more important than legislation is the instruction and guidance in political affairs which the people might receive from a body which kept all national concerns suffused in a broad daylight of discussion."[52] Over one hundred years later, members of Congress recognize that one of their most powerful instruments for shaping foreign policy is their ability to change the climate of opinion that gave rise to it. As the Bush administration's about-face on the issue of aid to the Iraqi Kurds following the Gulf War attests, what the public and the press think about U.S. foreign policy influences the choices presidents make.[53] And the way members influence public and elite opinion is by framing: packaging an issue in a way that attracts media and executive branch attention, places the issue on the agenda, and puts the administration or a foreign government on the defensive.[54]

As Wilson's remark suggests, congressional efforts to shape public and elite opinion on foreign policy are by no means a recent invention. In 1934 the Senate set up a special committee, headed by Sen. Gerald P. Nye (R-N.Dak.), to investigate claims that U.S. arms manufacturers had maneuvered the United States into World War I. Although the Nye Committee never managed to substantiate the so-called merchants of death thesis, its highly publicized hearings played a major role in fueling isolationist sentiment in the United States on the eve of World War II. When war broke out, the Senate Special Committee to Investigate the National Defense Program, under the leadership of Sen. Harry Truman (D-Mo.), conducted wide-ranging hearings and inquiries into the U.S. war effort. "Fear of investigation or public exposure by the committee was enough in itself to cause countless people in industry, government, and the military to do their jobs right, thereby, in the long run, saving thousands of lives."[55] In 1966 and 1967, the Senate Foreign Relations Committee held a series of televised hearings on the Vietnam War that, as Sen. Frank Church (D-Idaho) later noted, took "Senate questioning of policy out of executive session, where the administration retained control, to the public forum, where the president had no control."[56] The hearings gave critics of Lyndon Johnson's policies a national platform and helped to fuel the nascent antiwar movement.

What is new about congressional attempts to frame public opinion on foreign policy is their prevalence. The increased willingness of members of Congress to target public opinion is due to two factors. One is technology. With the advent of satellite transmissions, video cameras, and cable channels, it is now far easier for members to reach the American public than it was fifty or even twenty-five years ago. The other factor behind the increased prevalence of framing is the erosion of congressional inhibitions against using outside strategies. For much of the twentieth century members who appealed directly to the public were derided on Capitol Hill as showhorses, and they were frequently penalized by the workhorses who dominated the congressional leadership. But with the last three decades having seen the dispersion of authority in Congress, the weakening of party discipline, and the politicization of foreign policy, outside strategies have gained new respect on Capitol Hill.[57]

Members of Congress use many different tools in their efforts to frame opinion. One such vehicle is a bill that is unlikely to become law but that highlights the perceived ills of administration policy. Rep. Nancy Pelosi (D-Calif.) described one legislative effort to punish China for its continued suppression of dissent as "a bill that is hard to veto and easy for the public to understand."[58] Congressional hearings offer another convenient vehicle for shaping opinion. Following President Bush's surprise decision in November 1990 to double the number of U.S. troops in Saudi Arabia, Sen. Sam Nunn (D-Ga.) chaired highly publicized hearings by the Senate Armed Services Committee that featured a parade of former administration officials who criticized the administration's decision to use force to liberate Kuwait. Members may also use reports to attract attention to a cause they support. To pressure the Bush administration into taking a harder line in dealing with the government of El Salvador after the murder of six Jesuit priests in 1989, the special House task force created to investigate the killings issued several reports critical of U.S. policy. Even speeches on the floor can come in handy in shaping opinion, especially now that both the House and Senate allow television cameras into their chambers. In 1990, Senate Majority Leader George Mitchell (D-Maine) gave a series of speeches on the floor of the Senate to draw attention to the resurgence of the Khmer Rouge in Cambodia.

Framing may also involve efforts outside of Congress. Some members of Congress write opinion pieces for major newspapers to float policy proposals or to influence elite opinion. Radio and television are perhaps even more popular vehicles. Members regularly make themselves available for radio and television appearances whenever a crisis breaks or a major vote takes place in order to define for the public the issue that is at stake. Members even resort to political theater in their efforts to shape elite and public opinion. During the controversy in the early 1980s over the Defense Department's policies on the pricing of spare parts, several members put up a Christmas tree decorated with thousand-dollar bolts and seven-hundred-dollar stool caps. The news media, unable to pass up a gripping visual image, gave the tree, and the issue of wasteful defense spending, extensive coverage.

That framing constitutes a strategy for influencing policy may come as a surprise. Critics typically dismiss framing as grandstanding precisely because it involves efforts to attract media coverage. To be sure, members thinking solely of their electoral interest sometimes run to the media with an issue. Senator Church, for example, sounded the tocsin on the Soviet brigade in Cuba in 1979 less to influence President Carter than to ingratiate himself with voters back home.[59] Much the same occurred in 1977 during the neutron bomb controversy. The substance of the floor debates suggests that many opponents did not understand the weapon they were criticizing.[60]

And framing efforts can bring enormous political profit to members of Congress. The most obvious benefit of media attention is public exposure. Exposure can help a member if the position taken pleases constituents, interest groups, or campaign donors, or it may help simply by giving the member more visibility. The career of Rep. Stephen Solarz (D-N.Y.) attests to the personal benefits of framing efforts. When the Philippines became a focal point of U.S. foreign policy in the mid-1980s, he worked the news media assiduously. "By his staff's count, he appeared on thirty-four radio and television shows and was quoted in eighty articles in *The New York Times, The Washington Post,* and *The Wall Street Journal* in a five month period."[61] Solarz soon found that his visibility led to an influx of campaign donations, many of them from outside his district.[62]

But the fact that some members of Congress manipulate the press for purely cynical reasons and others benefit from their association with major issues does not diminish the importance of framing to members who wish to change policy. For policy entrepreneurs, playing to the galleries is an essential tool for leveling the playing field in contests with the White House.[63] Members understand far better than their critics E. E. Schattschneider's point that increasing the scope of the decision-making arena may change the ultimate decision.[64] The media, especially television, give members the means to overcome the obstacles that block attempts to shape policy through legislation. The glare of the spotlight is often a member's best weapon for forcing the administration to reverse its course of action or to build public support for new policy initiatives.

Nor is framing any less useful a technique because it typically invokes simple, if not simplistic, arguments. Dismissing a Christmas tree adorned with bolts and stool caps as a stunt misses the point. Not only do presidents themselves indulge in simple and dramatic appeals—recall Ronald Reagan's

Star Wars speech—such appeals are essential to winning the support of the average citizen. A simple, well-framed charge that anyone can understand puts the burden of proof on the administration to justify its policies.[65]

Sometimes framing is the work of a single member of Congress, usually one who occupies a key post on Capitol Hill. Party leaders such as Senator Mitchell and committee chairs such as Senator Nunn draw the lion's share of news coverage, largely because the media presume both that they speak for other members and are more influential in Congress.[66] But being a party leader or committee chair is not necessary for drawing media attention. Representative Solarz turned up on so many television screens during the crisis in the Philippines because he painstakingly cultivated his contacts with journalists.

Although individual members of Congress at times play a crucial role in changing public and administration opinion on foreign policy, framing results more often from the actions of groups of legislators in Congress. When Congress and the Bush administration parted ways over how to deal with the Chinese government after Tiananmen Square, members who were angered over what they saw as a timid U.S. policy introduced legislation calling for trade sanctions, gave emotional floor speeches, and met with Chinese dissidents, all in an effort to "put political pressure on the administration to take stronger stands."[67] In 1990 and 1991, many members of Congress believed the Bush administration was moving too slowly in responding to the enormous changes sweeping the Soviet bloc. Members favoring a more conciliatory policy toward the Soviet Union introduced bills, gave speeches, appeared on TV talk shows, and issued press releases and staff reports, all in a bid to pressure the administration to act.

Framing efforts are aimed at one of three audiences. At the most general level, members of Congress seek to change public opinion in order to change both presidential and congressional behavior. Writing thirty years ago, Warner Schilling argued that legislators who wanted to influence defense policy should "change their policy target from the budget to the climate of opinion that shaped it."[68] In the mid-1980s, Sen. Charles Grassley (R-Iowa) showed the wisdom of Schilling's advice. Rather than attacking individual defense programs, Grassley released information that the air force had paid nearly one thousand dollars to purchase a small plastic cap for the leg of a navigator's stool. The story captured national headlines, and soon other members were scrambling to reveal stories of waste, fraud, and abuse in the Pentagon budget. As *The Almanac of American Politics* described Grassley's efforts: "He has shown the capacity to change the terms of the debate, and future historians may date the end of the Reagan Administration's huge increases in defense spending to Grassley's initiative."[69]

A second audience for framing efforts is the White House itself. In making the rounds of television and radio news shows during the Philippines crisis in 1986, for example, Senator Lugar clearly hoped that his media blitz would persuade President Reagan to drop his support for Ferdinand Marcos. In a similar vein, then-Sen. Albert Gore, Jr. (D-Tenn.) tried to embarrass the Bush administration into embracing the fight against global warming. When a government scientist complained that administration officials had forced him to tone down testimony he was scheduled to give to Congress on the need to combat global warming, Gore played the story to the hilt with the media. The Bush White House suddenly found itself under a barrage of criticism for bending scientific research to conform to its political agenda. Bowing to public pressure, "the White House announced it would hold a workshop on global warming to prepare for negotiations on an international treaty."[70]

The third possible target of framing is another country. Members of Congress often want to send signals to friends and foes. Take the case where a subsidiary of the Toshiba Corporation illegally sold machinery that enabled the Soviet navy to make its submarines far quieter and thus harder to detect. The government of Japan initially ignored the problem. Then the matter reached Capitol Hill. On 20 June 1987, five members of Congress stood on the grounds of the United States Capitol and used a sledgehammer to smash a radio/cassette player made by Toshiba to bits. Although the protest was a blatant publicity ploy, the news media on both sides of the Pacific gladly went along.

> The video clip was replayed again and again on Japanese television. One day later, the chairman and president of Toshiba Corporation announced their resignations. On July 20, the Toshiba Corporation ran a full-page ad in dozens of American newspapers apologizing for the actions of its subsidiary. By the end of July, a memorandum between MITI and the Japanese Foreign Ministry provided for ministerial review of sensitive exports, thus raising export control to a higher government level. On July 31, the Japanese government sent a tougher export control law to the Diet; the bill passed in early September. In a series of talks over the summer and fall, the Japanese agreed to become partners with the US in a new program to develop anti-submarine warfare technology. Japanese companies, led by Toshiba Corp., began formulating their own COCOM [Coordinating Committee for Multilateral Export Controls] compliance regulations.[71]

Thus, what many observers initially dismissed as a crass stunt by five publicity-hungry members of Congress succeeded in pushing Toshiba's transgressions to center-stage in U.S.-Japanese relations and thereby moved the government of Japan to action.

Operation Desert Shield offers another example of framing efforts aimed at other countries. Germany and Japan initially balked at providing aid. In September, the House began consideration of the annual defense authorization bill, including an amendment that sought to require the Japanese government to pay the full cost of stationing U.S. troops in Japan. The debate on the provision unleashed "a storm of animosity, extraordinary in its extent and intensity," over the reluctance of Germany and Japan to help support the multinational force.[72] The burden-sharing amendment, which almost surely would have lost had it been considered before the Iraqi invasion of Kuwait, passed the House by an overwhelming margin of 370 to 53. Bonn and Tokyo did not miss the powerful political signal being sent by the House. Within two days of the debate, Germany agreed to contribute to the gulf effort, and Japan quadrupled its aid offer.[73]

Framing offers members of Congress a powerful tool for shaping policy. If presidents fail to react quickly or move contrary to public opinion, they may find themselves suddenly compelled to change their policies. Yet framing does not always work. Presidents may be willing to pay a high political cost to advance their policy agenda or they may deflate congressional pressure by changing the style and not the substance of their policies. President Nixon reacted to opposition to Vietnam, for example, by taking the war underground.[74] When congressional and public criticism of U.S. policy toward El Salvador escalated in 1981, "administration officials simply stopped talking about Central America to reporters and . . . news coverage, especially on television, immediately dried up."[75] When President Bush came under attack in late 1991 for devoting too much attention to foreign policy, he responded by holding several highly publicized meetings with bankers, business executives, and economic advisers. The meetings were "meant more for public consumption near the start of the election campaign than as a genuine effort to bring about political changes."[76] And foreign countries can and do dismiss the symbolic actions of Congress.

Even when presidents and foreign countries change their substantive behavior, it is difficult to establish that Congress's efforts are responsible. Public support for high levels of defense spending may have fallen without the efforts of Senator Grassley and his imitators. The Reagan administration might have dropped its support for Ferdinand Marcos even without being pushed by Senator Lugar and others. And Germany and Japan might have increased their financial support for Operation Desert Shield even in the absence of bitter congressional debate. Still, it is hard to deny the conclusion that members of Congress often focus the glare of the public spotlight on foreign policy issues and that sometimes the results matter. Far from injecting politics into an otherwise technocratic decision making process, framing enables members to counter, at least partially, the president's inherent advantages in setting foreign policy.

CONCLUSION

The natural temptation when thinking of Congress's role in foreign policy is to think of legislation. After all, Congress is the country's supreme lawmaking body, and members of Congress fashion themselves as lawmakers. But to limit any discussion of congressional activism on foreign policy to legislation, whether of a substantive or procedural kind, misses a good deal of what Congress does in foreign policy. The very difficulties inherent in crafting and passing legislation, combined with the breathtaking speed with which international events can occur, encourage members to use nonlegislative means to influence the substance of policy.

Congressional diplomacy, executive-legislative consultations, and attempts to frame opinion draw varying degrees of approval from observers. In the case of congressional diplomacy, most observers agree that members of Congress are well within their rights to conduct fact-finding trips abroad and to meet with foreign officials. Attempts at Lone Ranger diplomacy, on the other hand, are almost universally condemned, regardless of whether they are undertaken by a member as prominent as Jim Wright or one as obscure as George Hansen. The belief that only the president should negotiate on behalf of the United States is deeply rooted in both elite and public opinion. The intensity of the inevitable criticism usually undercuts any attempt at alternative diplomacy.

In contrast to Lone Ranger diplomacy, commentators typically applaud instances of executive-legislative consultation as responsible leadership by the president and Congress. But what might be the most responsible course of action for members of Congress to follow is also often the most ineffective. Members can consult only so long as the president wants to solicit advice. And given the deep-seated policy differences that presidents frequently have with Congress, they often choose to inform rather than consult. When the president refuses to consult with Congress, members are forced to choose between acquiescence and action.

Because many in Congress today refuse to acquiesce in policies they believe to be unwise and because the obstacles to legislative success are so daunting, members increasingly turn to framing opinion in order to push foreign policy closer to their preferences. Of course, critics typically dismiss framing as political posturing. To be sure, many members of Congress are drawn to framing because it can be politically profitable. But to require members of Congress to be pure of motive is to impose a double standard. Presidents often use foreign policy to promote their political self-interest, going so far as to plan trips abroad around photo opportunities that will burnish their image as commander in chief and, in turn, boost their public approval ratings.[77]

The deeper lesson, however, is that efforts to frame opinion are crucial to advancing any policy, foreign or domestic. Whether Operation Desert Storm is defined as resisting naked aggression or as trading blood for oil, whether the debate over U.S.-Japan relations is cast in terms of free trade or fair trade, or whether global warming is seen as an economic or an environmental issue profoundly colors the course of political debate. And in American politics today the president enjoys considerable inherent advantages in dealing with Congress. If members of Congress allow the president to define the terms of debate, the inherent advantages grow even more formidable. Conversely, when members succeed in defining the terms of debate in their favor, the contest between the two branches of government is more nearly equal.

IN 1973, A CONGRESS appalled by the excesses of the imperial presidency
and spurred on by the abuses of Watergate passed the War Powers Resolution.
Supporters hailed the legislation for restoring the traditional balance of
power between Congress and the president on questions of war and peace.
Two decades later, however, the war power remains firmly lodged in the Oval
Office. Presidents have repeatedly refused to invoke the core provisions of the
War Powers Resolution, and few members of Congress believe that the law
can be made workable over the opposition of the White House. As Sen. Sam
Nunn (D-Ga.), chair of the Senate Armed Services Committee, puts it: The
War Powers Resolution has "never worked in the past [and] it's never going to
work."[1]

The failure of the War Powers Resolution illustrates an important lesson
about congressional involvement in foreign policy: greater activism by no
means guarantees Congress greater influence. Capitol Hill is littered with
bills that die in committees, reports that go unread, and speeches that are
quickly forgotten. Even when Congress passes laws designed to increase its
influence, foreign policy may retain a distinctly presidential imprint.

Of course, a gap between activism and influence typifies all congressional
decision making. By most accounts, however, the gap is greater when it
comes to foreign policy. Congress's problem in shaping foreign policy results
in part from congressional timidity, as some members doubt their competence to decide foreign policy issues and others fear that challenging the
president will hurt them at the polls. But it also reflects the greater obstacles
that members face in making their preferences felt on foreign policy. Presidents enjoy numerous advantages over Congress when it comes to foreign
affairs, and the Supreme Court has enhanced these inherent advantages by
deferring to the president on foreign policy. In contrast, the tools of lawmak-

ing and oversight that serve members so well in domestic policy often prove inadequate in foreign affairs.

While Congress enjoys greater success in influencing domestic policy, it remains an important force in the making of foreign policy. The extent of congressional influence, however, varies greatly across the wide range of foreign policy issues. While Congress seldom influences decisions to use military force, it frequently shapes the broad goals of foreign policy and it exercises tremendous influence over how resources will be allocated among specific programs. Congress's influence varies across what has been called crisis, strategic, and structural policy because the electoral costs of challenging the White House, the relative advantages of the two branches, and the extent of judicial deference vary with each policy area.[2]

TWO PRESIDENCIES

No one seriously doubts that Congress matters in the making of domestic policy. Whether the president is proposing to increase spending on education, reform the health care system, or raise taxes, observers inevitably ask how members of Congress will react. The same can not be said of foreign policy. Most scholarly work relegates members of Congress to the margins of decision making on foreign policy. Indeed, political scientists often speak of how the United States has "two presidencies," an embattled one at home and a triumphant one abroad.[3]

Efforts to explain why presidents get more of what they want and members get less of what they want on foreign policy usually point to congressional timidity. The historian Arthur Schlesinger, for example, argues that "in foreign policy the inclination is to let the Presidency have the responsibility—and the power."[4] Morton Halperin argues that on major foreign policy issues "members of Congress prefer to avoid the responsibility."[5] I. M. Destler, Leslie Gelb, and Anthony Lake complain that members have "little capacity or taste for making responsible decisions and accepting their consequences."[6]

What accounts for congressional timidity on foreign policy? In part it is attributed to norms about institutional competence. As Schlesinger writes, in domestic affairs members of Congress "have ample confidence in their own information and judgment. They do not lightly surrender power to the executive. In domestic policy, the republic is all Missouri: it has to be shown. But confronted by presidential initiatives abroad, [members of] Congress . . . generally lack confidence in their own information and judgment."[7] The doubts members have about their competence in foreign policy stem partly from their lack of expertise. But the doubts are also fueled by a lingering sense of institutional guilt over the failure of members more than a half-century ago to recognize the fascist threat in Europe and the Pacific.

The second and more commonly offered reason for congressional timidity is simple political expediency: challenging the president on foreign policy poses far greater electoral risks than does a similar challenge in domestic policy. Voters may see foreign policy challenges as undercutting the president and endangering the national interest. If a foreign policy issue lacks a constituency, which often happens because so few Americans care about international affairs, members will not face the potential for offsetting gains. In comparison, domestic issues do not generate a rally-'round-the-flag effect and they often excite greater constituent passion. Because the path of least electoral risk in foreign policy lies in avoiding an outright challenge to the president, many members prefer to posture rather than to take responsibility for foreign policy decisions.

As popular as arguments about congressional timidity may be, they should not be pushed too far. Even if members of Congress were confident electoral altruists, they would still have greater difficulty in making their preferences felt on foreign policy than they do in domestic policy. The reason is that the balance of power between the two branches of government shifts in favor of the president when the debate moves from domestic to foreign policy. Not only do presidents have greater formal and informal powers in foreign policy than in domestic policy, the Supreme Court's deference to the executive branch in foreign affairs intensifies the inherent disadvantages Congress faces when it tries to put its stamp on policy.

Presidents hold an edge over Congress in foreign affairs in part because in foreign policy they enjoy formal powers denied them in domestic policy. The Constitution designates the president as commander in chief, a position that has no analogy in domestic affairs. Although the framers saw the post as no more than the office at the top of the military hierarchy, over the course of two hundred years presidents have succeeded in transforming the commander-in-chief clause into an independent source of authority.[8] Likewise, since the days of George Washington it has been firmly established that the president alone has the authority to receive ambassadors, to recognize other states, and to negotiate on behalf of the United States.

Presidents also benefit from the fact that the inherent advantages of their office are at a maximum in foreign policy. Foremost among these advantages is the ability to initiate policy. In domestic affairs, changing policy usually requires writing new laws, and, as a result, presidential discretion is limited.

Presidents can propose tax hikes or health-care reform, but their proposals will not become policy *until* Congress approves.

In foreign policy, however, the reverse is true. As Woodrow Wilson recognized long before he became president, "The initiative in foreign affairs, which the President possesses without any restriction whatever, is virtually the power to control them absolutely."[9] The last twenty-five years abound with examples in which presidents used their initiative to make foreign policy: the opening to China, the grain embargo, the invasions of Grenada and Panama, and the dispatch of troops to Lebanon and Saudi Arabia, to name just a few. Of course, in many areas of foreign policy Congress has the constitutional authority to overturn a presidential initiative, but even here the policy stands *unless* Congress acts otherwise. And given the president's power to veto legislation, no congressional challenge will succeed in the absence of widespread consensus on Capitol Hill.

Secrecy is another inherent advantage held by the president on foreign policy. Public disclosure is the norm in domestic politics, but in foreign policy there is an inescapable need to keep some matters secret. In theory, members of Congress could claim a greater role for themselves in determining which matters will be kept secret, but the resulting workload would quickly overwhelm the institution. And the need to delegate to the executive branch the responsibility for handling secrets immediately puts members at the mercy of the executive's willingness to share information.

Presidents and their subordinates have shown themselves quite willing to use secrecy to deflect congressional challenges to their policy preferences. As the Iran-contra affair attests, administrations may go so far as to lie to Congress. Far more often, though, executive branch officials merely refuse to volunteer information that would help their opponents on Capitol Hill. In testimony before the Senate Intelligence Committee in 1984, for example, CIA Director William Casey flatly denied that the CIA had mined Nicaragua's harbors. "Only later did senators discover this was merely a subterfuge. Casey had relied on a technical distinction: the CIA had mined *piers* within the harbors."[10] Other foreign policy agencies also mislead members of Congress when it serves their interests. Rep. William Dickinson (R-Ala.) complains about the Defense Department: "You have to be pretty smart to know what the question is that will get the answer you are seeking. And I don't think for a minute that the Services knock themselves out trying to help you ask the right questions, unless they are anxious to have you ask that question."[11] And during the Reagan and Bush administrations, the State Department regularly downplayed human rights abuses by American allies.[12]

The president's advantages over Congress in foreign policy have been enhanced by the Supreme Court. For nearly two hundred years the Court has accorded the president broad powers to act overseas, powers it has explicitly refused him at home. The distinction between foreign and domestic policy is seen most clearly in the 1936 case *U.S. v. Curtiss-Wright Export Corporation,* perhaps the most frequently cited legal opinion on presidential authority in foreign affairs. Writing on behalf of a near-unanimous Court, Justice George Sutherland held that "the President [operates] as the sole organ of the federal government in the field of international relations" and that "within the international field [Congress] must often accord to the President a degree of discretion and freedom from statutory restriction which would not be admissible were domestic affairs alone involved."[13]

Legal scholars have long questioned the reasoning Sutherland used in deciding *Curtiss-Wright,* and in subsequent opinions other justices have dismissed his arguments about presidential authority as mere *dicta.*[14] Nonetheless, the Court continues to give the president great leeway to conduct foreign policy. In 1978, for instance, Congress sought to overcome a presidential reluctance to punish countries that violated international rules on whaling by passing a law imposing mandatory sanctions. In the early 1980s, Japan violated the rules but the Reagan administration refused to impose sanctions. The Supreme Court subsequently ruled that the president had the authority to waive the sanctions in return for a Japanese pledge to restrict whaling in the future. As Justice Thurgood Marshall recognized in his dissent to *Japan Whaling Association v. American Cetacean Society,* the Court's ruling significantly diminished congressional influence over foreign policy: "This Court now renders illusory the mandatory language of the statutory scheme, and finds permissible exactly the result that Congress sought to prevent."[15]

If the Supreme Court has done much to weaken congressional influence over foreign policy making with its rulings on the merits of cases, it has perhaps done even more to enhance presidential authority with its willingness to dismiss many congressional challenges on the grounds that the contested issues are not ripe for judicial decision or that they raise political and not legal questions.[16] (Why the courts find some foreign policy issues justiciable and others not remains unknown.) "Not one case contesting the constitutionality of the war in Vietnam ever came before the Supreme Court, and the lower courts consistently dismissed such actions, citing the doctrine of political questions."[17] In 1979 the Supreme Court dismissed a legal challenge to President Carter's decision to terminate the mutual defense treaty with Taiwan, with a plurality of the Court explicitly saying it was legally bound to dismiss the case "because it involves the authority of the President in the conduct of our country's foreign relations."[18]

The pro-executive branch bias of the Supreme Court exacerbates Congress's inherent disadvantages. One problem facing Congress is that much of foreign policy lies beyond legislation. No matter how much members of Congress might wish to, they cannot legislate an arms control treaty with Russia or ban human rights abuses in East Timor. Indeed, what the president will negotiate, or even if he will negotiate, lies beyond the reach of legislation. And as Chapter 4 discussed, even where legislation is feasible the speed with which events can change overseas and the need for flexibility and secrecy frequently render it an ineffectual tool for shaping policy.

At the same time, members of Congress face greater obstacles in overseeing foreign policy than domestic policy. Part of the problem is secrecy. In domestic policy, members rely heavily on constituents to alert them of instances in which the executive branch has violated existing legislation. As noted earlier, many laws are designed to create so-called fire alarms, systems of rules, procedures, and practices designed to make it easier for constituents to detect and notify Congress of executive branch transgressions. In foreign policy, however, the need to keep information secret limits the utility of fire alarms and greatly increases members' difficulties in monitoring the executive branch.

Foreign policy oversight also poses problems for members of Congress because it involves sovereign nations that have no obligation to cooperate. Congress can subpoena American citizens to testify, but it cannot, for example, compel the Japanese government to produce internal memorandums on its efforts to open up the Japanese market to American firms. Congress's limited ability to oversee foreign policy extends even to cases where a nation receives U.S. aid. As Joseph White points out, "Other nations are sovereign, so [a] committee 'can't go in and cut projects,' even if they are turkeys. In other cases, like that of Israel, aid is not project based and 'could be used for *anything.*'"[19]

Besides the difficulties posed by secrecy and sovereignty, members of Congress face problems in establishing the efficacy of foreign policy programs. Many domestic agencies and programs will over time produce clear evidence of their effectiveness. To take a hypothetical example, when the Department of Agriculture implements a new price support program designed to reduce government subsidies to cotton farmers, evidence will begin to accumulate within a year or two on whether subsidies actually have fallen. Of course, observers may (and usually do) argue over what the evidence means, but typically some undisputed evidence exists.

In contrast, in foreign policy it is usually far more difficult to relate means to ends. Opinions abound on the wisdom of Ronald Reagan's policy toward

Nicaragua, for example, but no one knows for sure whether or not the Sandinistas would have agreed to democratic elections in the absence of aid to the contras. The fundamental problem is that assessing the efficacy of many foreign policy programs requires knowledge about the preferences of foreign leaders, knowledge that usually is in short supply.

Defense policy presents similar difficulties in relating means to ends, though here the problem is usually one of judging the relationship in prospect rather than retrospect.[20] As a former chairman of the Joint Chiefs of Staff once put it, the Defense Department "lacks an easily calculated 'bottom line' to force needed change."[21] So long as the country remains out of war, the effectiveness of most weapons and tactics remains open to dispute. The services do subject individual weapons systems to operational testing, but an adversary would have a much greater incentive, namely survival, to find ways to defeat U.S. weapons. And even actual combat may leave questions unanswered. Following the Gulf War, for instance, considerable dispute arose over whether the Patriot missile had been as successful as the army had claimed.[22]

The difficulties members of Congress face in relating means to ends on foreign policy benefit the executive branch. Because many members agree with John Kennedy's claim that "domestic policy can only defeat us; foreign policy can kill us," the burden of proof in foreign policy usually rests with the president's critics.[23] But members who wish to challenge the president often find it difficult to build an airtight case. By necessity, much of their challenge is based on speculation rather than on hard evidence. But presidents can usually negate such challenges by responding with speculation of their own—speculation made all the more impressive because it bears the imprimatur of the administration's foreign policy experts.

Up to this point, the emphasis has been on the obstacles that members of Congress must surmount in order to influence foreign policy. But to what extent do members actually succeed in injecting their preferences into policy? As the next three sections show, the answer depends on the type of foreign policy issue at stake. The reason why congressional influence varies from crisis to strategic to structural policy is that the electoral costs of challenging the White House, the relative advantages of the two branches, and the extent of judicial deference vary with each policy type.

CRISIS POLICY

The most visible though least common category of foreign policy issues is crisis policy: situations in which officials perceive an immediate threat to U.S. national interests and are actively considering whether to use military force. Although international crises raise the possibility of war, members of Congress find themselves excluded from decisions on crisis policy. Presidents insist they have independent authority to initiate the use of force, a position that has been implicitly buttressed by the reluctance of the courts to confront the war powers issue. In turn, practical, normative, and electoral concerns generally leave members of Congress with little choice but to follow the president's lead.

To judge by the text of the Constitution and the debate that went into its drafting, members of Congress should play a key role in the making of crisis policy.[24] Article I, section 8 states that "the Congress shall have the power to declare War." In recognition that not all armed conflict reaches the level of full-scale war, the Constitution further assigns to Congress the power to "grant Letters of Marque and Reprisal." In assigning the war power to Congress, the delegates to the Constitutional Convention explicitly rejected proposals to lodge the authority to make war in the executive branch. When Pierce Butler moved to vest "the power in the President, who will have all the requisite qualities, and will not make war but when the nation will support it," none of the other delegates seconded his motion.[25]

Regardless of what the framers intended, by the middle of the twentieth century members of Congress found themselves on the outside looking in on crisis decision making. In Korea in 1950, Cuba in 1962, the Dominican Republic in 1965, and Cambodia in 1970, presidents ordered U.S. troops into actual or imminent hostilities without the benefit of specific congressional authorization. Indeed, in the case of Korea, several senior members of Congress actually urged Truman not to involve Congress, arguing that he could dispatch the troops on his own authority.[26] In Lebanon in 1958 and Vietnam in 1964, Congress gave Dwight Eisenhower and Lyndon Johnson unlimited discretion to use force. In the case of Vietnam, that discretion led to a war that few, if any, members had anticipated when they voted for the Gulf of Tonkin Resolution.[27]

The debacle in Vietnam, and especially Richard Nixon's unilateral decision to invade Cambodia, led members of Congress to attempt to reclaim the war power. The chosen vehicle was the War Powers Resolution, which was passed in November 1973 over Nixon's veto. Supporters of the law hoped it would deter presidents from sending troops into combat without first consulting with Congress. To give the request for greater executive-legislative consultations bite, the resolution has two key requirements. Section 4(a) requires the president to submit a report to Congress within forty-eight hours whenever troops are introduced "(1) into hostilities or situations where imminent involvement in hostilities is clearly indicated by the circumstances; (2) into the territory, airspace or waters of a foreign nation, while equipped for combat, except for deployments which relate solely to supply, replacement, repair or training of such forces; or (3) in numbers which substantially enlarge United States armed forces equipped for combat already located in a foreign nation."[28] Section 5(b) stipulates that if U.S. armed forces have been sent into situations of actual or imminent hostilities the president must remove the troops within sixty days—ninety days if he requests a delay—unless Congress declares war or otherwise authorizes the use of force. The resolution also provides that Congress can compel the president to withdraw the troops at any time by passing a concurrent resolution. (After the Supreme Court in 1983 invalidated most uses of the legislative veto in *I.N.S. v. Chadha,* Congress passed separate legislation substituting a joint resolution for the concurrent resolution.)

Despite the hopes of its supporters, the War Powers Resolution has proved to be no more than what Arthur Schlesinger has called "a toy handcuff."[29] The sixty-day clock has never been tested, and many members seem almost pained by the fact that the resolution exists. When Ronald Reagan sent the marines to Lebanon in September 1982 to act as peacekeepers in the Lebanese civil war, for example, nine months elapsed before Congress went so far as to direct the president to "obtain statutory authorization from Congress with respect to any substantial expansion in the number or role in Lebanon of United States Armed Forces."[30] Congress finally invoked the War Powers Resolution in late September 1983, but only after several marines were killed and U.S. forces intervened in the civil war in support of the Lebanese government. Even then, Congress gave Reagan authority to act under the resolution for eighteen months and to use "such protective measures as may be necessary to secure the safety of the Multinational Force in Lebanon."[31]

As timid as Congress's actions on Lebanon were, they might have set an important precedent. But such was not the case. In 1987 the Reagan administration sent the U.S. Navy into the Persian Gulf to protect Kuwaiti shipping from attacks by Iran. Although the Defense Department paid "imminent danger" bonuses to U.S. personnel in the gulf and U.S. forces attacked Iranian ships and staging areas, motions to invoke the War Powers

Resolution died on the floor of Congress. Members showed even less enthusiasm for invoking the War Powers Resolution after George Bush sent U.S. troops to Saudi Arabia following the Iraqi invasion of Kuwait in August 1990. Congress adjourned for the year in late October without considering any motions to invoke the War Powers Resolution. The same pattern repeated itself in 1993 after several U.S. soldiers were killed in a peacekeeping effort in Somalia. The House and Senate both passed nonbinding resolutions asking President Bill Clinton to consult with Congress about the controversial deployment, but neither chamber moved to invoke the War Powers Resolution.[32]

Reasons for the failure of the War Powers Resolution abound.[33] One is that Congress is of many minds when it comes to the wisdom of the resolution. Some members, "reflecting their constituencies, are loath to second-guess the president or to do anything that might be perceived as undercutting American forces, especially if the administration could blame them for the loss of life."[34] Other members doubt the resolution's constitutionality or are happy to ignore its provisions if they agree with the president's decision to deploy troops. These attitudes give members who doubt the wisdom of the policy or the president's authority to order it good reason to conclude that any effort to invoke the resolution will be futile.

A second reason the War Powers Resolution has failed is that with the exception of Jimmy Carter every president since Richard Nixon has denied its constitutionality. Some have gone so far as to ignore the resolution in situations where it would seem to apply. In the early 1980s, for instance, Ronald Reagan refused to file a report on the activities of U.S. military advisers in El Salvador, even after several were killed, on the grounds that hostilities were not imminent. More generally, presidents have avoided taking any step that might be construed as acknowledging the constitutionality of the War Powers Resolution. Thus, when Ronald Reagan signed the resolution authorizing the presence of marines in Lebanon, he stated that the signing should not "be viewed as any acknowledgment that the President's constitutional authority can be impermissibly infringed by statute, that congressional authorization would be required if and when the period specified in Section 5(b) of the War Powers Resolution might be deemed to have been triggered and the period had expired."[35] In rejecting the constitutionality of the War Powers Resolution, presidents have stated repeatedly that the commander-in-chief clause gives them independent authority to make war.

The ability of presidents to disregard the War Powers Resolution has been made easier by the law's imprecision. The text of the resolution does not define what constitutes imminent or actual hostilities, thereby enabling presidents to skirt the law by denying that U.S. troops face a military danger. The resolution also fails to require presidents to state if they are filing their report under the provision that triggers the sixty-day clock. Thus, while presidents filed more than twenty reports to Congress in the first two decades the resolution was in effect, only Gerald Ford during the *Mayaguez* crisis filed a report that specified section 4(a)(1). (Since Ford submitted his report after U.S. forces had been withdrawn, he conceded little to Congress.) In every other instance, presidents have submitted their reports without mentioning any specific sections of the resolution, thereby shifting the burden of starting the clock onto Congress.

The War Powers Resolution also has been weakened by the deference the courts pay to the president in foreign policy. In the four instances in which members of Congress asked the courts to force the president to abide by the resolution, the suits were dismissed as nonjusticiable. In dismissing congressional challenges, the courts set a high standard for considering such a suit justiciable. In *Lowry v. Reagan,* for example, a federal district court ruled it would hear the dispute over President Reagan's authority to order the navy to protect Kuwaiti shipping only if there were a "true confrontation between the Executive and a unified Congress, as evidenced by its passage of legislation to enforce the [War Powers] Resolution."[36] Likewise, in *Dellums v. Bush,* a case in which 110 members challenged President Bush's authority to liberate Kuwait without congressional authorization, a federal district court ruled it would act only if "the plaintiffs in an action of this kind be or represent the majority of the members of Congress."[37] Since a declaration of war requires the approval of both houses of Congress, the courts have effectively shifted the burden of proof from a war's proponents, which is where the Constitution placed it, to a war's opponents.

The failure of the War Powers Resolution has prompted several reform proposals. In 1989, a bipartisan group of senators led by Robert Byrd (D-W. V.), John Warner (R-Va.), and Sam Nunn (D-Ga.) urged replacing the provision mandating the sixty-day clock with one stipulating that a resolution to reverse a presidential decision to send troops into imminent or actual hostilities would be accorded expedited attention in both chambers.[38] The Byrd-Nunn-Warner proposal sought to reverse the presumption of the War Powers Resolution that troops should be withdrawn unless Congress gave its permission. In 1993, Sen. Joseph Biden (D-Del.) proposed extending the sixty-day period and granting the president limited authority in advance to use force to implement United Nations resolutions.[39]

Reform efforts such as the Byrd-Nunn-Warner and Biden proposals face a dim future. Any attempt to revise the War Powers Resolution is likely to spark bitter debate on the floor, and many conservatives will use the opportunity to try to repeal the resolution outright. As Secretary of Defense Les Aspin observed during his confirmation hearings in 1993: "It's always been assumed that to try and amend [the Resolution] would be such a humongous fight and raise such enormous hackles, and in the end it's not clear whether you'd get anything much better."[40]

Even if political feasibility were not an issue, no reform can solve the fundamental problems that prevent members of Congress from having a say in the making of crisis policy. No law can prevent presidents from sending troops abroad without notice and thereby presenting Congress with a *fait accompli*. If the deployment turns out to be for a short duration, as happened in Grenada, Libya, and Panama (among other instances), members have no practical recourse against the president for having acted without congressional authorization. If the deployment turns out to be lengthy, however, the main recourse members have is the politically and morally difficult one of cutting off funds to troops who may be fighting for their lives.

Legislative restrictions might appear more appropriate for situations such as the Gulf War in which the decision to use force is made over the course of several weeks or months. Even here, though, the utility of legislative strictures is weak. One problem is that while legislation can urge, request, and demand that the president consult with members of Congress on decisions to use force, it cannot compel him to follow any of the advice that members might care to offer. Moreover, as Chapter 6 pointed out, the willingness of presidents to consult with members of Congress varies directly with the amount of agreement between both ends of Pennsylvania Avenue. As a result, executive-legislative consultation is most likely when it is least meaningful and least likely when it would be most meaningful.

At the same time, even the most precisely drafted law cannot overcome the limitations inherent in legislation as an instrument for influencing crisis policy. As an institution Congress can do no more than give or withhold its permission to use force. Conditional authorizations are impractical, so once members authorize the president to send U.S. troops into combat they cede control over policy to the executive branch. Members are free to hope that the president will use the authority wisely, but as the Gulf of Tonkin Resolution showed, once given the authority to use force a president is not bound by the expectations members might have about the conditions under which he will use it.[41] The "use it and lose it" quality of congressional authorizations makes many members leery about acting on crises until events have made armed conflict likely. By delaying, however, members virtually guarantee, as Sen. Arthur Vandenberg once put it, that crises will "never reach Congress until they have developed to a point where Congressional discretion is pathetically restricted."[42]

The evolution of Desert Shield into Desert Storm illustrates the problem facing members of Congress. When George Bush sent U.S. troops to the Persian Gulf in August 1990, some observers urged Congress to strengthen the president's bargaining position by authorizing him to use force against Iraq. At the beginning of October the House and Senate both passed non-binding resolutions expressing support for the actions Bush had taken, but neither chamber moved to give him authority to act against Iraq.[43] For members, such a resolution had two distinct disadvantages: defeating it would have undercut the president's bargaining leverage, while passing it would have relieved him of any need to include Congress in future decisions on the crisis. Since Bush's stated policy was to rely on economic sanctions to compel Iraq to withdraw from Kuwait, most members believed that any debate over authorizing the use of force would be premature. So long as the president refused to discuss the possibility of liberating Kuwait by force, members were content to accept the status quo.

All that changed in November when Bush announced that the United States was prepared to use force to liberate Kuwait. Although numerous observers urged Congress to convene in special session, the proposal foundered over two problems. One was that no one knew if war was likely; if Iraq backed down when threatened with force, as many in the administration claimed it would, then congressional authorization would be unnecessary. The other problem was that if members voted in November or December to authorize the use of force, they would have lost control of policy. While there were conditions under which a majority was prepared to vote in December for war, there were also conditions under which a majority would have voted against war. And no one knew which set of circumstances would prevail. Thus, as Rep. Dan Glickman (D-Kans.) put it at the time, "No one is interested in a hypothetical vote, and I don't want a hypothetical special session."[44]

By early January 1991 the question of whether to use force was no longer hypothetical. The Iraqi government had steadfastly refused to make even symbolic concessions, and the Bush administration had given in to public pressure and requested that Congress formally authorize the use of force. At the same time, however, members had only two options. They could either grant the president the authority he requested and thereby risk a costly war, or deny his request and thereby deal him a humiliating public rebuff and perhaps make war more likely. In the end, practical, normative, and electoral calculations led a majority of Congress, albeit a small one in the Senate, to grant the president authority to wage war.

None of the foregoing is to say that Congress can never figure in crisis policy. Members of Congress may succeed in shaping crisis decision making if a president, for reasons of political expediency or philosophy, chooses to solicit their views or to request their authorization. Similarly, as the effort to cut off funding for Vietnam during the dying days of the war and the grumbling in late 1993 over the peacekeeping effort in Somalia both suggest, Congress may become active once troops are deployed if the policy is unpopular with the public, the deployment is limited, the costs of withdrawal are small, or the administration vacillates in its commitment to the policy. Outside of these circumstances, however, Congress plays at best a small role in crisis policy. The hopes of the framers to the contrary, members of Congress have not found the means by which to keep the war power vested in the legislative branch.

STRATEGIC POLICY

Although crisis policy rivets the attention of practitioners and scholars alike, far more foreign policy issues constitute what can be called strategic policy. At its most essential, strategic policy outlines the basic goals and tactics of foreign policy. In diplomatic matters, strategic policy stipulates the nature of U.S. relations with other countries, such as whether the United States will pressure China to improve its human rights record or encourage Israel to trade land for peace. In defense matters, strategic policy establishes the basic mix and missions of military forces, such as the extent to which the Pentagon should continue to rely on reserve forces and whether nuclear strategy should emphasize defensive systems over offensive ones.

Instances in which Congress plays a substantial role in the making of strategic policy far exceed those for crisis policy. In Uganda in 1978, the Philippines and South Africa in 1986, and Russia in 1991, members of Congress, acting both as individuals and as an institution, forced administrations to reverse U.S. policy. In the late 1980s, members pushed the Reagan and Bush administrations to take a tougher stance with Japan on trade policy. And during the Reagan years, Congress frustrated attempts by the White House to overthrow the Sandinistas and to gut the major arms control treaties of the 1970s.

The reason for Congress's greater success in shaping strategic policy is due partly to the fact that challenging the president on strategic issues poses less of an electoral risk. The charge of being disloyal or unpatriotic carries less weight when leveled against a member who criticizes a president for acting slowly in response to the collapse of the Soviet Union than when leveled against a member who criticizes a president for ordering an invasion of Panama. Involvement in strategic policy may even bring members electoral credit. Interest groups are likely to reward members who champion their causes. Identification with a major foreign policy issue may also bring members greater media attention and, in turn, greater visibility back home.

At the same time, congressional influence over strategic policy is greater than that over crisis policy because there are clear limits on the president's authority to make strategic decisions. Unlike crisis policy, where presidents claim they can order the use of force on their own authority, many strategic decisions clearly require congressional assent. Foremost among these is the requirement that two-thirds of the Senate consent to any treaty. As Jimmy Carter discovered with both the Panama Canal and SALT II treaties, the ability of senators to withhold their consent gives them leverage over strategic policy.

Congress also has a powerful tool with which to influence strategic policy in its commerce power. Trade agreements such as the North American Free-Trade Agreement (NAFTA) must ultimately be approved by Congress, which gives the executive branch strong incentive to incorporate congressional views into the final agreement. The ability to grant or withhold most-favored-nation trading status also gives members influence. Members of Congress can also initiate trade legislation, as they did in 1978 in imposing a trade embargo on Uganda and again in 1986 in imposing sanctions on South Africa.

Strategic policy also is more susceptible to indirect congressional influence than is crisis policy. Many procedural reforms, for instance, are designed to build congressional preferences into the strategic policy choices the administration makes. This is especially true of efforts to create new agencies in the executive branch and to restructure the existing decision-making process. As Chapter 5 argued, the logic behind creating agencies such as the USTR and requiring the Commerce Department to participate in decisions on weapons co-production agreements is that the new participants will champion the preferences of many on Capitol Hill.

Framing provides another indirect means by which members can shape strategic policy. Early in 1990, for example, George Bush came under fire on Capitol Hill for allegedly failing to propose a fiscal 1991 defense budget that reflected the collapse of the Berlin Wall.[45] In the Senate, Sam Nunn

(D-Ga.) and other members of the Armed Services Committee criticized what they saw as business as usual, and they used committee hearings to air their proposals for overhauling the military. Criticism was equally harsh in the House. A special panel of the House Armed Services Committee issued a report concluding that the "Bush administration has been overly cautious, even grudging, in its appreciation of how the Soviet threat is changing."[46] Although the administration claimed that its budget proposal did reflect the new political map in Europe, opinion polls showed that many Americans were coming to agree with the critics on Capitol Hill. Finally, in August 1990, President Bush unveiled his plan for the post–cold war military. Quite noticeably, his proposal included many of the changes that his critics on Capitol Hill had urged months before.

Although Congress exercises more influence over strategic policy than over crisis policy, the president still retains decided advantages. The biggest is that much of strategic policy lies beyond the reach of legislation. Whether to recognize the government of Bosnia, to push other industrialized democracies to increase aid to Russia, or to accept the European Community's proposal on reducing farm subsidies are all decisions Congress cannot affect through legislation.

Presidents can also blunt congressional efforts to legislate strategic policy. In the realm of international negotiations, the president's power to conclude executive agreements diminishes the treaty power of the Senate. When members of Congress try to put their own strategic preferences into law, the president's power to veto legislation frustrates the work of an institution whose partisan, ideological, and regional differences incline it toward inertia.

Even in instances in which members of Congress succeed in legislating their preferences on strategic policy, presidents are well-situated to derail congressional activism. Congress depends on the willingness of the executive branch to implement its directives, and, as Rep. David Obey (D-Wis.), chair of the House Foreign Operations Subcommittee, once observed, "There isn't any way on God's green earth that [Congress] can instill in the Administration a will which is not there."[47] As the Reagan administration's response to Japan's violation of international whaling rules attests, presidents and their subordinates show considerable willingness to read discretion into foreign policy laws. At the same time, the executive branch can manipulate bureaucratic regulations and thereby undercut congressional directives. For example, when a Reagan administration proposal to sell military cargo trucks to Guatemala in 1981 foundered over a law banning the private sale of defense items to countries with poor human rights records, administration officials circumvented the ban by removing the trucks from the list of controlled exports.[48]

The president also enjoys a decided advantage over Congress when it comes to efforts to frame public and elite opinion. No member of Congress can command the attention of the media and the public in the way the president can. At the same time, most Americans are inclined to grant greater foreign policy expertise to the president and his advisers than to any member of Congress. The result is that so long as presidents choose to respond to world events, they are well-positioned to counter challenges to their strategic policy choices. Presidents only forfeit their inherent advantage when, as happened with George Bush on defense policy in 1990, they fail to react to changing world events and thereby create a policy vacuum their congressional critics can fill.[49]

STRUCTURAL POLICY

Structural policy constitutes the third major category of foreign policy issues. It governs how American resources will be used to achieve foreign policy goals. As such, it most closely resembles decision making on domestic distributive policies. In foreign affairs, structural policy answers questions such as which countries will receive how much foreign aid, what rules will govern immigration, and how much money will be given to international organizations. In the case of defense, structural policy determines the procurement, deployment, and organization of military personnel and materiel.

When it comes to structural decisions, congressional influence over foreign policy is at its greatest and presidential influence is at its weakest. The extent to which Congress influences structural policy is clear when it comes to foreign assistance, where the record is not merely one "of congressional participation but, indeed, of congressional dominance."[50] Members of Congress exercise similar influence over export subsidies and immigration policy.

Congress also plays a major role in shaping structural decisions on defense policy. As former secretary of the navy John Lehman observes, members of Congress have saved and expanded many defense programs over the objections of the executive branch.

> Without Congress, the executive would almost certainly have reduced the reserve components of the services to nearly zero. It was Congress that forced, upon a reluctant executive in the late 1970s, the personnel policies

and pay raises that have made the all-volunteer force a success. It was Congress that overruled the executive in 1980 and forced the Carter administration to continue to maintain a force of nuclear aircraft carriers; it was Congress that through six administrations built the nuclear submarine navy under Admiral Rickover, despite frequent vacillation from the executive; it was Congress that forced the most successful aircraft program in postwar naval history, the F-14 Tomcat, upon an executive wedded to the disastrous TFX, and it is Congress that has kept alive the revolutionary V-22 tiltrotor technology.[51]

Congress also has a substantial record of denying and scaling back defense programs. In the 1980s, Congress forced Jimmy Carter to abandon his plan to develop cruise missile carrier airplanes, stopped the navy from modernizing its tactical nuclear weapons, barred the army from developing a nuclear-armed version of the ATACMS missile, banned operational testing of satellite interceptors and thereby effectively killed the antisatellite weapon, limited the Reagan administration's plans for deploying the MX missile, and forced the Bush administration to reduce the procurement of the B-2 bomber from 132 planes to fewer than 25.[52]

Congress's considerable say in structural policy gives it indirect leverage over strategic policy. The reason, of course, is that implementation of many strategic policy decisions requires money. Thus, Congress denied the Reagan administration the chance to carry out its strategic policy of toppling the Sandinista government when it refused to appropriate funds to aid the contras. Congress similarly blocked the Reagan administration's plans to reinterpret the ABM treaty and to violate the (unratified) SALT II treaty by refusing to fund the structural programs needed to fulfill these strategic policy decisions. At the same time, Congress's decisions on structural issues may also push strategic policy in a direction opposed by the president, as happened when Congress directed the air force to develop both cruise and Midgetman missiles.

Congress's greater influence over structural policy stems partly from electoral factors. Members generally run the least electoral risk when they challenge presidents on the structural aspects of foreign policy. Indeed, if members are fighting to cut foreign aid or to save a weapons program that employs their constituents, challenging administration policy may be an electoral plus. At the same time, decisions on structural policy are dominated by subgovernments composed of federal agencies, congressional committees, and interest groups. Members of the subgovernments cooperate to serve their clients, and they make many decisions on the basis of mutual noninterference and logrolling. They are also highly motivated to protect their domain from intrusions by outsiders, whether it be the president, the secretary of defense, or a congressional party leader.[53]

Congress's greater influence over structural policy also stems from the fact that in structural policy the president's inherent advantages, particularly the ability to initiate policy, are nullified. Most decisions on structural policy involve appropriations, and presidents cannot spend money that Congress refuses to appropriate. As a result, in structural policy the burden rests with the executive to persuade members to support its programs; hence, inertia generally works to the advantage of Congress and not the president.

The power of the purse also enables members to initiate programs that the executive branch opposes. Of course, presidents can veto appropriations bills that contain provisions they dislike. Yet the fact that an objectionable funding decision usually is one of thousands in an appropriations bill the president almost always wants to see passed makes the veto difficult to wield. Moreover, unlike the case with the war power, when it comes to ignoring Congress's power of the purse, presidents gain little support from the courts. As Chapter 4 noted, the Supreme Court has never struck down any use of the appropriations power as an unconstitutional infringement on executive authority.

Although members of Congress have considerable say in structural policy, they by no means control it. One obstacle confronting members of Congress is that they depend on the executive branch to implement their directives. Because congressional oversight is spotty even under the best of circumstances, the executive branch has ample opportunity to undercut congressional directives by twisting legal interpretations to meet its needs. The extreme example, of course, came during the Iran-contra affair when the Reagan administration circumvented the Boland amendments by shifting responsibility for aiding the contras to the National Security Council staff, which it claimed was not covered by the ban.

A second obstacle members of Congress face in their efforts to set structural policy is that it is far easier to bar policies and programs than to compel the executive branch to embrace new ones. As is the case with strategic policy, Congress cannot instill in the administration a will that is not there, and executive branch agencies can drag their feet when implementing programs they dislike. Where administrations allow congressionally mandated programs to fail, congressional critics may be hard pressed to prove the executive is responsible. As a result, the success of congressional efforts to enact new programs ultimately hinges on the existence of sympathetic constituencies within the executive branch. The armed services committees succeeded in convincing the air force to develop cruise missiles in the 1970s because the program had supporters in the military (if not among air force generals). In contrast, the effort in the mid-1980s to force the air force to develop the Midgetman foundered over the air force's staunch opposition to a single-warhead missile.

For similar reasons, members of Congress find it far easier to use structural policy to bar certain types of strategic policy than to initiate new ones. For example, members prevented the Reagan administration from gutting the ABM and SALT II treaties, but they could not force it to conclude a new arms control treaty. In the same vein, Congress in the 1980s repeatedly limited spending on military construction in Europe on the ground that America's allies were not bearing their fair share of the military burden. Successive administrations concerned with maintaining a unified front against the Soviet Union just as predictably declined to press their NATO partners to pay more of the cost of basing U.S. troops in Europe.

The third obstacle facing members of Congress is that even though they have tremendous say over structural decisions, this by no means guarantees that structural policy will yield the results they anticipate. As Joseph White points out, Congress, like the executive branch, cannot escape the frustration created by simple incompetence:

> Even on a purely structural, entirely visible item such as the army's Divisional Air Defense (DIVAD) system, Congress may be thwarted because there is no way to force the army to get something right. Nor would punishing the State Department for allowing the Soviets to build eavesdropping equipment into its walls in Moscow produce a functioning embassy. Defunding a program does not help if the program's mission is essential. The problem of incompetence in the Philippine government and its misuse of U.S. aid would not be solved by cutting off funds but it would damage the U.S. mission of support for that government.[54]

In short, members often find that employing their powers of the purse on structural policy will simply generate new problems.

CONCLUSION

The ability of Congress to influence foreign policy varies greatly from issue to issue. In crisis policy Congress operates on the fringes of power. Members can suggest policies to the president, implore him to avoid others, and threaten him with political harm in the future, but ultimately the president decides whom he will and will not consult on decisions to use force. In strategic policy congressional influence increases, but even here the president's constitutional powers and the practical difficulties of reversing presidential initiatives hamper congressional influence. In structural policy Congress operates at its greatest advantage. By virtue of its control of the purse strings alone, members of Congress must be involved in structural policy.

The failure of Congress to dominate foreign policy is due partly to congressional timidity. Some members believe as a matter of principle that Congress should defer to the president, and others fear that second-guessing the president in foreign affairs will alienate voters. But congressional timidity tells only part of the story. Members of Congress also face considerable institutional obstacles. In foreign policy, the formal powers of the president and the inherent advantages of the presidency are at their maximum. The Supreme Court in turn has reinforced the president's advantages both with its rulings on the merits and its habit of dismissing congressional challenges to the executive as not ripe for judicial decision or as raising political and not legal questions. Finally, in foreign affairs Congress's inherent disadvantages in policy making are at their maximum. Congress lacks all the attributes of "decision, activity, secrecy, and dispatch" that Alexander Hamilton long ago hailed as the great virtues of the presidency.[55]

The institutional obstacles that confront members who want to put their imprint on foreign policy highlight why talk of Congress's ability to control foreign policy is misguided, at least insofar as the word "control" is used in the positive sense of directing or commanding policy. The frequent claims by Irreconcilables of an "Imperial Congress" and "foreign policy by Congress" notwithstanding, members are institutionally ill-equipped to wrest control of foreign policy from the president.

VICES AND
VIRTUES

CONGRESSIONAL ACTIVISM on foreign policy elicits considerable commentary, most of it negative.[1] Irreconcilables claim that Congress has usurped presidential prerogatives on foreign policy. Eugene Rostow, former director of the Arms Control and Disarmament Agency, goes so far as to argue that we are witnessing the transformation of "the President into a ceremonial figurehead graciously presiding over the activities of an omnipotent Congress."[2] Although Skeptics dismiss such claims as gross exaggerations, they too seem to long for the supposedly idyllic days of bipartisanship. I. M. Destler, Leslie Gelb, and Anthony Lake lament, for example, that Congress has made the foreign policy debate "*more* ideological and unreal."[3]

Complaints that congressional activism harms U.S. foreign policy have a long and respected intellectual pedigree. Alexis de Tocqueville warned in his survey of American political life that "foreign policy does not require the use of any of the good qualities peculiar to democracy but does demand the cultivation of almost all of those which it lacks."[4] George Kennan worried that when it comes to foreign affairs, a democracy is like "one of those prehistoric monsters with a body as long as this room and a brain the size of a pin."[5] Even a scholar as devoted to democratic governance as Robert Dahl wrote of Congress's role in foreign affairs that "the great weapon of free government has misfired. Separation of powers between President and Congress has proved to be less productive of freedom than of conflict, patronage, inefficiency, and irresponsibility."[6]

The prominence of Congress's critics and the persistence of their criticisms provide a powerful indictment of congressional activism. But an indictment is not a conviction. For all the complaints, does the record support claims that congressional activism harms U.S. foreign policy? Or are there virtues to congressional activism that the critics fail to see?

Any attempt to assess the vices and virtues of Congress's role in foreign policy presents problems. One must first avoid the temptation to judge congressional activism in terms of one's views of the merits of a particular president's policies, a temptation best captured by former secretary of the navy John Lehman's observation that "I have been a 'strong president man' when in the executive branch and a 'strong Congress man' when out of the government in political opposition."[7] At the same time, no agreed upon standard exists for judging whether foreign policy powers are properly allocated between Congress and the president or for measuring whether the policies actually chosen advance the "national interest." Thus, Bruce Jentleson's claim that "the experiences in El Salvador and especially the Philippines should dispel the generalization that deference by Congress always is beneficial to U.S. diplomacy" may be true, but it will hardly persuade Ronald Reagan's supporters.[8]

In the absence of an agreed-upon standard for judging Congress, debates over the merits of congressional activism in foreign policy usually devolve into something akin to judging the flavor of ice cream—it's all a matter of taste. Yet even without assuming a nonexistent consensus on the appropriate level of congressional activism, something can be said about the accuracy of four major criticisms of Congress: that it meddles too much in the details of foreign policy, that it allows its committees to duplicate each other's work, that it is too parochial, and that it undermines the ability of the president to negotiate with other countries. To be sure, each of these complaints contains an element of truth—Congress at times does become mired in minutiae, it can be inefficient and parochial, and it can undercut presidential diplomacy. On the whole, however, the complaints are greatly exaggerated. Despite much fretting by Irreconcilables and Skeptics alike about the dangers of congressional activism, evidence that Congress seriously harms U.S. foreign policy is sorely lacking.

Besides being exaggerated, complaints about the vices of congressional activism overlook its virtues. One is that members of Congress frequently strengthen the president's hand in international negotiations. Members also bring different values and perspectives to bear on policy debates, views that provide a useful political scrub for administration proposals. Last, the active participation of members in decision making helps to legitimize U.S. foreign policy both at home and abroad. Precisely because the United States is a democracy it is important that policy decisions be made democratically.

MICROMANAGEMENT

Complaints about excessive congressional involvement in the details of administration—commonly known as micromanagement—have become a standard criticism of Congress's efforts on defense and foreign policy. On becoming president, for example, George Bush vowed to reverse what he saw as excessive congressional involvement in foreign policy. Secretary of Defense Dick Cheney once held a news conference featuring two ceiling-high stacks of paper to highlight Pentagon complaints that Congress required the Defense Department to conduct too many studies.[9] Observers with no ideological axe to grind worry that the foreign aid bill attracts too many amendments, that the reports issued by congressional committees have too many pages, and that Congress burdens the executive branch with detailed and often inconsistent advice.[10] Even members of Congress fear that the institution has abandoned its duty to provide guidance on major issues in its efforts to provide detailed programmatic advice.[11]

Critics argue that micromanagement increases program costs and prevents smooth policy formulation and execution. In the case of defense policy, critics argue that Congress's passion for changing hundreds of line items in the budget, coupled with the often divergent recommendations of the committees involved, undermines the Pentagon's ability to plan. In turn, defense contractors cannot schedule their production lines efficiently because the size and character of a "buy" may change annually or even monthly. The end result is waste and inefficiency. In the case of foreign policy, critics argue that the myriad of congressional directives robs the president of the discretion he needs. As Secretary of State James Baker lamented in testimony before the Senate Foreign Relations Committee in 1989: "We do not have the flexibility to adapt to differing diplomatic and foreign policy situations and events that take place."[12]

Does congressional micromanagement seriously threaten the quality of foreign policy? Anyone who watches Congress can quickly turn up examples of what appear to be excessive legislative concern for details. One might reasonably wonder, for example, if members of Congress are playing to their strength when they offer floor amendments seeking to regulate drug and lie detector testing of State Department personnel, as happened during consideration of the 1987 State Department Authorization Act. Nor is it hard to find instances in which members display a zest for the trivial. In recent years, for example, Congress has ordered the air force to buy fewer garbage trucks, suggested that the navy name a ship after Bob Hope, and changed the number of muzzle bore sights the army could purchase.[13]

But for all the huffing and puffing, micromanagement is nowhere near as serious a problem as the critics claim. One reason is that the executive branch needs no lessons from Congress on excessive and even downright silly rule making. It is the Pentagon, after all, and not Congress that took fourteen pages to lay out the requirements for an acceptable fruitcake, including the provision that "the presence of vanilla flavoring shall be organoleptically detected."[14] And while Congress identified thirty-three policy objectives for foreign aid programs in the Foreign Assistance Authorization Act, the Agency for International Development expanded these to seventy-five.[15] Anyone who assumes that foreign policy would suddenly become more consistent and effective if only members of Congress behaved themselves misunderstands the realities of bureaucratic life. What appears to distinguish silly congressional directives from silly executive ones is that members do more of their work in the public eye and thus are more easily ridiculed.

A second problem with complaints about micromanagement is that much of what passes for congressional micromanagement actually originates in the executive branch. As Chapter 4 noted, a good deal of congressional legislation on foreign policy comes at the behest of the administration and not in spite of it. The earmarks contained in the foreign aid bills provide a case in point. Many of the specific provisions for Egypt, El Salvador, Greece, Israel, the Philippines, Pakistan, and Turkey—all among the ten largest recipients of American aid—have "been very much the case of the executive branch proposing and the legislature disposing."[16] Executive branch complaints about the burdens imposed by reporting requirements are surprising for a similar reason. The administration often encourages members of Congress to request reports and studies as a way of derailing more intrusive congressional action on foreign policy.

A third problem with arguments about micromanagement is that many of the claims the critics make are misleading. Some commonly offered indicators of congressional activism are meaningless. Although the number of floor amendments to the defense and foreign aid bills might interest people who value a tidy legislative process, it does not affect U.S. interests abroad, especially since, as the critics continually point out, so many amendments deal with minor matters. Similar skepticism should be accorded to complaints about the number of pages in committee reports. The quality of U.S. foreign policy making would not suddenly improve if the committees omitted the explanations for their decisions and thereby shortened the length of their reports.

Other claims made about congressional activism are simply wrong. For all the complaints that Congress places more and more demands on the Defense

Department each year, table 4 shows that in several areas Congress actually places fewer demands on the Pentagon today than it did in the 1960s. The most notable change is in the number of appearances by Defense Department officials before congressional committees. By the early 1980s, Pentagon officials spent two-thirds fewer hours testifying on Capitol Hill than they did fifteen years earlier. In other areas, such as the number of hearings and the number of witnesses called, congressional demands on the Defense Department have remained relatively stable.

One area in which Congress's interest in the details of foreign policy has risen is the budget. As figure 1 shows, the number of changes Congress made in the defense budget increased substantially during the 1980s. The increased number of line-item adjustments would seem to support complaints about budgetary micromanagement. Yet these complaints miss two crucial points. One is that Congress changes budget line items primarily to bring the president's budget request into line with what a majority of members is willing to spend.[17] When presidents submit politically realistic budgets Congress makes fewer changes, which is precisely what happened in the late 1980s. The other point is that when congressional budgeteers do tinker with the budget, they often follow the advice of military officials on which programs to cut.

Another area in which congressional demands on the executive branch have increased is requests for reports and studies. The Defense Department, for example, saw congressional requests for reports and studies rise from 223 in 1980 to 733 in 1991, a more than threefold increase.[18] Not surprisingly, defense officials have criticized the increased workload, claiming that it costs $50 million per year to comply with the reporting requirements. Yet the complaints are vastly overblown. In a defense budget of more than $250 billion, $50 million amounts to less than .02 percent of spending. Moreover, much of the money would be spent even if Congress repealed every reporting requirement; many of the reports contain information that is needed to run the Pentagon. That is why despite the claims by Secretary Cheney and others that Congress is drowning the Pentagon in paper, defense officials have been slow to eliminate reports. When invited in 1990 to propose an overhaul of the reporting system, the Pentagon suggested only 71 reports for termination or modification.[19]

Complaints about the burden that reporting requirements place on the State Department are similarly overblown. A 1988 study conducted by the Congressional Research Service on behalf of the House Foreign Affairs Committee surveyed 383 reports required of the State Department and its affiliated agencies. The study found that 63 percent of the reports served a useful

Table 4
Congressional Requests for Information from the Department of Defense

	Annual Average					
	1965– 1968	1969– 1972	1973– 1976	1977– 1980	1981– 1984	1986– 1991
Number of hearings	363	513	407	496[a]	456	411[a]
Number of witnesses	720	1,983	1,171	1,744	1,306	n.a.
Hours of testimony by defense officials	3,770	2,107	2,515	1,443	1,420	n.a.
Hours of testimony by secretary of defense	90	82	67	67	46	n.a.
Written inquiries	156,629[a]	187,739[a]	145,940	95,185	101,305	111,839
Telephone inquiries	402,589[a]	698,103[a]	660,385	389,336[a]	593,163	n.a.

Sources: Data for 1965–1984 are taken from U.S. Government Accounting Office, "Legislative Oversight: Congressional Requests for Information on Defense Activities," GAO/NSIAD-86-65BR, February 1986. Data for 1986–1991 were supplied by Leonard G. Campbell, director for Plans and Systems, Office of the Comptroller of the Department of Defense, 12 February 1992.

Note: [a]The average is based on three years of data.

purpose and that another 19 percent were dead letters that placed no demands on the executive branch. And the cost of producing the reports was small. Nearly half the reports "cost virtually nothing" to produce, and many other reports "consist of information or policy analysis the administration has or needs anyway so there should be little additional cost."[20]

The fourth problem with complaints about congressional micromanagement is also the most important: they rest on the mistaken assumption that members of Congress can shape the broad contours of policy without becoming enmeshed in the details of policy. Jeffrey Bergner, for example, argues that "Congress could do its greatest service by ceasing to try to micro-manage

Figure 1
Line-Item Changes to Annual Defense Bills, FY 1970–1990

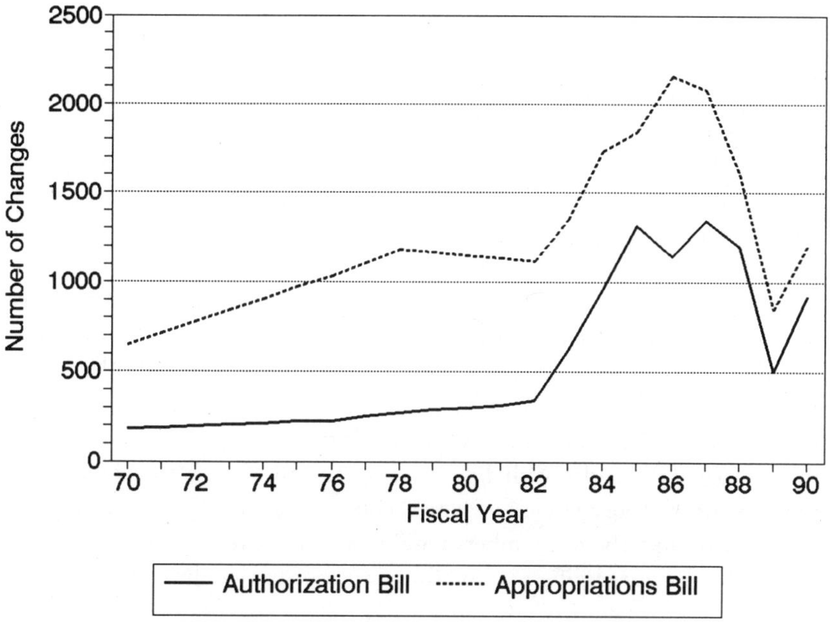

Sources: James M. Lindsay, "Congress and the Defense Budget," *Washington Quarterly* 11 (Winter 1988): 61, and "White Paper on the Department of Defense and the Congress," Report to the President by the Secretary of Defense, January 1990, p. 7.

the details of foreign policy and by compelling the executive branch to think together with the Congress about the principles which ought to guide U.S. foreign policy in the coming decade."[21] Howard Wiarda laments that Congress is no longer content "exercising the broad oversight it exercised in the past and leaving the details of policy up to the executive and the State Department."[22] And former Sen. J. William Fulbright (D-Ark.), the long-time chair of the Foreign Relations Committee, urges members to recognize that their role lies "in the authorization of military and major political commitments, and in advising broad policy directions, while leaving to the executive the necessary flexibility to conduct policy within the broad parameters approved by the legislature."[23]

Calls for Congress to focus on the broad sweep of foreign policy sound appealing, but they are politically naive. Because presidents are free to disregard any advice that members of Congress might offer, the ability of members to influence policy stems in large part from their ability to stipulate the details of policy, especially the details of budgetary decisions. Thus, when members disagreed with President Reagan over policy toward El Salvador and Nicaragua, over the goals of trade policy, and over the direction of arms control policy, they quickly found that nonbinding expressions of sentiment meant little to a president determined to have his own way. Only when members began to rewrite the details of policy did they succeed in moving policy in the direction they favored.

In truth, much of what critics dismiss as micromanagement is actually *macromanagement* through the control of the details of policy.[24] Congressional directives to rename ships after famous comedians may draw guffaws, but the very triviality of such actions makes them unworthy of the fuss made over them. What troubles the critics, especially those in the executive branch, is that members of Congress use the details of policy to impose their preferences on the executive branch. The cuts Congress made in aid to El Salvador in the early 1990s, the changes it made in the procedures for authorizing intelligence activities in 1991, and the changes it made in defense spending after the collapse of the Berlin Wall did not result from the mere whim of members or the work of overeager congressional staffers. In each of these cases, and in many others like them, members fought over the details of policy because they had deep-seated differences with the administration over the substance of policy.

Critics are right, though, in noting that congressional interventions lead, over time, to a patchwork of inconsistent and even contradictory statutory provisions.[25] But it is not clear why Congress, rather than the executive branch, should bear the blame for the hodgepodge of statutes. After all, most congressional directives of any consequence come only after a president tries to thwart, or succeeds in thwarting, the will of Congress on a policy issue. Moreover, if obsolete, convoluted, or inconsistent legislation is at the heart of executive branch complaints about micromanagement, the executive branch has not acquitted itself well. When congressional committees have offered to streamline existing legislation in exchange for administration pledges to take seriously members' concerns about major policy issues, the response from the executive branch has been tepid.[26]

In the end, the furor over micromanagement owes much to bureaucratic self-interest. Officials in the executive branch complain about Congress for much the same reason professors complain about deans: Congress and deans both say no. For the executive branch Congress is an obstacle, an obstacle made all the more annoying by the fact that for a brief time in the 1950s and 1960s it was relatively easy to surmount. But appeals for members of Congress to shift their sights from minutiae to the broad sweep of policy will not change things. Members see these appeals for what they are: disguised attempts to move Congress back to a posture of deference. Until presidents agree to work with rather than against Capitol Hill, members' preoccupation with the details of foreign policy will persist.

COMMITTEE DUPLICATION

Complaints about congressional micromanagement often go hand in hand with complaints that too many congressional committees claim jurisdiction over foreign policy. The committees duplicate much of each other's work, which breeds turf battles and sends conflicting signals to the foreign policy bureaucracy. In the 1980s, for example, the Senate Armed Services Committee fought with the Appropriations Committee over the extent to which authorization decisions limit what can be appropriated, and it fought with the Intelligence Committee over who should authorize the intelligence activities of the Defense Department.[27] In the view of the critics, Congress could minimize turf battles and improve its deliberations by consolidating the committee system.

The preoccupation with overlapping committee jurisdictions is in some respects puzzling. No cries are heard that responsibility for foreign policy is even more widely dispersed in the executive branch. Foreign aid programs are developed and administered by the Agency for International Development, the State Department, the Department of Agriculture, the Treasury Department, the Defense Department, the Peace Corps, the U.S. Information Agency, and the Environmental Protection Agency (EPA).[28] The intelligence community comprises the CIA, the Defense Intelligence Agency, the Federal Bureau of Investigation, the Drug Enforcement Agency, Army Intelligence, Navy Intelligence, Marine Corps Intelligence, Air Force Intelligence, and bureaus within the Departments of State, Energy, and Treasury. Planning for U.S. participation at the 1992 Earth Summit involved EPA, the Vice-President's Council on Competitiveness, the National Security Council Staff, the White House Staff, and the Departments of State, Treasury, Defense, Interior, and Energy.[29] The executive branch would seem to be in even more dire need of reorganization than Congress if jurisdictional duplication in fact impeded sound policy.

At the same time, committee duplication often fails to produce the ills attributed to it. Much is made, for example, of the delays created by the need to coordinate the activities of multiple committees. Yet the Omnibus Trade and Competitiveness Act of 1988, which involved the work of five committees in the Senate and eight in the House, sailed through Congress. And many times executive branch agencies benefit from the committee duplication they routinely denounce. When the authorizing and appropriations committees issue conflicting directives, for example, agencies follow the directives they prefer.[30]

The truth is that the preoccupation with overlapping committee jurisdictions is misplaced. As Chapter 3 argued, statistics on the number of committees with formal jurisdiction over foreign policy greatly exaggerate the extent and level of committee involvement. Most committees that have formal jurisdiction operate on the margins of policy. Moreover, overlap and duplication are inherent in policy making rather than merely a symptom of willful organizational inefficiency on the part of members of Congress. As the organization of the foreign policy bureaucracy attests, the complexity and diversity of foreign policy issues makes it difficult to divide them into a small set of mutually exclusive policy areas. At the same time, the fact that Congress is a bicameral legislature ensures (and was designed to ensure) duplication.

The preoccupation with overlapping committee jurisdictions also overlooks how committee rivalries often improve the quality of Congress's deliberations. They do so first by prodding committees to discharge their duties. One of the great dangers of the committee system is that committees will become advocates for, rather than overseers of, the bureaucracy. At the same time, a cardinal rule of life on Capitol Hill is that committees that cede turf soon become inconsequential. As a result, the threat of poaching helps counter the tendency of committees to become captured by the very agencies they are intended to oversee.

The longstanding tensions between the Senate Armed Services Committee and the Senate Foreign Relations Committee highlight the value of turf battles. During the first major debate over the Safeguard ABM system, members of Foreign Relations took to the floor to question their counterparts on Armed Services. "It quickly became apparent that [SASC's] members did not understand the questions, much less know the answers."[31] Having been embarrassed on the floor, SASC's interest in ABM suddenly blossomed. Two decades later, Armed Services returned the favor. The prominence of SASC during debate over Operation Desert Storm convinced members of Foreign Relations of the need to revitalize their committee.

Turf battles with domestic policy committees also push the foreign policy committees to discharge their duties. During the mid-1980s, for instance, the House Armed Services Committee took a critical interest in the procurement of the B-1B, an interest that was "driven not only by strong feelings about the aircraft's technical problems, but also by the need to outflank

Representative John Dingell, who . . . used his position on the House Energy and Commerce Committee to criticize acquisition."[32] The investigation by Rep. Henry Gonzalez (D-Tex.), chair of the House Banking Committee, into the Banca Nazionale del Lavoro scandal played a similar role in stimulating congressional interest in the Bush administration's prewar policy toward Iraq. When Gonzalez produced evidence that Iraq had used commodity credit loans backed by the U.S. government to purchase military technology, the House Foreign Affairs Committee investigated U.S. military ties with Iraq and the Senate Intelligence Committee examined what the intelligence community knew about the misuse of the commodity loan program.[33]

Besides creating incentives for committees to discharge their duties, jurisdictional duplication inhibits congressional parochialism. The need to secure the approval of several committees makes it harder for members of Congress to deliver parochial benefits than would be the case if they had to deal with only one or two committees in pushing their pet projects. Victory in the authorization bill does not guarantee victory in the appropriations bill, and victory on one side of Capitol Hill does not guarantee a victory on the other. Senators move more quickly against pork barrel projects in House bills than in Senate bills, and representatives return the favor. A consolidated committee system, on the other hand, would make it easier for members on the remaining committees to enact their pet projects into law and thereby increase the instances of congressional parochialism.

None of the foregoing is to say that committee rivalries produce efficient decision making. They don't. Pushing legislation through the committee system requires considerable time and effort, which is a source of tremendous frustration and irritation for the people who work on Capitol Hill and in the executive branch. Members of Congress rankle at being forced to navigate their proposals through a gauntlet of committees, congressional staff complain about their unending workload, and executive branch officials resent being asked to testify on the same issue before multiple committees.

As understandable as these frustrations are, the standard for evaluating committee duplication should not be whether it enables government officials to enjoy their working life. Rather, it should be whether or not committee duplication hurts policy making more than it helps. And on that score, what critics take to be a great weakness of Congress is in fact a great strength. Simply put, rivalries among committees help to compel Congress to discharge its duties because ambition is made to counteract ambition.[34] Although committee rivalries by no means guarantee that Congress will choose wisely or expeditiously, more congressional oversight is likely to result from committee duplication than from the "rational" decision-making structures so favored by reformers. In this respect, critics would do well to reconsider the wisdom of their calls for a consolidated committee system. When Congress attempted to rationalize its decision making in the 1870s by uniting the functions of oversight, authorization, and appropriation in a single committee for each policy domain, the new committees became captives of the very agencies they were intended to oversee.[35]

PAROCHIALISM

A third criticism of Congress's involvement in foreign policy is that members of Congress are too parochial in their outlook. As Tocqueville argued, "In politics the tendency of a democracy [is] to obey its feelings rather than its calculations and to abandon a long-matured plan to satisfy a momentary passion."[36] Many members of Congress agree. Senator Fulbright complains: "Congressmen are acutely sensitive to the influence of private pressure and to excesses and inadequacies of a public opinion that is all to often ignorant of the needs, the dangers, and the opportunities in our foreign relations."[37] Pushed by the whims of shifting public sentiment, a Congress left to its own devices is said to produce a foreign policy fraught by fragmentation, inconsistency, particularism, and volatility.

No one can say anything intelligent about Congress without acknowledging that members are sensitive to constituent opinion. That sensitivity is by design. The authors of the Constitution gave members of the House two-year terms precisely because they believed the legislature should be responsive to the citizenry. And while the Senate was originally intended to be the saucer where the passions of politics cooled, the shift to the direct election of senators has made that body sensitive to public opinion as well. The result is that members ignore their constituents at their peril. Even members driven by concerns of good policy know they need to win reelection if they hope to advance their policy goals.

The real issue, though, is the extent to which parochialism distorts the substance of foreign policy. And here the complaints of the critics are less than compelling. For all the anecdotes about congressional parochialism and claims of impending doom, the hard evidence suggests that congressional parochialism is far less pervasive and far less catastrophic in its consequences than folklore contends.

As Chapter 2 discussed, study after study finds that constituents' economic interests play a minor role in congressional decision making on weapons systems. Most congressional decisions on defense, and particularly on major programs, appear to be driven by ideological concerns. In some respects, the limited reach of the parochial imperative on weapons systems should not be surprising. For all the legislative bragging about bringing home the bacon, much of defense procurement regulation is designed to keep politics out.[38] The one area of defense policy where parochialism is substantial is military basing and operations and maintenance.[39] Not surprisingly, these are also programs where the question before Congress almost always is not *what* to build but *who* should build it.

Parochialism is also far less extensive in foreign policy than is commonly assumed. As Eileen Burgin's research shows, perceptions of constituent opinion clearly influence whether members choose to be active on an issue.[40] But once members decide to act, constituent opinion fades as a motive for intensity of action. And in Congress intensity of action greatly affects the likelihood that legislation will grab the attention of the White House or win the support of a majority of members. At the same time, much is made of the influence that ethnic lobbies wield on Capitol Hill. Observers like to point to the clout enjoyed by the Jewish lobby and to the success the Greek lobby had in persuading Congress first to impose an embargo on military sales to Turkey and then to tie the amount of military aid given to Greece to the amount given to Turkey. But aside from Jewish and Greek Americans, most studies of ethnic lobbies find that such groups have little influence on Congress.[41]

The one area of foreign policy where congressional parochialism is prominent is trade policy. Members of Congress from Michigan demand quotas on Japanese automobiles, those from North and South Carolina fight against the influx of inexpensive textiles from China, and those from the Pacific Northwest rail against unfair competition by Canadian loggers. But despite the explosion of the American trade deficit in the 1980s and the concomitant rise in protectionist pressures on Congress, U.S. trade policy remains remarkably open. Each year numerous trade bills are introduced in Congress, but most of the protectionist measures, and particularly the more extreme ones, never leave the floor. The failure of Congress to return to the days of Smoot-Hawley is due partly to the widespread, albeit weakening, commitment on Capitol Hill and elsewhere in American political life to the belief in free trade. It is also due to the difficulty of building a legislative coalition in favor of protectionism. While the parochial imperative impels some members to devise protectionist measures that favor local businesses, it impels other members to fight legislation that would harm local businesses that depend on imports.[42]

If too much attention and credit are given to congressional parochialism, executive branch parochialism is downplayed. The implicit and sometimes explicit assumption in many discussions of the vices of congressional activism is that policies that emerge from the executive represent the national interest. Most discussions hail the president's greater distance from the electorate, the superior information sources available to the executive branch, and the technical expertise of foreign policy officials. In contrast, the changes Congress makes in the president's policies are seen as something akin to a fall from a state of grace.

The portrait of the rational, dispassionate bureaucracy runs contrary to how decisions actually are made in the executive branch. Although public opinion holds little sway in the foreign policy bureaucracy, the entire literature on bureaucratic politics shows that a parochialism of a different sort infects agency decisions.[43] The air force neglects to buy sufficient numbers of close air support aircraft, preferring instead the more glamorous fighter planes and strategic bombers. The navy spends hundreds of millions of dollars refurbishing battleships even though most defense analysts agree that the money would be better spent on sealift. The State Department preoccupies itself with the concerns of other countries and neglects U.S. interests. And to further complicate matters, decisions that emerge from the bureaucracy are often compromises stitched together with an eye more toward satisfying different government constituencies than toward promoting the national interest.

The White House also cannot claim the mantle of dispassionate and rational decision making. Several studies have linked presidential decision making on foreign policy with changes in public opinion and with the ebb and flow of the electoral cycle.[44] President Carter's shift toward more hawkish defense and foreign policies in the second half of his term was caused as much by public opinion polls and electoral calculations as by judgments about U.S. interests abroad. Several of Carter's advisers admitted that they viewed the Iran hostage crisis in terms of what it would do to "the President's image and his prospects for re-election."[45] The Reagan administration charted its foreign policy with a keen eye poised on what the American public would and would not tolerate.[46] George Bush canceled a trip to Asia in December 1991 because of complaints he was devoting too much attention to foreign affairs and not enough time to domestic matters. He eventually rescheduled the trip, recasting it as an effort to promote American exports and jobs.

Besides exaggerating the rationality and wisdom of decisions made in the executive branch, critics of Congress err in assuming that congressional parochialism is always a vice. The assumption flows from an unquestioned belief that policy making can and should be a technocratic matter, with decisions by experts based purely on merit. Such a view is antithetical to the entire American political system, which is predicated on the belief that self-interest will motivate legislators. As James Madison put it Federalist No. 51, the best way to promote the public good is to create a system in which "the private interest of every individual may be a sentinel over the public rights."[47]

Two examples illustrate the positive contributions that congressional parochialism can make. The first involves the A-10 close air support aircraft. Rep. Joseph Addabbo (D-N.Y.), the chair of the House Appropriations Defense Subcommittee and the representative for the district in which the plane was built, forced the air force to buy A-10s on several occasions in the early 1980s. Although critics decried Addabbo's move at the time as rank parochialism, the plane distinguished itself in the Gulf War, where it killed more tanks than any other aircraft and had a higher operational availability rate than other, more sophisticated ground attack aircraft.[48] The second example involves a fire-support system known as LTACFIRE. In the mid-1980s, Rep. Bill Chappell (D-Fla.), Addabbo's successor as chair of the Appropriations Defense Subcommittee, overrode the army's objections and forced the Pentagon to buy LTACFIRE. During the Gulf War, LTACFIRE proved vital, with one army unit reporting that "it couldn't have done its job without it."[49] In an all too common irony, the army took credit for developing the system.

The positive benefits of congressional parochialism are harder to see in foreign policy, if only because it is difficult to measure the effect of any specific foreign policy. (At least planes and tanks can be tested even when not actually used). But in many instances where public opinion encouraged, if not sparked, congressional activism, history appears to vindicate Congress. Whether the issue is apartheid in South Africa, support for Ferdinand Marcos in the Philippines, the civil war in El Salvador, or the political changes sweeping the Soviet bloc, members of Congress recognized long before the administration the need for changes in American policy. By most accounts, the changes that members lobbied for in these and other cases succeeded in promoting U.S. interests. And in several instances where members lost the policy debate, as happened most notably over the question of what policy toward China should look like in the wake of the massacre at Tiananmen Square, the policies favored by the administration did not distinguish themselves.

PRESIDENTIAL BARGAINING

A fourth criticism leveled against Congress's involvement in foreign policy is that congressional activism curtails the president's bargaining leverage and thereby hurts the national interest. Officials in the Reagan administration made just this argument when members of Congress criticized their handling of START and Nicaragua. The argument gained even greater currency in the months leading up to the Gulf War. Many observers claimed that congressional debate over the U.S. presence in the gulf would have the perverse effect of making war more likely by convincing Iraq that it could outlast the United States. Underlying the bargaining leverage argument, of course, is the assumption that the president's policy advances the national interest, an assumption many would dispute when the hypothetical is made concrete.

Whether congressional activism undermines the president's negotiating stance is a more complex issue than might seem to be the case at first glance. Often overlooked is the question of how the preferences of Congress and the president are distributed. Most discussions of the bargaining leverage argument assume that a majority of Congress prefers a policy that lies between what the president and the foreign country prefer, as happened with both START and Nicaragua during the Reagan years and again with Operation Desert Storm. When Congress prefers a more conciliatory policy option it seems safe to say that congressional activism doesn't help the president's negotiating position.[50] To the extent that foreign leaders follow and understand political divisions in Washington—which is far from always the case— they know the president faces domestic pressure to compromise.[51]

Whether the conciliatory stance of Congress forces the White House to compromise, however, depends on another factor, namely, how the president values a compromise outcome relative to the status quo. If the president prefers the status quo to compromise, then no compromise will be forthcoming, regardless of the level of congressional activism. This is what happened at the START talks during the Reagan administration. Members pleaded with the administration and for a time held the MX missile program hostage, but in the end they could not force Reagan to bargain enthusiastically. The only exception to the general rule that members cannot force the president to accept a compromise are those few issues, primarily involving trade, where Congress has constitutional authority to legislate policy.

Of course, critics worry not just that the president might concede under pressure from Capitol Hill but that members of Congress might prevent him from achieving his diplomatic objectives. Debate in Congress may convince foreign leaders to stand firm in the face of U.S. demands. Executive-legislative squabbling may also persuade foreign leaders that they can gain simply by waiting, since time might bring concessions from the administration.

As appealing as this logic is, it rests on the implicit assumption that foreign leaders are willing to accept the conciliatory position favored by members of Congress. When this is the case, foreign leaders have an incentive to wait. But frequently foreign leaders reject the policy positions of both the president and Congress. When this occurs, nothing that happens on Capitol Hill affects the outcome of negotiations. The Gulf War provides a textbook example. Many members of Congress and a good many political pundits worried that the public debate over the resolution authorizing the use of force against Iraq would embolden Saddam Hussein. The fact that Hussein refused to capitulate to U.S. demands, even after Iraq suffered more than thirty days of heavy bombing, makes it hard to sustain the argument that President Bush's attempt at coercive diplomacy would have worked if only he had enjoyed the enthusiastic support of Congress.

Instances where many members of Congress want the president to compromise garner considerable attention. But many times a majority in Congress opposes compromise. This happens when Congress prefers an outcome more extreme than what the president prefers. In situations such as these, congressional activism actually *strengthens* the president's bargaining position. Again, to the extent that foreign leaders follow executive-legislative conflict, they know that the president's ability to compromise is limited. In turn, they know they must be willing to compromise if an agreement is to be reached. Just such a dynamic governed the Carter administration's negotiations over the future of the Panama Canal.[52] Hardline congressional attitudes also regularly manifest themselves on trade, basing rights, foreign aid, and human rights.[53]

The fact that a hardline Congress strengthens the president's bargaining position explains why administrations sometimes encourage congressional activism. When administrations want to put pressure on another country but do not want to be seen doing so, Congress provides a convenient villain. Former secretary of the treasury John Connally observes that the Nixon administration regularly "used Congress as our bargaining lever."[54] When the Nixon administration wanted additional concessions from the government of Japan in trade talks, for example, it asked Wilbur Mills, the chair of the Ways and Means Committee, to introduce a bill on textile quotas.[55] More recently, the Reagan administration encouraged Rep. William Broomfield (R-Mich.) to introduce a bill penalizing New Zealand for its decision to adopt a nuclear-free weapons policy. Fearful that any steps it took would be counterproductive, the administration hoped that Broomfield's bill would serve as a useful prod to Wellington.[56]

More often, however, the president and Congress fall naturally into the roles of good cop and bad cop. The danger inherent in Congress's assuming the role of the bad cop on its own is that it will prevent presidents from conducting a policy they think will advance the national interest. In the aftermath of the massacre at Tiananmen Square, for example, President Bush argued that the hardline policy favored by most in Congress would be counterproductive. Again, one may doubt whether the president's policy made sense. But putting this complaint aside, presidents enjoy the upper hand when faced with congressional pressure to alter their policies. When many in Congress opposed the Panama Canal treaties, for example, the Carter administration launched a nationwide speech and media campaign that successfully turned the tide of public and congressional opinion.[57] Likewise, despite substantial criticism from Capitol Hill, President Bush made only cosmetic changes in his China policy.

VIRTUES

Although congressional involvement in foreign policy is far from perfect, members of Congress are hardly the villains that their critics paint them to be. But to say someone isn't ugly is not to say he is handsome. Are there virtues to found in Congress's active involvement in defense and foreign policy? In a word, yes. Congressional debate strengthens the president's bargaining leverage abroad in some circumstances, subjects administration proposals to a useful political scrub, and legitimizes whichever policies are eventually chosen.

As the last section suggested, one of the virtues of congressional activism is that a Congress that favors hardline policies strengthens the president's hand in the international arena. Some critics recognize this virtue of congressional activism but wish that Congress played the bad cop role only when asked. But such congressional deference diminishes the boost to the president's negotiating leverage. It is precisely the fear that the president cannot control Congress and that members will impose unilateral solutions if their concerns are not addressed that makes the good cop/bad cop scenario believable and effective.

The bad cop role that members of Congress take upon themselves provides the president with an additional advantage: a scapegoat. When presidents decide, for diplomatic or political reasons, that they cannot satisfy the demands of other countries but don't wish to bear the blame for the decision, Congress provides a ready-made excuse. To take just one example, presidents historically have used Congress as an excuse when they want to avoid providing U.S. aid to other countries.[58] Again, the excuse is believable precisely because members of Congress are active on foreign policy. Congressional activism also provides the president with a scapegoat in domestic politics. When members want the president to moderate his policies, he can blame foreign policy failures on congressional obstructionism, as Ronald Reagan frequently did.[59]

A second virtue of Congress's involvement in foreign policy is that members bring different values and perspectives to bear on policy issues. Sometimes members are driven by parochial concerns, as happened with the A-10 and LTACFIRE and as happens regularly with trade issues. At other times they are driven primarily by party or ideology. Whatever the impetus, congressional debate provides a useful political scrub that forces administrations to justify and, where needed, to revise their initiatives. As Rep. Lee Hamilton (D-Ind.) writes:

> Debate, tension, review can lead to decisions and actions which stand a better chance in serving the American national interest, and reflecting the values of the American people. Total cooperation should not be regarded as the essential condition of sound foreign policy. The concern of the Congress should be to strike a reasonable balance between responsible criticism on the one hand, based on measured oversight of the executive branch, and responsible cooperation on the other hand, stimulated by good and sound procedures of consultation between the President and members of Congress.[60]

Of course, congressional activism does not ensure sensible policy. As the rejection of the Treaty of Versailles and the refusal to recognize the rise of fascism in Germany and Japan both attest, Congress has no monopoly on wisdom. But the fact that members bring different values and perspectives to the debate makes it far more likely that administration proposals will be examined thoroughly.

In bringing different values and perspectives to bear on policy debates, members of Congress have a decided advantage over the executive branch in terms of policy innovation.[61] The foreign policy bureaucracy typically has a vested interest in existing policies, and its hierarchical structure makes it easy for suborganizations to block new initiatives. In contrast, because members often have no vested interest in the status quo and because the decentralized structure of Congress encourages policy entrepreneurship, members can float new policy ideas with ease. Such entrepreneurial capabilities were clearly in evidence in 1990 when members of the armed services committees moved far more quickly than the Bush administration to propose major changes in defense policy in response to the fall of the Berlin Wall. Indeed, the administration succeeded in producing its own proposal only after it excluded the leadership of the army, navy, and air force from deliberations on the plan.[62]

Critics worry, of course, that members of Congress have gone beyond responsible criticism and have turned the virtues of debate into a vice. An especially common refrain is that Congress takes too long to make decisions and that even then it reopens questions once thought settled. If Congress were less active, so the argument goes, the U.S. role abroad would be more resolute, and the national interest would benefit.

The fear that Congress breeds conflict and stalemate on foreign policy is curious in several respects. One is that the critics exaggerate the degree of delay and vacillation on Capitol Hill. For all the attention given to such lengthy congressional debates as the one over aid to the contras, relatively few issues split Congress so nearly down the middle. Moreover, when a foreign policy issue becomes mired in stalemate, responsibility for the impasse usually rests as much, if not more, with the executive branch as with Congress. For example, the debate over contra aid lasted as long as it did not because liberal Democrats delighted in challenging a popular president but because the Reagan administration refused for several years to accept Congress's refusal to support the overthrow of the Sandinista government. Indeed, some administration officials "scorned attempts at negotiation with Congress, believing instead that Congress could be strong-armed into acquiescence with if not support for [White House] policy."[63]

Complaints about delay and vacillation on Capitol Hill also fail to make it clear why it is preferable to pursue resolutely a policy that deeply divides the country. Again, while a less active Congress would make U.S. foreign policy making more efficient, efficiency does not necessarily mean better decisions. As Alexander Hamilton, himself a strong president man, observed in Federalist No. 70, "In the legislature, promptitude of decision is oftener an evil than a benefit. The differences of opinion, and the jarrings of parties in that department of the government, though they may sometimes obstruct salutary plans, yet often promote deliberation and circumspection; and serve to check excesses of the majority."[64] Perhaps not surprisingly, the three biggest foreign policy blunders of the past fifty years—the Bay of Pigs, Vietnam, and Iran-contra—resulted from too little debate, not too much. Analogous examples in which congressional debate—as opposed to the policy choice made by Congress—unambiguously damaged U.S. interests are far harder to find.

If critics worry that members of Congress have turned the virtues of debate into a vice, they also worry that members lack the expertise needed to make foreign policy decisions. Such criticisms conveniently forget that many senior foreign policy officials arrive in Washington with little or no foreign policy expertise—recall National Security Adviser William Clark and Secretary of State James Baker—and that it was the "best and the brightest" who gave America Vietnam. Nor are administration experts infallible. After all, as late as 1 August 1990, the Bush administration opposed a bill to impose sanctions on Iraq on the ground that the United States needed to be conciliatory in its dealings with Saddam Hussein. The expertise critique also forgets that while members of Congress themselves may not be foreign policy experts, they too can draw on the advice of experts. Members in need turn to congressional staff (many of whom used to hold positions in the executive branch), disaffected officials in the executive branch (some of whom use Congress to communicate with senior administration officials), scholars in think tanks and universities (who see members of Congress as entrepreneurs for their policy ideas), and interest groups (who provide information and policy rationales to advance their interests).

But in a larger sense the focus on expertise misses what is at stake in the struggle between Congress and the president over foreign policy. Expertise matters most on scientific and technical issues, but these are the issues least likely to be at the core of the debate between the two ends of Pennsylvania Avenue. Congress and the president struggle far more often over what are essentially *political* judgments. Which is more likely to produce political reform in China, the carrot or the stick? Should the United States play a vigorous role in rebuilding the economies of the former Soviet republics or should it leave them to their own devices? What size military does the United States need in the post–cold war world? Answers to questions such as these turn on judgments about goals and values and on beliefs about the way the world works, areas in which experts are no better off than members of Congress.[65] And anyone who doubts the fallibility of foreign policy experts should check the record of their writings on America's op-ed pages as well as the repeated failures of CIA analysts to divine the future.

Critics worry as well that debate in Congress leads to leaks that unravel carefully constructed diplomatic efforts. Fears that no secret is safe on Capitol Hill are as old as the republic—while serving as secretary of state, Thomas Jefferson declined to discuss an issue involving Great Britain with members of Congress because "if the Senate should be consulted & consequently apprized of our line, it would become known to Hammond [the British minister]."[66] Yet for all their longevity, complaints about congressional leaks have an air of unreality about them—if Congress leaks information, the executive branch gushes it.[67] Indeed, as the Tower Commission concluded after interviewing cabinet officials from several administrations, executive branch officials blame Congress disproportionately for leaks of classified information because it provides "a convenient excuse for Presidents to avoid Congressional consultation."[68] When congressional leaks do occur, what often matters most is not that secrets have been lost but how the White House handles the issue. The Carter administration, for example, was rocked by leaks regarding the neutron bomb program and the Soviet brigade in Cuba. In both instances, Carter's bungled response to the leak greatly magnified the problem.[69] And secrecy is not a blessing when policies are ill-conceived. As Iran-contra attests, U.S. interests at times benefit from less rather than more secrecy.

The third virtue of Congress's activism is that it legitimizes whichever policies are eventually chosen. As Robert Pastor observes, "The inclusion of other views or interests not only increases the prospects of avoiding mistakes and forging a better policy, but it also gives groups a stake in the policy's success."[70] Especially important in this regard is the impact of congressional debate on public opinion. The Vietnam War taught us at great cost that no foreign policy can be sustained without the firm support of the American public. Debates in Congress, be they on the merits of aid to Russia, free-trade arrangements with Mexico, or using U.S. troops to enforce the resolutions of the Security Council, present valuable opportunities to educate the American public about U.S. interests in the world.[71] Presidents who cannot win such battles for public opinion would do well to rethink the wisdom of their policies.

Of course, it has become habit whenever American foreign policy making is discussed to invoke Tocqueville's lament that democracy is ill-suited to foreign affairs. Whatever the merits of Tocqueville's argument—he was describing a political system quite different from the one we know today—the United States is a democracy. That is the source of its great strength. And as Michael Walzer observers, "The test of a democracy is not that the right side wins the political battle but that there is a political battle."[72] Policies that pass through public debate and inspection emerge all the stronger for it, because they enjoy greater respect both at home and abroad.

CONCLUSION

Congressional activism on foreign policy is a fact of life in the 1990s. If anything, the collapse of the Soviet Union, the intensifying economic rivalry with Europe and Japan, and the emergence of issues such as global warming will continue to encourage congressional activism. At the same time, the press of economic and social problems at home will fuel neo-isolationist sentiments, making it likely that some in Congress will push for the United States to turn inward.

Congress's involvement in foreign policy does have costs. The institution often dawdles when making decisions, and on occasion it reverses course once it does decide. Sometimes members of Congress delve too deeply into budgetary details. Committee turf battles prove enormously frustrating to members and administration officials alike. Congressional activism on occasion turns into abuse, as when senators hold up ambassadorial appointments to punish foreign service officers for the policies of previous administrations. And congressional activism by no means guarantees that the United States will have a wise foreign policy. Like officials in the executive branch, members of Congress may choose policies that will prove to be ineffective or naive.

Even in combination, however, these vices do not constitute a crisis in U.S. foreign policy making. To be sure, if Congress did run foreign policy, its inefficiencies would imperil the national interest. But congressional activism today remains a far cry from what it was a century ago when Congress dominated foreign policy. Congress today does not run foreign policy, and the inherent advantages the president enjoys in the modern international arena make it unlikely that it ever will again. It is also clear that Congress's activism makes it harder for the president to achieve his foreign policy goals. That is why administration officials who survey the state of executive-legislative relations continually lament a paradise lost. But the duty facing members of Congress is not to make the president's job easier but to make the country's policies better. And they can only do that by challenging the president.

When alarms about "congressional overreaching" are sounded—as they invariably will be in the future—it is worth remembering that conflict between the executive and the legislature is designed into the American political system. In Richard Neustadt's famous formulation, the Constitution provides for "separated institutions *sharing* power."[73] So long as ideology and party divide the two ends of Pennsylvania Avenue, Congress and the president will struggle over foreign policy. Of course, the prospect of executive-legislative conflict worries many observers, some because they favor the president's policies and others because they fear the country suffers when politics goes beyond the water's edge. The latter worry is the more troubling, but for all the concern expressed, instances in which congressional activism clearly hurts the national interest or the cause of good policy are in short supply.

The wisdom of the framers' belief that separate institutions sharing power would promote the common good becomes clear once one recognizes that neither the president nor Congress monopolizes "correct" policy positions. In this respect, the Irreconcilables who denounced Congress for obstructing the foreign policies of Presidents Reagan and Bush quickly rediscovered the virtues of congressional activism with Bill Clinton in the White House. By the same token, liberals who praised Congress for contesting the policies of Reagan and Bush will have to remember that lesson with one of their own in the Oval Office.

Instead of seeing executive-legislative conflict over foreign policy as a cause for dismay, we should recognize that healthy democracies argue over the wisdom of policies. Debate is what, ultimately, produces better policy. Unfortunately, the particular institutional arrangements of the American political system sometimes obscure the fact that real issues are being argued. Irreconcilables and Skeptics assume that "politics" produces *only* other— disreputable, illegitimate, and harmful—disputes. Sometimes congressional activism represents "noise" and sometimes it hurts American interests. But many times congressional activism focuses on real issues and produces desirable outcomes. Congressional activism, at its best, advances the discussion over the wisest course of action in foreign policy.

NOTES

INTRODUCTION

1. "The Colonel Presents His Case: His Beliefs, His Work, and His Grievances," *New York Times,* 10 July 1987.

2. See, for example, Paul N. Stockton, "The New Game on the Hill: The Politics of Arms Control and Strategic Force Modernization," *International Security* 16 (Fall 1991): 146–70.

3. For an extensive review of the literature on Congress and foreign policy, see James M. Lindsay and Randall B. Ripley, "Foreign and Defense Policy in Congress: A Research Agenda for the 1990s," *Legislative Studies Quarterly* 17 (August 1992): 417–49. The classic studies of Congress and foreign policy include Holbert N. Carroll, *The House of Representatives and Foreign Affairs,* rev. ed. (Boston: Little, Brown, 1966); Robert Dahl, *Congress and Foreign Policy* (New York: Harcourt, Brace, 1950); George L. Grassmuck, *Sectional Biases in Congress on Foreign Policy,* Johns Hopkins University Studies in Historical and Political Science, ser. 68, no. 3 (Baltimore: Johns Hopkins Press, 1951); Malcolm E. Jewell, *Senatorial Politics and Foreign Policy* (Lexington: University of Kentucky Press, 1962); and James Robinson, *Congress and Foreign Policy Making,* rev. ed. (Homewood, Ill.: Dorsey Press, 1967).

4. Among others see Dick Cheney, "Congressional Overreaching in Foreign Policy," in *Foreign Policy and the Constitution,* ed. Robert A. Goldwin and Robert A. Licht (Washington, D.C.: American Enterprise Institute, 1990); L. Gordon Crovitz, "Micromanaging Foreign Policy," *Public Interest* 100 (Summer 1990): 102–15; L. Gordon Crovitz and Jeremy A. Rabkin, eds., *The Fettered Presidency: Legal Constraints on the Executive Branch* (Washington, D.C.: American Enterprise Institute, 1989); Peter W. Rodman, "The Imperial Congress," *National Interest* 1 (Fall 1985): 26–35; Eugene V. Rostow, *President, Prime Minister, or Constitutional Monarch?* McNair Papers, no. 3 (Washington, D.C.: National Defense University, 1989); George Szamuely, "The Imperial Congress," *Commentary,* September 1987, pp. 27–32; Howard J. Wiarda, *Foreign Policy without Illusion: How Foreign Policy-Making Works and Fails to Work in the United States* (Glenview, Ill.: Scott, Foresman/Little, Brown, 1990); and Jay Winik, "The Quest for Bipartisanship: A New Beginning for a New World Order," *Washington Quarterly* 14 (Autumn 1991): 115–30.

5. Harold Hongju Koh, "Why the President (Almost) Always Wins in Foreign Affairs: Lessons of the Iran-Contra Affair," *Yale Law Journal* 97 (June 1988): 1255–1342. See also I. M. Destler, Leslie H. Gelb, and Anthony Lake, *Our Own Worst Enemy: The Unmaking of American Foreign Policy* (New York: Simon and Schuster, 1984); Barbara Hinckley, *Less Than Meets the Eye: Congress, the President, and Foreign Policy* (Chicago: University of Chicago Press, 1994); Charles W. Kegley, Jr., and Eugene R. Wittkopf,

American Foreign Policy: Pattern and Process, 4th ed. (New York: St. Martin's Press, 1991); and Harold Hongju Koh, *The National Security Constitution: Sharing Power after the Iran-Contra Affair* (New Haven: Yale University Press, 1990).

6. William D. Rogers, "Who's in Charge of Foreign Policy?" *New York Times Magazine,* 9 September 1979, p. 49.

7. Frank E. Smith, *Congressman from Mississippi* (New York: Random House, 1964), p. 127.

8. See Thomas E. Mann, *Unsafe at Any Margin: Interpreting Congressional Elections* (Washington, D.C.: American Enterprise Institute, 1978).

9. Senator Church later admitted that "he had erred badly by seizing this issue in the way that he had." Quoted in F. Forrester Church, *Father and Son: A Personal Biography of Senator Frank Church* (New York: Harper and Row, 1985), p. 141.

10. David R. Mayhew, *Congress: The Electoral Connection* (New Haven: Yale University Press, 1974), p. 115.

11. Ibid., p. 147.

12. Robert J. Art, "Congress and the Defense Budget: Enhancing Policy Oversight," *Political Science Quarterly* 100 (Summer 1985): 240.

13. Wiarda, *Foreign Policy without Illusion,* p. 221.

14. Mathew D. McCubbins and Thomas Schwartz, "Congressional Oversight Overlooked: Police Patrol versus Fire Alarms," *American Journal of Political Science* 28 (February 1984): 165–79.

15. For a splendid elaboration of this point, see Stanley J. Heginbotham, "Congress and Defense Policymaking: Toward Realistic Expectations in a System of Countervailing Parochialisms," in *National Security Policy: The Decision-Making Process,* ed. Robert L. Pfaltzgraff, Jr., and Uri Ra'anan (Hamden, Conn.: Archon Books, 1984).

16. See Steve Hoadley, "The US Congress and the New Zealand Military Preference Elimination Bill," *Political Science* 43 (July 1991): 47–60.

17. See Kenneth A. Shepsle, "Congress Is a 'They,' Not an 'It': Legislative Intent As Oxymoron," *International Review of Law and Economics* 12 (June 1992): 239–56.

18. Dan Caldwell, *The Dynamics of Domestic Politics and Arms Control: The SALT II Treaty Ratification Debate* (Columbia: University of South Carolina Press, 1991); Dan Caldwell, "The SALT II Treaty," in *The Politics of Arms Control Treaty Ratification,* ed. Michael Krepon and Dan Caldwell (New York: St. Martin's Press, 1991); and Stephen J. Flanagan, "The Domestic Politics of SALT II: Implications for the Foreign Policy Process," in *Congress, the Presidency, and American Foreign Policy,* ed. John Spanier and Joseph Nogee (New York: Pergamon Press, 1981).

19. Gregory F. Treverton, "Intelligence: Welcome to the American Government," in *A Question of Balance: The President, the Congress, and Foreign Policy,* ed. Thomas E. Mann (Washington, D.C.: Brookings Institution, 1990), p. 98.

20. Eric Schmitt, "U.S. Hopes to Sell F-15s to Saudis, but Delicately," *New York Times,* 26 February 1992.

21. Quoted in Joseph White, "Decision Making in the Appropriations Subcommittees on Defense and Foreign Operations," in *Congress Resurgent: Foreign and Defense Policy on Capitol Hill,* ed. Randall B. Ripley and James M. Lindsay (Ann Arbor: University of Michigan Press, 1993), p. 200 (emphasis in the original).

CHAPTER 1. FOREIGN POLICY
ON CAPITOL HILL

1. "President Bush Delivers Inaugural Address," *Congressional Quarterly Weekly Report,* 21 January 1989, pp. 142–43.

2. Edward S. Corwin, *The President: Office and Powers, 1787–1957,* 4th rev. ed. (New York: New York University Press, 1957), p. 171.

3. Jay Winik, "The Quest for Bipartisanship: A New Beginning for a New World Order," *Washington Quarterly* 14 (Autumn 1991): 118.

4. See David Gray Adler, "The Constitution and Presidential Warmaking," *Political Science Quarterly* 103 (Spring 1988): 8–13; Alexander Hamilton, "Federalist No. 69," in Alexander Hamilton, James Madison, and John Jay, *The Federalist Papers,* ed. Garry Wills (New York: Bantam Books, 1982); and Louis Henkin, *Foreign Affairs and the Constitution* (Mineola, N.Y.: Foundation Press, 1972), pp. 50–51.

5. Louis Henkin, *Constitutionalism, Democracy, and Foreign Affairs* (New York: Columbia University Press, 1990), p. 19.

6. Quoted in Jean E. Smith, *The Constitution and American Foreign Policy* (St. Paul, Minn.: West Publishing, 1989), pp. 52 and 55.

7. The literature on the foreign policy powers of Congress and the president is immense. Two recent contributions are Michael J. Glennon, *Constitutional Diplomacy* (Princeton: Princeton University Press, 1990), and Harold Hongju Koh, *The National Security Constitution: Sharing Power after the Iran-Contra Affair* (New Haven: Yale University Press, 1990).

8. On the activities of the war hawks, see Richard B. Cheney and Lynne V. Cheney, *Kings of the Hill: Power and Personality in the House of Representatives* (New York: Continuum, 1983), pp. 1–21.

9. Arthur M. Schlesinger, Jr., *The Imperial Presidency* (Boston: Houghton Mifflin, 1989), p. 27.

10. Quoted in ibid., p. 42.

11. Daniel S. Cheever and H. Field Haviland, Jr., *American Foreign Policy and the Separation of Powers* (Cambridge: Harvard University Press, 1952), p. 48; W. Stull Holt, *Treaties Defeated in the Senate* (Baltimore: Johns Hopkins Press, 1933), p. 121; Gerard Felix Warburg, *Conflict and Consensus: The Struggle between Congress and the President over Foreign Policymaking* (New York: Harper and Row, 1989), p. 20; and Woodrow Wilson, *Congressional Government: A Study in American Politics* (Gloucester, Mass.: Peter Smith, 1973).

12. See Royden J. Dangerfield, *In Defense of the Senate: A Study in Treaty Making* (Norman: University of Oklahoma Press, 1933), pp. 183–252, and Holt, *Treaties Defeated in the Senate,* pp. 121–77.

13. William Roscoe Thayer, *The Life and Letters of John Hay, Volume II* (Boston: Houghton Mifflin, 1915), p. 170.

14. Quoted in Cecil V. Crabb, Jr., *Bipartisan Foreign Policy: Myth or Reality?* (Evanston, Ill.: Row, Peterson, 1957), p. 37.

15. Wilson, *Congressional Government,* p. 52 (emphasis in the original).

16. Woodrow Wilson, *Constitutional Government in the United States* (New York: Columbia University Press, 1961), pp. 139–40.

17. For discussions of the Senate debate over the Treaty of Versailles, see Cheever and Haviland, *Foreign Policy and Separation of Powers,* pp. 68–81; Holt, *Treaties Defeated in the*

Senate, pp. 249–307; Ralph Stone, *The Irreconcilables: The Fight against the League of Nations* (Lexington: University of Kentucky Press, 1970); John Chalmers Vinson, *Referendum for Isolation: Defeat of Article Ten of the League of Nations Covenant* (Athens: University of Georgia Press, 1961); and William C. Widenor, "The League of Nations Component of the Versailles Treaty," in *The Politics of Arms Control Treaty Ratification,* ed. Michael Krepon and Dan Caldwell (New York: St. Martin's Press, 1991).

18. For discussions of executive-legislative relations during the interwar years, see Thomas H. Buckley, "The Washington Naval Treaties," in Krepon and Caldwell, *Politics of Arms Control Treaty Ratification;* George L. Grassmuck, *Sectional Biases in Congress on Foreign Policy,* Johns Hopkins University Studies in Historical and Political Science, ser. 68, no. 3 (Baltimore: Johns Hopkins Press, 1951); Rodney J. McElroy, "The Geneva Protocol of 1925," in Krepon and Caldwell, *Politics of Arms Control Treaty Ratification;* and Albert C. Westphal, *The House Committee on Foreign Affairs* (New York: Columbia University Press, 1942).

19. Richard Dean Burns and W. Addams Dixon, "Foreign Policy and the 'Democratic Myth': The Debate on the Ludlow Amendment," *Mid-America* 47 (October 1965): 288–306.

20. Quoted in William L. Langer and S. Everett Gleason, *The Challenge of Isolation* (New York: Harper and Bros., 1952), p. 144.

21. Robert H. Ferrell, *American Diplomacy: A History,* 3d ed. (New York: Norton, 1975), p. 549.

22. On executive-legislative relations in the two years preceding Pearl Harbor, see William L. Langer and S. Everett Gleason, *The Undeclared War: 1940–1941* (New York: Harper and Bros., 1953), pp. 257–84 and 570–74.

23. Ferrell, *American Diplomacy,* p. 560.

24. Sol Bloom, *The Autobiography of Sol Bloom* (New York: Putnam, 1948), pp. 243–44.

25. Alexis de Tocqueville, *Democracy in America* (New York: Anchor Books, 1969), p. 126.

26. See Schlesinger, *Imperial Presidency,* esp. pp. 127–207.

27. For general overviews of executive-legislative relations on foreign policy during the first three decades after World War II, see Philip J. Briggs, *Making American Foreign Policy: President-Congress Relations from the Second World War to Vietnam* (Lanham, Md.: University Press of America, 1991), and John Rourke, *Congress and the Presidency in U.S. Foreign Policymaking: A Study of Interaction and Influence, 1945–1982* (Boulder, Colo.: Westview Press, 1983).

28. See Cheever and Haviland, *Foreign Policy and Separation of Powers,* pp. 97–100; H. Bradford Westerfield, *Foreign Policy and Party Politics: Pearl Harbor to Korea* (New Haven: Yale University Press, 1955), pp. 153–55; and Roland Young, *Congressional Politics in the Second World War* (New York: Columbia University Press, 1956), pp. 184–87.

29. Cheever and Haviland, *Foreign Policy and Separation of Powers,* p. 128.

30. Dean Acheson, *Present at the Creation: My Years in the State Department* (New York: Norton, 1987), pp. 413–14.

31. See Cheever and Haviland, *Foreign Policy and Separation of Powers,* pp. 146–57; Crabb, *Bipartisan Foreign Policy,* pp. 98–115; and Westerfield, *Foreign Policy and Party Politics,* pp. 240–68 and 343–69.

32. Holbert N. Carroll, *The House of Representatives and Foreign Affairs,* rev. ed. (Boston: Little, Brown, 1966), p. 268.

33. For discussions of the Great Debate of 1951, see Acheson, *Present at the Creation,* pp. 488–96; Crabb, *Bipartisan Foreign Policy,* pp. 87–94; and Schlesinger, *Imperial Presidency,* pp. 135–40.

34. Quoted in Schlesinger, *Imperial Presidency,* p. 136.

35. Acheson, *Present at the Creation,* p. 496.

36. The most detailed discussion of the debate over the Bricker Amendment is Duane Tananbaum, *The Bricker Amendment Controversy: A Test of Eisenhower's Political Leadership* (Ithaca, N.Y.: Cornell University Press, 1988).

37. Cathal J. Nolan, "The Last Hurrah of Conservative Isolationism: Eisenhower, Congress, and the Bricker Amendment," *Presidential Studies Quarterly* 22 (Spring 1992): 337–49.

38. Quoted in James L. Sundquist, *The Decline and Resurgence of Congress* (Washington, D.C.: Brookings Institution, 1981), p. 116.

39. On Congress and foreign aid during the second postwar decade, see John D. Montgomery, *The Politics of Foreign Aid* (New York: Praeger, 1962). On Congress and defense policy, see Raymond H. Dawson, "Congressional Innovation and Intervention in Defense Policy: Legislative Authorization of Weapons Systems," *American Political Science Review* 56 (March 1962): 42–57; Bernard K. Gordon, "The Military Budget: Congressional Phase," *Journal of Politics* 23 (November 1961): 689–710; and Edward A. Kolodziej, *The Uncommon Defense and Congress, 1945–1963* (Columbus: Ohio State University Press, 1966).

40. For pessimistic assessments of congressional influence over defense and foreign policy in the late 1950s and early 1960s, see Carroll, *House of Representatives,* esp. pp. 363–68; Lewis Anthony Dexter, "Congressmen and the Making of Military Policy," in *New Perspectives on the House of Representatives,* ed. Robert L. Peabody and Nelson W. Polsby (Chicago: Rand McNally, 1968); Samuel P. Huntington, *The Common Defense: Strategic Programs in National Politics* (New York: Columbia University Press, 1961); James A. Robinson, *Congress and Foreign Policy-Making: A Study in Legislative Influence and Initiative,* rev. ed. (Homewood, Ill.: Dorsey Press, 1967); and H. Bradford Westerfield, "Congress and Closed Politics in National Security Affairs," *Orbis* 10 (Fall 1966): 737–53.

41. Quoted in Schlesinger, *Imperial Presidency,* p. 160.

42. See, for example, the questions raised during committee hearings by Sen. Mike Mansfield (D-Mont.) and others in U.S. Congress, Senate Committees on Foreign Relations and Armed Services, *The President's Proposal on the Middle East, Part 1,* 85th Cong., 1st sess., 1957, esp. p. 118.

43. Shortly before the Cuban missile crisis began, Congress passed a resolution expressing the determination of the United States "to prevent in Cuba the creation or use of an externally supported military capability endangering the security of the United States." The resolution did not, however, authorize Kennedy to use force, and he did not refer to the resolution when he imposed the naval quarantine on Cuba. See "Cuba Resolution," *Congressional Quarterly Weekly Report,* 21 September 1962, p. 1565; "House Passes Cuba Resolution, 384-7," *Congressional Quarterly Weekly Report,* 28 September 1962, p. 1691; and Schlesinger, *Imperial Presidency,* pp. 173–75.

44. The figures on troop deployments are from John E. Mueller, *War, Presidents, and Public Opinion* (New York: Wiley, 1973), p. 28.

45. Sundquist, *Decline and Resurgence of Congress,* p. 116.

46. See George C. Herring, *America's Longest War: The United States and Vietnam, 1950–1975*, 2d ed. (New York: Knopf, 1986), pp. 122–23.

47. The text of the Gulf of Tonkin Resolution is reprinted in John Hart Ely, *War and Responsibility: Constitutional Lessons of Vietnam and Its Aftermath* (Princeton: Princeton University Press, 1993), p. 16, and Smith, *Constitution and Foreign Policy*, pp. 254–55.

48. Smith, *Constitution and Foreign Policy*, p. 235.

49. Quoted in Sundquist, *Decline and Resurgence of Congress*, p. 125.

50. Quoted in Adam Yarmolinsky, *The Military Establishment: Its Impacts on American Society* (New York: Harper and Row, 1971), p. 53.

51. For evidence that ideological differences on foreign policy cut across rather than along party lines in the 1950s and 1960s, see Malcolm E. Jewell, *Senatorial Politics and Foreign Policy* (Lexington: University of Kentucky Press, 1962), pp. 10–52; James M. McCormick and Eugene R. Wittkopf, "Bipartisanship, Partisanship, and Ideology in Congressional-Executive Foreign Policy Relations, 1947–88," *Journal of Politics* 52 (November 1990): 1077–1100; James M. McCormick and Eugene R. Wittkopf, "Bush and Bipartisanship: The Past as Prologue?" *Washington Quarterly* 13 (Winter 1990): 5–16; Leroy N. Rieselbach, *The Roots of Isolationism: Congressional Voting and Presidential Leadership in Foreign Policy* (Indianapolis, Ind.: Bobbs-Merrill, 1966); and Peter Trubowitz, "Ideology, Party, and U.S. Foreign and Defense Policy: An Analysis of Senate Voting, 1947–1984," Ph.D. diss., Massachusetts Institute of Technology, 1986.

52. Nolan, "Last Hurrah of Conservative Isolationism," p. 337.

53. For evidence that congressional debate on defense and foreign policy took on increasingly partisan tones in the 1980s, see McCormick and Wittkopf, "Bipartisanship, Partisanship, and Ideology," pp. 1077–1100; McCormick and Wittkopf, "Bush and Bipartisanship," pp. 5–16; and David W. Rohde, "Partisan Leadership and Congressional Assertiveness in Foreign and Defense Policy," in *The New Politics of American Foreign Policy*, ed. David A. Deese (New York: St. Martin's Press, 1994).

54. See Cynthia J. Arnson, *Crossroads: Congress, the Reagan Administration, and Central America* (New York: Pantheon Books, 1989); Philip Brenner and William M. LeoGrande, "Congress and Nicaragua: The Limits of Alternative Policy Making," in *Divided Government: Cooperation and Conflict between the President and Congress*, ed. James Thurber (Washington, D.C.: CQ Press, 1991); William M. LeoGrande, "The Controversy over Contra Aid, 1981–90: A Historical Narrative," in *Public Opinion in U.S. Foreign Policy: The Controversy over Contra Aid*, ed. Richard Sobel (Lanham, Md.: Rowman and Littlefield, 1993); Robert A. Pastor, *Condemned to Repetition: The United States and Nicaragua* (Princeton: Princeton University Press, 1987); and Robert A. Pastor, "The War between the Branches: Explaining U.S. Policy toward Nicaragua, 1979–89," in Sobel, *Public Opinion in U.S. Foreign Policy*.

55. James M. Lindsay, "Congress and Defense Policy: 1961 to 1986," *Armed Forces and Society* 13 (Spring 1987): 371–401.

56. See Arthur M. Schlesinger, Jr., *A Thousand Days: John F. Kennedy in the White House* (New York: Greenwich House, 1983), pp. 251–52.

57. Theodore C. Sorenson, *Kennedy* (New York: Harper and Row, 1965), pp. 347–48.

58. Frank J. Smist, *Congress Oversees the United States Intelligence Community, 1947–1989* (Knoxville: University of Tennessee Press, 1990), p. 7.

59. J. William Fulbright, "American Foreign Policy in the 20th Century under an 18th-Century Constitution," *Cornell Law Quarterly* 47 (Fall 1961): 2.

60. Lindsay, "Congress and Defense Policy," pp. 382–85.

61. See Norman Ornstein, "Interest Groups, Congress, and American Foreign Policy," in *American Foreign Policy in an Uncertain World,* ed. David P. Forsythe (Lincoln: University of Nebraska Press, 1984); John T. Tierney, "Congressional Activism in Foreign Policy: Its Varied Forms and Stimuli," in Deese, *New Politics of American Foreign Policy;* and John T. Tierney, "Interest Group Involvement in Congressional Foreign and Defense Policy," in *Congress Resurgent: Foreign and Defense Policy on Capitol Hill,* ed. Randall B. Ripley and James M. Lindsay (Ann Arbor: University of Michigan Press, 1993).

62. The literature on ethnic lobbies is large. Among others, see Mohammed E. Ahrari, ed., *Ethnic Groups and U.S. Foreign Policy* (New York: Greenwood Press, 1987); Mitchell Bard, *The Water's Edge and Beyond: Defining the Limits to Domestic Influence on United States Middle East Policy* (New Brunswick, N.J.: Transaction Publishers, 1991); David Howard Goldberg, *Foreign Policy and Ethnic Interest Groups* (Westport, Conn.: Greenwood Press, 1990); F. Chidozie Ogene, *Interest Groups and the Shaping of Foreign Policy: Four Case Studies of United States African Policy* (New York: St. Martin's Press, 1983); Eric Uslaner, "A Tower of Babel on Foreign Policy?" in *Interest Group Politics,* 3d ed., ed. Allan J. Cigler and Burdett A. Loomis (Washington, D.C.: CQ Press, 1991); and Paul Y. Watanabe, *Ethnic Groups, Congress, and American Foreign Policy* (Westport, Conn.: Greenwood Press, 1984).

63. See John D. Isaacs and Katherine Magraw, "The Lobbyist and the MX," *Bulletin of the Atomic Scientists* 39 (February 1983): 56–57, and Michael Pertschuk, *Giant Killers* (New York: Norton, 1986), pp. 181–228.

64. Tierney, "Interest Group Involvement," p. 95.

65. See John R. MacArthur, *Second Front: Censorship and Propaganda in the Gulf War* (New York: Hill and Wang, 1992).

66. Rochelle L. Stanfield, "Balkan Wars on K Street," *National Journal,* 15 August 1992, pp. 1903–4.

67. Harold W. Stanley and Richard G. Niemi, *Vital Statistics on American Politics* (Washington, D.C.: CQ Press, 1992), p. 278.

68. Joe Martin, *My First Fifty Years in Politics* (New York: McGraw-Hill, 1960), p. 49.

69. Bloom, *Autobiography,* pp. 308–14.

CHAPTER 2. LEGISLATIVE MOTIVATION AND FOREIGN POLICY

1. Thomas M. Franck and Edward Weisband, *Foreign Policy by Congress* (New York: Oxford University Press, 1979), p. 277.

2. For a discussion of why electoral explanations are popular with journalists, see Edward J. Epstein, *News from Nowhere* (New York: Random House, 1973), pp. 215–25.

3. See, for instance, Elaine Sciolino, "Senator Tries to Balance Party and Constituency," *New York Times,* 11 January 1991, and Martin Tolchin, "Southern Democrats Are Torn As Vote Nears," *New York Times,* 12 January 1991.

4. Keith Bradsher, "Senate Backs Curbs on Beijing's Access to Markets in U.S.," *New York Times,* 26 February 1992.

5. David R. Mayhew, *Congress: The Electoral Connection* (New Haven: Yale University Press, 1974). Although Mayhew emphasized that he was assuming that members of

Congress act *as if* they were single-minded seekers of reelection, some political scientists continue to misread Mayhew as arguing that members of Congress in fact care only about reelection. See, for instance, Daniel Wirls, "Congress and the Politics of Military Reform," *Armed Forces and Society* 17 (Summer 1991): 512.

6. Quoted in Mitchell Stephens, *A History of News* (New York: Penguin Books, 1988), p. 45. On the public's interest in foreign policy, see Gabriel Almond, *The American People and Foreign Policy* (New York: Harcourt, Brace, 1950); Lloyd A. Cantril and Hadley Cantril, *The Political Beliefs of Americans: A Study of Public Opinion* (New York: Clarion Book, 1968); John E. Reilly, ed., *American Public Opinion and U.S. Foreign Policy* (Chicago: Chicago Council on Foreign Relations, 1991); and Richard Sobel, "Public Opinion about United States Intervention in El Salvador and Nicaragua," *Public Opinion Quarterly* 53 (Spring 1989): 114–28.

7. Quoted in R. W. Apple, Jr., "War Clouds, No Thunder," *New York Times*, 6 November 1990.

8. See, for example, Robert J. Art, "Congress and the Defense Budget: Enhancing Policy Oversight," *Political Science Quarterly* 100 (Summer 1985): 227–49.

9. Mayhew, *Congress*, pp. 61–73.

10. See Anna M. Warrock and Howard Husock, "Taking Toshiba Public," Case C15-88-858.0, Harvard University, John F. Kennedy School of Government, 1988, pp. 11–12.

11. On advertising as an electorally useful activity for members of Congress, see Mayhew, *Congress*, pp. 48–52.

12. Kenneth R. Mayer, *The Political Economy of Defense Contracting* (New Haven: Yale University Press, 1991), p. 134.

13. Mayhew, *Congress*, pp. 52–61.

14. See John H. Aldrich, John L. Sullivan, and Eugene Borgida, "Foreign Affairs and Issue Voting: Do Presidential Candidates 'Waltz before a Blind Audience?'" *American Political Science Review* 83 (March 1989): 123–42.

15. Les Aspin, "The Defense Budget and Foreign Policy: The Role of Congress," *Daedalus* 104 (Summer 1975): 155.

16. George D. Moffett III, *The Limits of Victory: The Ratification of the Panama Canal Treaties* (Ithaca, N.Y.: Cornell University Press, 1985), pp. 209–14.

17. *Gallup Report* 220–21 (January–February 1984): 14; Louis Harris, "Doubts Arise over U.S. Military Involvement in Lebanon," *The Harris Survey*, no. 76, 22 September 1983; and Philip J. Powlick, "Foreign Policy Decisions and Public Opinion: The Case of the Lebanon Intervention," Paper presented at the 1988 annual meeting of the American Political Science Association, Washington, D.C.

18. See Richard Sobel, "Public Opinion about U.S. Intervention in Nicaragua: A Polling Addendum," in *Public Opinion in U.S. Foreign Policy: The Controversy over Contra Aid*, ed. Richard Sobel (Lanham, Md.: Rowman and Littlefield, 1993).

19. Warren E. Miller and Donald E. Stokes, "Constituency Influence in Congress," *American Political Science Review* 57 (March 1963): 45–56.

20. L. Marvin Overby, "Assessing Constituency Influence: Congressional Voting on the Nuclear Freeze, 1982–83" *Legislative Studies Quarterly* 16 (May 1991): 297–312.

21. Larry M. Bartels, "Constituency Opinion and Congressional Policy Making: The Reagan Defense Buildup," *American Political Science Review* 85 (June 1991): 457–74.

22. See John W. Kingdon, *Congressmen's Voting Decisions,* 3d ed. (Ann Arbor: University of Michigan Press, 1989).

23. See William P. Avery and David P. Forsythe, "Human Rights, National Security, and the U.S. Senate," *International Studies Quarterly* 23 (June 1979): 303–20; William M. LeoGrande, "Did the Public Matter? The Impact of Public Opinion on Congressional Support for Ronald Reagan's Nicaragua Policy," in Sobel, *Public Opinion in U.S. Foreign Policy;* William M. LeoGrande and Philip Brenner, "The House Divided: Ideological Polarization over Aid to the Nicaraguan 'Contras,'" *Legislative Studies Quarterly* 18 (February 1993): 105–36; James M. McCormick, "Congressional Voting on the Nuclear Freeze Resolution," *American Politics Quarterly* 13 (January 1985): 122–36; and James M. McCormick and Michael Black, "Ideology and Senate Voting on the Panama Canal Treaties," *Legislative Studies Quarterly* 8 (February 1983): 45–63.

24. Among the more recent contributions are Richard Fleisher, "Economic Benefit, Ideology, and Senate Voting on the B-1 Bomber," *American Politics Quarterly* 13 (April 1985): 200–211; James M. Lindsay, "Parochialism, Policy, and Constituency Constraints: Congressional Voting on Strategic Weapons Systems," *American Journal of Political Science* 34 (November 1990): 936–60; James M. Lindsay, "Testing the Parochial Hypothesis: Congress and the Strategic Defense Initiative," *Journal of Politics* 53 (August 1991): 860–76; Mayer, *Political Economy of Defense Contracting,* pp. 98–132; Peter Navarro, *The Policy Game: How Special Interests and Ideologues Are Stealing America* (New York: Wiley, 1984); Bruce A. Ray, "Defense Department Spending and 'Hawkish' Voting in the House of Representatives," *Western Political Quarterly* 34 (September 1981): 438–46; Frank Whelon Wayman, "Arms Control and Strategic Voting in the U.S. Senate," *Journal of Conflict Resolution* 29 (June 1985): 225–51. For a bibliography of studies published before 1980, see James M. Lindsay, "Congress and the Defense Budget: Parochialism or Policy?" in *Arms, Politics, and the Economy: Historical and Contemporary Perspectives,* ed. Robert Higgs (New York: Holmes and Meier, 1990), p. 197.

25. Eileen Burgin, "Representatives' Decisions on Participation in Foreign Policy Issues," *Legislative Studies Quarterly* 16 (November 1991): 521–46, and Eileen Burgin, "The Influence of Constituents: Congressional Decision Making on Issues of Defense and Foreign and Defense Policy," in *Congress Resurgent: Foreign and Defense Policy on Capitol Hill,* ed. Randall B. Ripley and James M. Lindsay (Ann Arbor: University of Michigan Press, 1993).

26. Eileen Burgin, "Congressional Voting on the Persian Gulf War," University of Vermont, typescript, 1993.

27. On the importance of the different types of constituencies a member of Congress must address, see Richard F. Fenno, Jr., *Home Style: House Members in Their Districts* (Boston: Little, Brown, 1978).

28. Chuck Alston, "Solarz Looks Abroad to Find Election Cash at Home," *Congressional Quarterly Weekly Report,* 11 March 1989, pp. 501–4.

29. Carroll J. Doherty, "Defending Serbia," *Congressional Quarterly Weekly Report,* 13 June 1992, p. 1715.

30. Burgin, "Representatives' Decisions," p. 526.

31. James M. Lindsay, *Congress and Nuclear Weapons* (Baltimore: Johns Hopkins University Press, 1991), p. 114.

32. See Mary Collins, "News of Congress by the Congress," *Washington Journalism*

Review, June 1990, pp. 30–34, and Hedrick Smith, *The Power Game: How Washington Works* (New York: Random House, 1988), pp. 20–40.

33. Quoted in Collins, "News of Congress," p. 30.

34. See Kingdon, *Congressmen's Voting Decisions,* esp. pp. 67–68.

35. Robert A. Dahl, *Congress and Foreign Policy* (New York: Harcourt, Brace, 1950), p. 42 (emphasis in the original).

36. For discussions of how members of Congress decide what position to take when an issue comes before Congress, see R. Douglas Arnold, *The Logic of Congressional Action* (New Haven: Yale University Press, 1990); William T. Bianco, *A Proper Responsibility: Trust between Representatives and Constituents* (Ann Arbor: University of Michigan Press, 1994); and Kingdon, *Congressmen's Voting Decisions.*

37. See, for example, the comments by Reps. Ike Skelton (D-Mo.), Mickey Edwards (R-Okla.), and Bill Richardson (D-N.M.) in "Public Opinion and Contra Aid: Congressional Commentaries," in Sobel, *Public Opinion in U.S. Foreign Policy,* pp. 241–65.

38. On the ability of members of Congress to construct a reelection constituency that mirrors their own policy views, see Raymond A. Bauer, Ithiel de Sola Pool, and Lewis Anthony Dexter, *American Business and Public Policy,* 2d ed. (Chicago: Aldine, Atherton, 1972), pp. 414–24; Lewis Anthony Dexter, "The Representative and His District," *Human Organization* 16 (Spring 1957): 2–13; Fenno, *Home Style,* pp. 1–30; and Keith T. Poole, "Recent Developments in Analytical Models of Voting in the U.S. Congress," *Legislative Studies Quarterly* 13 (February 1988): 117–33.

39. Kingdon, *Congressmen's Voting Decisions,* p. 277.

40. Lindsay, *Congress and Nuclear Weapons,* p. 58.

41. J. William Fulbright, "The Legislator as Educator," *Foreign Affairs* 57 (Spring 1979): 722–23.

42. William L. Langer and S. Everett Gleason, *The Undeclared War: 1940–1941* (New York: Harper and Bros., 1953), p. 574.

43. See Pamela Fessler, "Sponsors of Soviet Packages Scramble for Support," *Congressional Quarterly Weekly Report,* 23 November 1991, pp. 3466–67, and Pamela Fessler, "Congress Clears Soviet Aid Bill in Late Reversal of Sentiment," *Congressional Quarterly Weekly Report,* 30 November 1991, p. 3536.

44. Keith Bradsher, "Lawmakers Balk on I.M.F. Funds," *New York Times,* 22 July 1991.

45. On the desire of members of Congress to write legislation that protects them from constituent wrath, see Morris P. Fiorina, "Legislator Uncertainty, Legislative Control, and the Delegation of Legislative Power," *Journal of Law, Economics, and Organization* 33 (Spring 1986): 33–51, and R. Kent Weaver, "The Politics of Blame Avoidance," *Journal of Public Policy* 6 (October–December 1986): 371–98.

46. On the importance of procedural maneuvers to congressional decision making on foreign policy, see Aspin, "Defense Budget and Foreign Policy," pp. 163–67.

47. Pat Towell, "Bipartisan Alliance Leaves Mark on Pentagon Spending Bill," *Congressional Quarterly Weekly Report,* 6 June 1992, p. 1611.

48. Mark G. McDonough, "Panama Canal Treaty Negotiations (B): Concluding a Treaty," Case C14-79-224, Harvard University, John F. Kennedy School of Government, 1979, p. 12.

49. See Paul N. Stockton, "Congress and the Making of National Security Strategy for the Post–Cold War Era," in Ripley and Lindsay, *Congress Resurgent,* pp. 253–56.

50. For evidence on the geographical concentration of spending on major weapons systems, see Lindsay, *Congress and Nuclear Weapons*, p. 97.

51. See James M. Lindsay, "Congressional Oversight of the Department of Defense: Reconsidering the Conventional Wisdom," *Armed Forces and Society* 17 (Fall 1990): 18–20.

CHAPTER 3. DECISION MAKING IN CONGRESS

1. Mackubin Thomas Owens, "Micromanaging the Defense Budget," *Public Interest* 100 (Summer 1990): 132.

2. John Lehman, *Making War: The 200-Year-Old Battle between the President and Congress over How America Goes to War* (New York: Scribner, 1992), p. 214.

3. Quoted in Steven V. Roberts, "Foreign Policy: Lot of Table Thumping Going On," *New York Times,* 29 May 1985.

4. Quoted in Rochelle L. Stanfield, "Floating Power Centers," *National Journal,* 1 December 1990, p. 2916.

5. For descriptions of the Senate Foreign Relations Committee during its heyday, see David N. Farnsworth, *The Senate Committee on Foreign Relations* (Urbana: University of Illinois Press, 1961); Malcolm E. Jewell, *Senatorial Politics and Foreign Policy* (Lexington: University of Kentucky Press, 1962), pp. 110–45; and H. Bradford Westerfield, *Foreign Policy and Party Politics: Pearl Harbor to Korea* (New Haven: Yale University Press, 1955), esp. pp. 115–22.

6. Stanfield, "Floating Power Centers," p. 2916.

7. Quoted in Christopher Madison, "Awaiting a Wake-Up," *National Journal,* 28 March 1992, p. 750.

8. See James M. McCormick, "Decision Making in the Foreign Affairs and Foreign Relations Committees," in *Congress Resurgent: Foreign and Defense Policy on Capitol Hill,* ed. Randall B. Ripley and James M. Lindsay (Ann Arbor: University of Michigan Press, 1993), pp. 130–31.

9. For quantitative measures of the ideological polarization on Foreign Relations, see ibid., pp. 131–33, and Claire E. Noble, "Competing for Influence: The Foreign Policy Committees and Arms Sales," Ph.D diss., University of Iowa, 1993, pp. 62–71 and 171–77.

10. Stanfield, "Floating Power Centers," p. 2916; Madison, "Awaiting a Wake-Up," p. 754; McCormick, "Decision Making," p. 143; and Noble, "Competing for Influence," p. 103.

11. Quoted in Robert A. Dahl, *Congress and Foreign Policy* (New York: Harcourt, Brace, 1950), p. 147. See also Holbert N. Carroll, *The House of Representatives and Foreign Affairs,* rev. ed. (Boston: Little, Brown, 1966), pp. 90–138; Richard F. Fenno, Jr., *Congressmen in Committees* (Boston: Little, Brown, 1973), pp. 212–26; and Albert C. Westphal, *The House Committee on Foreign Affairs* (New York: Columbia University Press, 1942).

12. James A. Robinson, *Congress and Foreign Policy-Making: A Study in Legislative Influence and Initiative,* rev. ed. (Homewood, Ill.: Dorsey Press, 1967), p. 104.

13. Fred Kaiser, "Oversight of Foreign Policy: The U.S. House Committee on International Relations," *Legislative Studies Quarterly* 2 (August 1977): 261.

14. For extended discussions of the Foreign Affairs Committee, see James M. McCormick, "The Changing Role of the House Foreign Affairs Committee in the 1970s and 1980s," *Congress and the Presidency* 12 (Spring 1985): 1–20; McCormick, "Decision Making," esp. pp. 126–28; Noble, "Competing for Influence," esp. chap. 4; and Charles W. Whalen, Jr., *The House and Foreign Policy: The Irony of Reform* (Chapel Hill: University of North Carolina Press, 1982), pp. 26–77.

15. Quoted in Carroll J. Doherty, "Fascell Announces Retirement; Hamilton Likely to Ascend," *Congressional Quarterly Weekly Report*, 30 May 1992, p. 1546.

16. Quoted in Christopher Madison, "Paper Tiger," *National Journal*, 15 June 1991, p. 1434.

17. See McCormick, "Decision Making," p. 135.

18. Quoted in Richard E. Cohen, "Seeking a Bigger Piece of the Action," *National Journal*, 12 January 1991, p. 92.

19. *Congressional Record*, 98th Cong., 1st sess., 1983, 129, pt. 7:8376.

20. Christopher Madison, "No Blank Check," *National Journal*, 6 October 1990, p. 2397.

21. Lewis Anthony Dexter, "Congressmen and the Making of Military Policy," in *New Perspectives on the House of Representatives*, ed. Robert L. Peabody and Nelson W. Polsby (Chicago: Rand McNally, 1968), p. 181.

22. Quoted in Herbert W. Stephens, "The Role of the Legislative Committees in the Appropriations Process: A Study Focused on the Armed Services Committees," *Western Political Quarterly* 24 (March 1971): 147.

23. Bernard K. Gordon, "The Military Budget: Congressional Phase," *Journal of Politics* 23 (November 1961): 693.

24. For detailed discussions of the armed services committees, see Robert J. Art, "Congress and the Defense Budget: Enhancing Policy Oversight," *Political Science Quarterly* 100 (Summer 1985): 227–49; Christopher J. Deering, "Decision Making in the Armed Services Committees," in Ripley and Lindsay, *Congress Resurgent;* and James M. Lindsay, "Congress and Defense Policy: 1961 to 1986," *Armed Forces and Society* 13 (Spring 1987): 371–401.

25. William A. Lucas and Raymond A. Dawson, *The Organizational Politics of Defense* (Pittsburgh, Pa.: International Studies Association, 1974), p. 120.

26. See James M. Lindsay, *Congress and Nuclear Weapons* (Baltimore: Johns Hopkins University Press, 1991), p. 26.

27. For data on the amending activity on defense bills, see ibid., p. 374, and Steven S. Smith, *Call to Order: Floor Politics in the House and Senate* (Washington, D.C.: Brookings Institution, 1989), pp. 216–23.

28. David C. Morrison, "Sam Nunn Inc.," *National Journal*, 15 June 1991, pp. 1483–86.

29. David C. Morrison, "Sharing Command," *National Journal*, 13 June 1992, p. 1397.

30. The best discussions of the appropriations committees can be found in Joseph White, "Decision Making in the Appropriations Subcommittees on Defense and Foreign Operations," in Ripley and Lindsay, *Congress Resurgent;* and Joseph White, "The Functions and Power of the House Appropriations Committee," Ph.D. diss., University of California, Berkeley, 1989.

31. Quoted in Stanfield, "Floating Power Centers," p. 2917.

32. Quoted in Diane Granat, "House Appropriations Panel Doles Out Cold Federal Cash, Chafes at Budget Procedures," *Congressional Quarterly Weekly Report,* 18 June 1983, p. 1209.

33. See Lindsay, *Congress and Nuclear Weapons,* pp. 27–28, and Steven S. Smith and Christopher J. Deering, *Committees in Congress,* 2d ed. (Washington, D.C.: CQ Press, 1990), pp. 61–117.

34. White, "Decision Making in the Appropriations Subcommittees," p. 196.

35. See Barry M. Blechman, "The New Congressional Role in Arms Control," in *A Question of Balance: The President, the Congress, and Foreign Policy,* ed. Thomas E. Mann (Washington, D.C.: Brookings Institution, 1990), pp. 129–30.

36. Stanfield, "Floating Power Centers," p. 2917.

37. Carroll J. Doherty, "Lawmakers Seek Political Cover As Israel Aid Delay Runs Out," *Congressional Quarterly Weekly Report,* 18 January 1992, pp. 118–23.

38. White, "Decision Making in the Appropriations Subcommittees," p. 196 (emphasis in the original).

39. Quoted in ibid., p. 197.

40. See Loch K. Johnson, *America's Secret Power: The CIA in a Democratic Society* (New York: Oxford University Press, 1989); Thomas G. Paterson, "Oversight or Afterview?: Congress, the CIA, and Covert Actions since 1947," in *Congress and United States Foreign Policy,* ed. Michael Barnhart (Albany: State University of New York Press, 1987); and Frank J. Smist, Jr., *Congress Oversees the United States Intelligence Community, 1947–1989* (Knoxville: University of Tennessee Press, 1990).

41. Quoted in Gregory F. Treverton, "Intelligence: Welcome to the American Government," in Mann, *Question of Balance,* p. 74.

42. Stephen E. Ambrose, *Eisenhower: The President* (New York: Simon and Schuster, 1984), p. 135.

43. Treverton, "Intelligence," p. 74.

44. For discussions of the day-to-day operations of the intelligence committees, see Loch K. Johnson, "Covert Action and Accountability: Decision-Making for America's Secret Foreign Policy," *International Studies Quarterly* 33 (March 1989): 81–109, and Frederick M. Kaiser, "Congressional Rules and Conflict Resolution: Access to Information in the House Select Committee on Intelligence," *Congress and the Presidency* 15 (Spring 1988): 49–73.

45. See Johnson, *America's Secret Power,* pp. 247–48; Smist, *Congress Oversees Intelligence Community,* pp. 267–76; and Treverton, "Intelligence," p. 79.

46. Smist, *Congress Oversees Intelligence Community,* pp. 269–70.

47. Johnson, *America's Secret Power,* p. 247.

48. Johnson, "Covert Action," p. 100.

49. Philip Taubman, "Are U.S. Covert Activities Best Policy on Nicaragua?" *New York Times,* 15 June 1983.

50. "U.S. Invasion Ousts Noriega," *Congress Quarterly Almanac 1989* (Washington, D.C.: Congressional Quarterly, 1990), p. 603.

51. Gregory J. Bowens, "'Bad Rap' for the CIA?" *Congressional Quarterly Weekly Report,* 6 November 1993, p. 3061.

52. Robert M. Gates, "The CIA and American Foreign Policy," *Foreign Affairs* 66 (Winter 1987/88): 224.

53. Quoted in U.S. Congress, House Select Committee to Investigate Covert Arms Transactions with Iran, *Iran-Contra Affair,* 100th Cong., H. Rept. 433, 1987, p. 123.

54. Treverton, "Intelligence," pp. 94–95.

55. See Loch Johnson, "The U.S. Congress and the CIA: Monitoring the Dark Side of Government," *Legislative Studies Quarterly* 5 (November 1980): 480–82.

56. Smist, *Congress Oversees Intelligence Community,* p. 218.

57. Treverton, "Intelligence," p. 88.

58. On the limited electoral appeal of a seat on one of the intelligence committees, see Smist, *Congress Oversees Intelligence Community,* pp. 91–93.

59. Christopher Madison, "Opening the Doors," *National Journal,* 15 June 1991, p. 1462.

60. Susan Webb Hammond, "Congress in Foreign Policy," in *The President, the Congress, and Foreign Policy,* ed. Edmund S. Muskie, Kenneth Rush, and Kenneth W. Thompson (Lanham, Md.: University Press of America, 1986), p. 80.

61. Lindsay, "Congress and Defense Policy," p. 374, and Smith, *Call to Order,* p. 217.

62. Bruce W. Jentleson, "American Diplomacy: Around the World and along Pennsylvania Avenue," in Mann, *Question of Balance,* p. 168.

63. *Congressional Record,* 99th Cong., 1st sess., 1985, 131, pt. 18:253–51.

64. Douglas C. Waller, *Congress and the Nuclear Freeze: An Inside Look at the Politics of a Mass Movement* (Amherst: University of Massachusetts Press, 1987), p. 258.

65. Daniel Wirls, *Buildup: The Politics of Defense in the Reagan Era* (Ithaca, N.Y.: Cornell University Press, 1992), p. 110.

66. Ibid., p. 111.

67. Morrison, "Sharing Command," p. 1397.

68. Michael A. West, "The Role of Congress in the Defense Budget Process—A Positive View," *Naval War College Review* 32 (May–June 1979): 89.

69. See Lindsay, *Congress and Nuclear Weapons,* pp. 55–61.

70. See Jon R. Bond and Richard Fleisher, "Are There Two Presidencies? Yes, but Only for Republicans," *Journal of Politics* 50 (August 1988): 747–67; Stephen L. Hayes, Susan E. Howell, and John M. Flaxbeard, "Presidential Support among Senatorial Leaders and Followers," *American Politics Quarterly* 12 (April 1984): 195–209; and Jewell, *Senatorial Politics and Foreign Policy,* esp. pp. 53–83.

71. "Floor Tactics Disputed," *Congressional Quarterly Almanac, 1970* (Washington, D.C.: Congressional Quarterly, 1971), p. 948.

72. Quoted in James L. Sundquist, *The Decline and Resurgence of Congress* (Washington, D.C.: Brookings Institution, 1981).

73. Barbara Sinclair, "Congressional Party Leaders in the Foreign and Defense Policy Arena," in Ripley and Lindsay, *Congress Resurgent,* p. 220.

74. See Barry M. Blechman, *The Politics of National Security: Congress and U.S. Defense Policy* (New York: Oxford University Press, 1990), pp. 38–39, and Lindsay, *Congress and Nuclear Weapons,* pp. 58–59.

75. Sinclair, "Congressional Party Leaders," p. 224.

76. See Steven S. Smith, "Congressional Leaders and Foreign Policy," in *Congress and the Making of Foreign Policy,* ed. Paul E. Peterson (Norman: University of Oklahoma Press, 1994).

77. Sinclair, "Congressional Party Leaders," p. 217.

78. Lindsay, *Congress and Nuclear Weapons,* p. 58.

79. White, "Decision Making in the Appropriations Subcommittees," p. 186.

80. Quoted in ibid., p. 187.

81. Norman J. Ornstein, Thomas E. Mann, and Michael J. Malbin, *Vital Statistics on Congress, 1991–1992* (Washington, D.C.: CQ Press, 1992), p. 135.

82. Ibid., pp. 124 and 135.

83. See, for example, I. M. Destler, "Executive-Congressional Conflict in Foreign Policy: Explaining It, Coping with It," in *Congress Reconsidered*, 3d ed., ed. Lawrence C. Dodd and Bruce I. Oppenheimer (Washington, D.C.: CQ Press, 1985), pp. 350–51; Lehman, *Making War*, p. xv; and Howard J. Wiarda, *Foreign Policy without Illusion: How Foreign Policy-Making Works and Fails to Work in the United States* (Glenview, Ill.: Scott, Foresman/Little, Brown, 1990), pp. 207–8.

84. Whalen, *The House and Foreign Policy*, pp. 59–60. See also Mark Bisnow, *In the Shadow of the Dome: Chronicles of a Capitol Hill Aide* (New York: Morrow, 1990), pp. 307–8.

CHAPTER 4.
SUBSTANTIVE LEGISLATION

1. John Jay, "Federalist No. 64," in Alexander Hamilton, James Madison, and John Jay, *The Federalist Papers*, ed. Garry Wills (New York: Bantam Books, 1982), pp. 326–27.

2. George H. Haynes, *The Senate of the United States: Its History and Practice*, vol. 1 (New York: Russell and Russell, 1960), p. 66. See also Ralston Hayden, *The Senate and Treaties, 1789–1817* (London: Macmillan, 1920), pp. 16–26, and Charles C. Tansill, "The Treaty-Making Powers of the Senate," *American Journal of International Law* 18 (July 1924): 464–66.

3. For instances in which Washington solicited the advice of the Senate on treaty matters, see Tansill, "Treaty-Making Powers of the Senate," pp. 466–69.

4. *Congressional Record*, 90th Cong., 1st sess., 1967, 114, pt. 15:20703.

5. On the Geneva Protocol of 1925, see Rodney J. McElroy, "The Geneva Protocol of 1925," in *The Politics of Arms Control Treaty Ratification*, ed. Michael Krepon and Dan Caldwell (New York: St. Martin's Press, 1991).

6. Ellen C. Collier, "U.S. Senate Rejection of Treaties: A Brief Survey of Past Instances," Congressional Research Service, Report no. 87-305F, 30 March 1987, p. 3.

7. Ibid., pp. 5–11.

8. Carroll J. Doherty and Pat Towell, "Senate Panel Endorses Treaty to Cut Forces in Europe," *Congressional Quarterly Weekly Report*, 23 November 1991, p. 3473.

9. *Congressional Record*, 100th Cong., 1st sess., 1987, 133, pt. 17:23963.

10. Doherty and Towell, "Senate Panel Endorses Treaty," p. 3473.

11. Daniel S. Cheever and H. Field Haviland, Jr., *American Foreign Policy and the Separation of Powers* (Cambridge: Harvard University Press, 1952), p. 44.

12. Henry Cabot Lodge, *The Senate and the League of Nations* (New York: Scribner, 1925), p. 147.

13. The classic statement of the law of anticipated reactions is Carl J. Friedrich, *Constitutional Government and Democracy: Theory and Practice in Europe and America*, rev. ed. (Boston: Little, Brown, 1941), pp. 589–91. For an extended but unpersuasive attempt to

discount the importance of anticipated reactions, see Mark Peterson, *Legislating Together: The White House and Capitol Hill from Eisenhower to Reagan* (Cambridge: Harvard University Press, 1990), pp. 60–67.

14. For discussions of the status of executive agreements in U.S. law, see Michael J. Glennon, *Constitutional Diplomacy* (Princeton: Princeton University Press, 1990), pp. 164–91; Jean E. Smith, *The Constitution and American Foreign Policy* (St. Paul, Minn.: West Publishing, 1989), pp. 107–32; and U.S. Congress, Senate Committee on Foreign Relations, *Treaties and Other International Agreements: The Role of the United States Senate*, 98th Cong., 2d sess., S. Prt. 205, 1984.

15. See Cecil V. Crabb, Jr., and Pat M. Holt, *Invitation to Struggle: Congress, the President, and Foreign Policy*, 4th ed. (Washington, D.C.: CQ Press, 1992), p. 73.

16. Arthur M. Schlesinger, Jr., *The Imperial Presidency* (Boston: Houghton Mifflin, 1989), p. 104.

17. Circular 175 Procedures, 11 *Foreign Affairs Manual*, chap. 700, 25 October 1974. Reprinted in U.S. Congress, House Committee on International Relations, *Congressional Review of International Agreements*, 94th Cong., 2d sess., 1976, pp. 387–409.

18. Gerald F. Seib, "Chemical-Weapons Agreement with Soviets Spurs Discord As Senators Contend It Should Be a Treaty," *Wall Street Journal*, 5 July 1990.

19. See the remarks by Senator Fulbright in *Congressional Record*, 90th Cong., 1st sess., 1967, 113, pt. 15:20717.

20. James M. McCormick, *American Foreign Policy and Process*, 2d ed. (Itasca, Ill.: Peacock, 1992), p. 310.

21. See Robert Scigliano, "Politics, the Constitution, and the President's War Power," in *The New Politics of American Foreign Policy*, ed. David A. Deese (New York: St. Martin's Press, 1994), p. 151.

22. J. Terry Emerson, "War Powers Legislation," *West Virginia Law Review* 53 (August–November 1971): 88–119. For a list of instances of presidential decisions to use armed forces abroad, with or without congressional authorization, see "Instances of Use of United States Armed Forces Abroad, 1798–1989," CRS Report for Congress, 4 December 1989, in *Congressional Record*, 10 January 1991, pp. S130–35.

23. On the issue of the war power, see, among others, David Gray Adler, "The Constitution and Presidential Warmaking: The Enduring Debate," *Political Science Quarterly* 103 (Spring 1988): 3–17; John Hart Ely, *War and Responsibility: Constitutional Lessons of Vietnam and Its Aftermath* (Princeton: Princeton University Press, 1993); Charles Lofgren, "War-Making under the Constitution," *Yale Law Journal* 81 (March 1972): 672–702; Schlesinger, *Imperial Presidency*, esp. chaps. 3–7; Scigliano, "Politics, the Constitution, and the President's War Power," pp. 148–65; J. Gregory Sidak, "To Declare War," *Duke Law Journal* 41 (September 1991): 27–121; Abraham D. Sofaer, *War, Foreign Affairs, and Constitutional Power: The Origins* (Cambridge, Mass.: Ballinger, 1976); and Francis D. Wormuth and Edwin B. Firmage, *To Chain the Dog of War: The War Powers of Congress in History and Law* (Dallas, Tex.: Southern Methodist University Press, 1986).

24. Carroll J. Doherty, "A Close Vote on War Powers," *Congressional Quarterly Weekly Report*, 6 November 1993, p. 3060; Carroll J. Doherty, "On Somalia, War Powers Law Becomes a GOP Weapon," *Congressional Quarterly Weekly Report*, 30 October 1993, pp. 2987–88; and Pat Towell, "Clinton's Policy Is Battered, But His Powers Are Intact," *Congressional Quarterly Weekly Report*, 23 October 1993, pp. 2896–2901.

25. Ralph D. Nurnberger, "The United States and Idi Amin: Congress to the Rescue," *African Studies Review* 25 (March 1982): 49–65.

26. John Felton, "Foreign Aid System Criticized As Cumbersome, Ineffective," *Congressional Quarterly Weekly Report*, 11 February 1989, p. 272.

27. For a discussion of the evolution of the legislation imposing limits on tests of the Strategic Defense Initiative, see Crabb and Holt, *Invitation to Struggle*, pp. 82–83.

28. Quoted in Smith, *Constitution and Foreign Policy*, p. 109.

29. Quoted in "A Billion Dollars to Give Away Panama Canal?" *U.S. News and World Report*, 19 March 1979, p. 46.

30. See "Panama Canal Implementation Bill Clears," *Congressional Quarterly Almanac, 1979* (Washington, D.C.: Congressional Quarterly, 1980), pp. 142–56.

31. For discussions of the limits of the appropriations power, see Harold Hongju Koh, *The National Security Constitution: Sharing Power after the Iran-Contra Affair* (New Haven: Yale University Press, 1990), pp. 129–31; Louis Henkin, *Constitutionalism, Democracy, and Foreign Affairs* (New York: Columbia University Press, 1990), pp. 31–32; and Kate Stith, "Congress' Power of the Purse," *Yale Law Journal* 97 (June 1988): 1360–63.

32. Thomas M. Franck and Clifford A. Bob, "The Return of Humpty-Dumpty: Foreign Relations Law after the Chadha Case," *American Journal of International Law* 79 (October 1985): 944, and Koh, *National Security Constitution*, p. 130.

33. Dick Cheney, "Congressional Overreaching in Foreign Policy," in *Foreign Policy and the Constitution*, ed. Robert A. Goldwin and Robert A. Licht (Washington, D.C.: American Enterprise Institute, 1991), p. 104.

34. See Barry M. Blechman, *The Politics of National Security: Congress and U.S. Defense Policy* (New York: Oxford University Press, 1990), and James M. Lindsay, *Congress and Nuclear Weapons* (Baltimore: Johns Hopkins University Press, 1991).

35. Christopher Madison, "Follow the Leader," *National Journal*, 12 January 1991, p. 104.

36. Quoted in McCormick, *American Foreign Policy and Process*, p. 272.

37. Richard Eliot Benedick, *Ozone Diplomacy: New Directions in Safeguarding the Planet* (Cambridge: Harvard University Press, 1991), pp. 173–74.

38. Claire E. Noble, "Competing for Influence: The Foreign Policy Committees and Arms Sales," Ph.D. diss., University of Iowa, 1993, p. 142.

39. Quoted in Pat Towell with Steven Pressman, "House Gives President the Go-Ahead on MX," *Congressional Quarterly Weekly Report*, 30 March 1985, p. 566.

40. Quoted in Pat Towell with Nadine Cohodas and Steven Pressman, "Senate Hands Reagan Victory on MX Missiles," *Congressional Quarterly Weekly Report*, 23 March 1985, p. 518.

41. Steve Hoadley, "The US Congress and the New Zealand Military Preference Elimination Bill," *Political Science* 43 (July 1991): 47–60.

42. Charles W. Whalen, Jr., *The House and Foreign Policy: The Irony of Reform* (Chapel Hill: University of North Carolina Press, 1982), p. 90.

43. See Carroll J. Doherty, "Foreign Policy Rules Riddled with Presidential Loopholes," *Congressional Quarterly Weekly Report*, 5 December 1992, pp. 3753–58.

44. I. M. Destler, Leslie H. Gelb, and Anthony Lake, *Our Own Worst Enemy: The Unmaking of American Foreign Policy* (New York: Simon and Schuster, 1984), pp. 158–59.

45. On the dispute over certifying the human rights record of the Salvadoran govern-

ment, see Cynthia J. Arnson, *Crossroads: Congress, the Reagan Administration, and Central America* (New York: Pantheon Books, 1989), pp. 81–98, 113–14, and 131–43.

46. John L. Jackley, *Hill Rat: Blowing the Lid Off Congress* (Washington, D.C.: Regnery Gateway, 1992), p. 147.

47. Pamela Fessler, "Senators Assail Decision to Sell Military Parts to Pakistan," *Congressional Quarterly Weekly Report,* 1 August 1992, p. 2295, and Steven Greenhouse, "Senators Seek Full Cutoff of Arms to Pakistan," *New York Times,* 8 March 1992.

48. See Thomas M. Franck and Edward Weisband, *Foreign Policy by Congress* (New York: Oxford University Press, 1979), p. 22.

49. Elizabeth Drew, "A Political Journal," *New Yorker,* 20 June 1983, p. 75.

50. Franck and Weisband, *Foreign Policy by Congress,* p. 56.

51. Quoted in Drew, "Political Journal," p. 69.

52. See Lindsay, *Congress and Nuclear Weapons,* pp. 145–48.

53. Robert A. Pastor, *Congress and the Politics of U.S. Foreign Economic Policy, 1929–1976* (Berkeley: University of California Press, 1980), p. 193.

54. Gerald M. Boyd, "Bush Urges Restraint by Canada," *New York Times,* 13 June 1986.

55. See Drew, "Political Journal," pp. 60–75, and Strobe Talbott, *Deadly Gambits: The Reagan Administration and the Stalemate in Nuclear Arms Control* (New York: Knopf, 1984), pp. 330–42.

56. Robert F. Drinan, S.J., and Teresa T. Kuo, "The 1991 Battle for Human Rights in China," *Human Rights Quarterly* 14 (February 1992): 39.

57. Glenn Tobin, "US-Canada Free Trade Negotiations: Gaining Approval to Proceed (B)," Case C16-8-786.0, Harvard University, John F. Kennedy School of Government, 1987, p. 8.

58. Stanley J. Heginbotham, "Dateline Washington: The Rules of the Game," *Foreign Policy* 53 (Winter 1983–84): 170.

CHAPTER 5.
PROCEDURAL LEGISLATION

1. See David S. Cloud, "Chemical Weapons Ban in Sight after Four-Year Hill Odyssey," *Congressional Quarterly Weekly Report,* 23 November 1991, p. 3467.

2. Les Aspin, "The Defense Budget and Foreign Policy: The Role of Congress," *Daedalus* 104 (Summer 1975): 168.

3. Morris P. Fiorina, "Congressional Control of the Bureaucracy: A Mismatch of Incentives and Capabilities," in *Congress Reconsidered,* 2d ed., ed. Lawrence C. Dodd and Bruce I. Oppenheimer (Washington, D.C.: Congressional Quarterly Press, 1981), p. 333.

4. Mathew D. McCubbins, Roger G. Noll, and Barry R. Weingast, "Administrative Procedures as Instruments of Political Control," *Journal of Law, Economics, and Organization* 3 (Fall 1987): 254.

5. Jerry L. Mashaw, *Bureaucratic Justice* (New Haven: Yale University Press, 1983), and Jerry L. Mashaw, *Due Process in the Administrative State* (New Haven: Yale University Press, 1985).

6. See Morris P. Fiorina, "Legislator Uncertainty, Legislative Control, and the Dele-

gation of Legislative Power," *Journal of Law, Economics, and Organization* 33 (Spring 1986): 33–51, and R. Kent Weaver, "The Politics of Blame Avoidance," *Journal of Public Policy* 6 (October–December 1986): 371–98.

7. Murray J. Horn and Kenneth A. Shepsle, "Commentary on 'Administrative Arrangements and the Political Control of Agencies': Administrative Process and Organizational Form As Legislative Responses to Agency Costs," *Virginia Law Review* 75 (March 1989): 505.

8. Mathew D. McCubbins and Thomas Schwartz, "Congressional Oversight Overlooked: Police Patrol versus Fire Alarms," *American Journal of Political Science* 28 (February 1984): 165–79.

9. Duncan Clarke, *Politics of Arms Control: The Role and Effectiveness of the U.S. Arms Control and Disarmament Agency* (New York: Free Press, 1979), p. x.

10. Robert A. Pastor, *Congress and the Politics of U.S. Foreign Economic Policy, 1929–1976* (Berkeley: University of California Press, 1980), p. 112.

11. See David P. Forsythe, *Human Rights and U.S. Foreign Policy: Congress Reconsidered* (Gainesville: University Presses of Florida, 1988), pp. 120–29, and Edward S. Maynard, "The Bureaucracy and Implementation of US Human Rights Policy," *Human Rights Quarterly* 11 (1989): 175–248.

12. Michael R. Gordon, "Help Wanted in Weapons Testing Office but Pentagon Slow to Fill Top Job," *National Journal*, 13 October 1984, pp. 1914–17, and U.S. Congress, Committee of Conference, *Department of Defense Authorization Act, 1984*, 98th Cong., 1st sess., H. Rept. 352, 1983, p. 258.

13. Pietro S. Nivola, "Trade Policy: Refereeing the Playing Field," in *A Question of Balance: The President, the Congress, and Foreign Policy*, ed. Thomas E. Mann (Washington, D.C.: Brookings Institution, 1990), p. 238.

14. U.S. Congress, Senate Committee on Armed Services, *National Defense Authorization Act for Fiscal Year 1989*, 100th Cong., 2d sess., S. Rept. 326, 1988, pp. 106–7.

15. Louis L. Ortmayer, "The Political Economy of National Security: The FSX Agreement," Paper presented at the 1990 annual meeting of the International Studies Association/South, Raleigh, North Carolina.

16. See Sharyn O'Halloran, "Congress and Foreign Trade Policy," in *Congress Resurgent: Foreign and Defense Policy on Capitol Hill*, ed. Randall B. Ripley and James M. Lindsay (Ann Arbor: University of Michigan Press, 1993), and Sharyn O'Halloran, *Politics, Process, and American Trade Policy* (Ann Arbor: University of Michigan Press, 1993).

17. See Margaret E. Galey, "Congress, Foreign Policy, and Human Rights Ten Years after Helsinki," *Human Rights Quarterly* 7 (August 1985): 334–72.

18. John Felton, "Bush Throws Down the Gauntlet on Provisions He Opposes," *Congressional Quarterly Weekly Report*, 24 February 1990, p. 604.

19. See Robert C. Cassidy, Jr., "Negotiating about Negotiations: The Geneva Multilateral Trade Talks," in *The Tethered Presidency: Congressional Restraints on Executive Power*, ed. Thomas M. Franck (New York: New York University Press, 1981); Jacques J. Gorlin, "Foreign Trade and the Constitution," in *Foreign Policy and the Constitution*, ed. Robert A. Goldwin and Robert A. Licht (Washington, D.C.: American Enterprise Institute, 1990); John Jackson, Jean-Victor Louis, and Mitsuo Matsushita, *Implementing the Tokyo Round: National Constitutions and International Economic Rules* (Ann Arbor: University of Michigan Press, 1984); James M. Lindsay, "Congress, Foreign Policy, and the New Institutional

ism," *International Studies Quarterly* 38 (June 1994): 281–304; and Joan E. Twiggs, *The Tokyo Round of Multilateral Trade Negotiations: A Case Study in Building Domestic Support for Diplomacy* (Lanham, Md.: University Press of America, 1987).

20. The text of President Bush's veto message appears in "Bush Vetoes Congress' Plan to Stall FS-X Program," *Congressional Quarterly Weekly Report,* 5 August 1989, p. 2071.

21. Ortmayer, "Political Economy of National Security," p. 19.

22. Felton, "Bush Throws Down the Gauntlet," p. 603.

23. Personal communication from Rep. James A. Leach (R-Iowa), 21 February 1992.

24. For discussions of the origins of the legislative veto, see Louis Fisher, *Constitutional Conflicts between Congress and the President* (Princeton: Princeton University Press, 1985), pp. 162–72, and Thomas M. Franck and Clifford A. Bob, "The Return of Humpty-Dumpty: Foreign Relations Law after the Chadha Case," *American Journal of International Law* 79 (October 1985): 912–60.

25. See Franck and Bob, "Return of Humpty-Dumpty," pp. 912–60; Martha Liebler Gibson, *Weapons of Influence: The Legislative Veto, American Foreign Policy, and the Irony of Reform* (Boulder, Colo.: Westview Press, 1992); and Robert S. Gilmour and Barbara Hinkson Craig, "After the Congressional Veto: Assessing the Alternatives," *Journal of Policy Analysis and Management* 3 (Spring 1984): 373–92.

26. See Vanessa Patton Sciarra, "Congress and Arms Sales: Tapping the Potential of the Fast-Track Guarantee Procedure," *Yale Law Journal* 97 (June 1988): 1447–48.

27. Franck and Bob, "Return of Humpty-Dumpty," pp. 942–44.

28. "Bush Asks to Stay on Fast Track," *Congressional Quarterly Weekly Report,* 2 March 1991, p. 531.

29. U.S. Congress, Conference Report to Accompany H.R. 3, *Omnibus Trade and Competitiveness Act of 1988,* 100th Cong., 2d sess., H. Rept. 576, 1988, p. 576.

30. Elizabeth E. King, "The Omnibus Trade Bill of 1988: 'Super 301' and Its Effects on the Multilateral Trade System under GATT," *University of Pennsylvania Journal of International Business Law* 12 (Summer 1991): 255–57; Nivola, "Trade Policy," pp. 235–39; and Sharyn O'Halloran, "Congress, the President, and U.S. Trade Policy: Process and Policy Outcomes," Paper presented at the 1990 annual meeting of the American Political Science Association, San Francisco, pp. 13–14.

31. Robert Dahl, *Congress and Foreign Policy* (New York: Harcourt, Brace, 1950), pp. 178–79.

32. See Charlotte Twight, "Institutional Underpinnings of Parochialism: The Case of Military Base Closures," *Cato Journal* 9 (Spring/Summer 1989): 73–105, and Charlotte Twight, "DoD Attempts to Close Military Bases: The Political Economy of Congressional Resistance," in *Arms, Politics, and the Economy: Historical and Contemporary Perspectives,* ed. Robert Higgs (New York: Holmes and Meier, 1990).

33. See Dan Caldwell, "The Jackson-Vanik Amendment," in *Congress, the Presidency and American Foreign Policy,* ed. John Spanier and Joseph Nogee (New York: Pergamon Press, 1981); Jessica Korn, "Institutional Reforms That Don't Matter: *Chadha* and the Legislative Veto in Jackson-Vanik," *Harvard Journal on Legislation* 29 (Summer 1992): 455–515; and Paula Stern, *Water's Edge: Domestic Politics and the Making of American Foreign Policy* (Westport, Conn.: Greenwood Press, 1979).

34. James M. Lindsay, *Congress and Nuclear Weapons* (Baltimore: Johns Hopkins University Press, 1991), p. 77.

35. See Tanya Broder and Bernard D. Lambek, "Military Aid to Guatemala: The

Failure of U.S. Human Rights Legislation," *Yale Journal of International Law* 13 (Winter 1988): 111–45; David P. Forsythe, "Congress and Human Rights in U.S. Foreign Policy: The Fate of General Legislation," *Human Rights Quarterly* 9 (August 1987): 382–404; and Forsythe, *Human Rights and U.S. Foreign Policy,* esp. chaps. 3–5.

36. Quoted in Forsythe, "Congress and Human Rights," p. 383.

37. Jeffrey A. Meyer, "Congressional Control of Foreign Assistance," *Yale Journal of International Law* 13 (Winter 1988): 86.

38. See Ellen C. Collier, "Foreign Policy by Reporting Requirement," *Washington Quarterly* 11 (Winter 1988): 75; John Felton, "Foreign Aid System Criticized As Cumbersome, Ineffective," *Congressional Quarterly Weekly Report,* 11 February 1989, p. 272; U.S. Congress, House Committee on Foreign Affairs, *Required Reports to Congress on Foreign Policy* (Washington, D.C.: U.S. Government Printing Office, 1988), p. iii; and U.S. Congress, House Committee on Foreign Affairs, *Foreign Assistance Reporting Requirements* (Washington, D.C.: U.S. Government Printing Office, 1989), pp. 2–3.

39. Figures on defense reports were derived from data provided in a personal communication from Leonard G. Campbell, director for Plans and Systems, Office of the Comptroller of the Department of Defense, 12 February 1992, and James M. Lindsay, "Congress and the Defense Budget," *Washington Quarterly* 11 (Winter 1988): 61.

40. *Foreign Assistance Reporting Requirements,* p. 3.

41. Pamela Fessler, "Complaints Are Stacking Up As Hill Piles on Reports," *Congressional Quarterly Weekly Report,* 7 September 1991, pp. 2562–66.

42. Quoted in "Counting Calls for Military Witnesses," *New York Times,* 4 March 1986.

43. Fessler, "Complaints Are Stacking Up," p. 2564.

44. Ibid., p. 2563.

45. Ibid., p. 2565.

46. Robert Lyle Butterworth, "Bureaucratic Politics and Congress' Role in Weapons Development," *Policy Studies Journal* 8 (Autumn 1979): 77, and U.S. Congress, House Committee on Foreign Affairs, *Fundamentals of Nuclear Arms Control: Part IX—The Congressional Role in Nuclear Arms Control,* 99th Cong., 2d sess., 1986, p. 21.

47. Janne E. Nolan, "The INF Treaty," in *The Politics of Arms Control Treaty Ratification,* ed. Michael Krepon and Dan Caldwell (New York: St. Martin's Press, 1991), pp. 369–70.

48. Robert M. Gates, "The CIA and Foreign Policy," *Foreign Affairs* 66 (Winter 1987/88): 224.

49. See, for example, I. M. Destler, Leslie H. Gelb, and Anthony Lake, *Our Own Worst Enemy: The Unmaking of American Foreign Policy* (New York: Simon and Schuster, 1984), p. 145.

50. Fessler, "Complaints Are Stacking Up," p. 2563.

51. Clarke, *Politics of Arms Control,* p. 97.

52. See Sarah Helm, " 'Resistance,' Not Reform, at Pentagon," *Washington Post,* 23 September 1987, and David C. Morrison, "Another Czar Bows Out," *National Journal,* 5 January 1991, p. 43.

53. See U.S. Congress, General Accounting Office, "DOD Needs to Plan and Conduct More Timely Operational Tests and Evaluation," GAO/NSIAD-90-107, May 1990; U.S. Congress, General Accounting Office, "Operational Test and Evaluation Oversight: Improving but More Is Needed," GAO/NSIAD-87-108BR, March 1987; U.S. Con-

gress, General Accounting Office, "Weapons Testing: Quality of DoD Operational Testing and Reporting," PEMD-88-32BR, July 1988.

54. Galey, "Congress, Foreign Policy, and Human Rights," p. 368.

55. Forsythe, "Congress and Human Rights," p. 386.

56. Cassidy, "Negotiating about Negotiations," pp. 264–82, and Lindsay, "Congress, Foreign Policy, and the New Institutionalism," pp. 291–92.

57. See Twight, "DoD Attempts to Close Military Bases, pp. 236–80, and Twight, "Institutional Underpinnings of Parochialism," pp. 73–105.

58. Gilmour and Craig, "After the Congressional Veto," pp. 375–76.

59. Bruce W. Jentleson, "American Diplomacy: Around the World and along Pennsylvania Avenue," in Mann, Question of Balance, p. 161.

60. Cecil V. Crabb and Pat M. Holt, Invitation to Struggle: Congress, the President, and Foreign Policy, 4th ed. (Washington, D.C.: CQ Press, 1992), pp. 113–15.

61. Rochelle L. Stanfield, "Weighing Arms for Saudis," National Journal, 12 January 1991, p. 79.

62. Ronald D. Elving, "Trade Mood Turns Hawkish As Frustration Builds," Congressional Quarterly Weekly Report, 31 March 1990, p. 969.

63. King, "Omnibus Trade Bill of 1988," p. 271.

64. Ronald D. Elving, "Members Score Bush Decision to Let Japan Off 'Hit List,'" Congressional Quarterly Weekly Report, 25 April 1990, pp. 1251–52.

65. Quoted in U.S. Congress, House Committee on Armed Services, Defense for a New Era: Lessons of the Persian Gulf War (Washington, D.C.: U.S. Government Printing Office, 1992), p. 41.

66. Loch K. Johnson, "Covert Action and Accountability: Decision-Making for America's Secret Foreign Policy," International Studies Quarterly 33 (March 1989): 101.

67. See "U.S. Invasion Ousts Panama's Noriega," Congress Quarterly Almanac, 1989 (Washington, D.C.: Congressional Quarterly, 1990), pp. 601–4. For similar complaints by officials in the Carter administration, see Thomas E. Cronin, "A Resurgent Congress and the Imperial Presidency," Political Science Quarterly 95 (Summer 1980): 220.

68. Gates, "CIA and Foreign Policy," pp. 224–25.

69. On the definitional problems that plague the War Powers Resolution, see Robert A. Katzmann, "War Powers: Toward a New Accommodation," in Mann, Question of Balance, pp. 49–52. On the use of presidential waivers in foreign policy legislation, see Carroll J. Doherty, "Foreign Policy Rules Riddled with Presidential Loopholes," Congressional Quarterly Weekly Report, 5 December 1992, pp. 3753–58.

70. See Lindsay, "Congress, Foreign Policy, and the New Institutionalism," pp. 288–89.

71. Forsythe, "Congress and Human Rights," p. 404, and U.S. Congress, General Accounting Office, "State Department's Commitment to Accurate Reporting Has Increased," GAP/NSIAD-90-224, September 1990.

72. The classic study of bureaucratic self-interest in foreign policy is Morton H. Halperin, Bureaucratic Politics and Foreign Policy (Washington, D.C.: Brookings Institution, 1974).

73. Broder and Lambek, "Military Aid to Guatemala," pp. 124–43, and Forsythe, "Congress and Human Rights," pp. 383–85.

CHAPTER 6. DIPLOMACY, CONSULTATIONS, AND FRAMING

1. See Richard G. Lugar, *Letters to the Next President* (New York: Simon and Schuster, 1988), pp. 149–63, and Hedrick Smith, *The Power Game: How Washington Works* (New York: Random House, 1988), pp. 43–44.

2. Quoted in Jean E. Smith, *The Constitution and American Foreign Policy* (St. Paul, Minn.: West Publishing, 1989), p. 163.

3. *United States v. Curtiss-Wright Export Corporation*, 299 U.S. 304, 319 (1936).

4. For discussions of Wright's mediation efforts, see Cynthia J. Arnson, *Crossroads: Congress, the Reagan Administration, and Central America* (New York: Pantheon Books, 1989), pp. 203–4; John M. Barry, *The Ambition and the Power* (New York: Penguin Books, 1990), pp. 493–515; and John Felton, "Nicaragua Peace Process Moves to Capitol Hill," *Congressional Quarterly Weekly Report*, 14 November 1987, pp. 2789–91.

5. Felton, "Nicaragua Peace Process," p. 2789.

6. David Johnston and Michael Wines, "Spying Data on Sandinistas Involved U.S. Congressmen, Ex-Officials Say," *New York Times*, 15 September 1991.

7. William D. Rogers, "Who's in Charge of Foreign Policy?" *New York Times Magazine*, 9 September 1979, p. 50.

8. John Felton, "Hansen's One-Man Mission to Iran . . . Reflects His Direct Approach to Issues," *Congressional Quarterly Weekly Report*, 1 December 1979, pp. 2704–5.

9. Dick Cheney, "Congressional Overreaching in Foreign Policy," in *Foreign Policy and the Constitution*, ed. Robert A. Goldwin and Robert A. Licht (Washington, D.C.: American Enterprise Institute, 1991), pp. 108–9, and Bruce Jentleson, "American Diplomacy: Around the World and along Pennsylvania Avenue," in *A Question of Balance: The President, the Congress, and Foreign Policy*, ed. Thomas E. Mann (Washington, D.C.: Brookings Institution, 1990), pp. 175–76.

10. John Lehman, *Making War: The 200-Year-Old Battle between the President and Congress over How America Goes to War* (New York: Scribner, 1992), p. 44.

11. U.S. Congress, House Committee on Armed Services, *Reports on Incremental Costs to the United States of the Persian Gulf Conflict and on Contributions by Foreign Countries in Response to the Conflict*, 102d Cong., 1st sess., H. Rept. 4, 1991, p. 8.

12. See Daniel S. Cheever and H. Field Haviland, Jr., *American Foreign Policy and the Separation of Powers* (Cambridge: Harvard University Press, 1952), p. 63; Thomas M. Franck and Edward Weisband, *Foreign Policy by Congress* (New York: Oxford University Press, 1979), p. 138; and W. Stull Holt, *Treaties Defeated in the Senate* (Baltimore: Johns Hopkins Press, 1933), pp. 180–81 and 263–64.

13. See Franck and Weisband, *Foreign Policy by Congress*, pp. 138–39.

14. See ibid., pp. 139–40.

15. See Cheever and Haviland, *Foreign Policy and Separation of Powers*, pp. 70–72, and Holt, *Treaties Defeated by the Senate*, pp. 304–5.

16. Lehman, *Making War*, p. 132.

17. Alan Platt, "The Anti-Ballistic Missile Treaty," in *The Politics of Arms Control Treaty Ratification*, ed. Michael Krepon and Dan Caldwell (New York: St. Martin's Press, 1991), pp. 237–38, and Alan Platt, *The U.S. Senate and Strategic Arms Policy, 1969–1977* (Boulder, Colo.: Westview Press, 1978), pp. 19–20.

18. Personal communication with Joseph Kruzel, member of the SALT I delegation, 22 September 1990 and 19 June 1991.

19. This figure is based on analysis of the *Federal Register* (Washington, D.C.: U.S. Government Printing Office, various years), which periodically publishes lists of the observers, advisers, and delegates to international conferences.

20. Barry M. Blechman, "The New Congressional Role in Arms Control," in Mann, *Question of Balance,* p. 122.

21. Strobe Talbott, *Endgame: The Inside Story of SALT II* (New York: Harper Torch-books, 1980), pp. 95–97.

22. Blechman, "Arms Control," p. 122. See also Michael Krepon, "Conclusions," in Krepon and Caldwell, *Politics of Arms Control Treaty Ratification,* pp. 444–45, and "U.S. Negotiators Head for Geneva," *Congressional Quarterly Weekly Report,* 9 March 1985, p. 438.

23. Janne E. Nolan, "The INF Treaty," in Krepon and Caldwell, *Politics of Arms Control Treaty Ratification,* p. 376.

24. John Tierney, "Interest Group Involvement in Congressional Foreign and Defense Policy," in *Congress Resurgent: Foreign and Defense Policy on Capitol Hill,* ed. Randall B. Ripley and James M. Lindsay (Ann Arbor: University of Michigan Press, 1993), p. 95.

25. Lee H. Hamilton, "Congress and the Presidency in American Foreign Policy," *Presidential Studies Quarterly* 18 (Summer 1988): 508.

26. U.S. Congress, House Committee on Foreign Affairs, *Historical Review of 95th–101st Congresses—Distinguished Visitors and Delegations Received* (Washington, D.C.: U.S. Government Printing Office, 1990), p. 19, and U.S. Congress, Senate Committee on Foreign Relations, *Legislative Activities Report of the Committee on Foreign Relations,* 102d Cong., 1st sess., S. Rept. 30, 1991, p. 158.

27. Samuel C. Patterson, "Congress and the Emerging Legislatures in New Democracies," Paper presented at the Conference on Congress and Foreign and Defense Policy Challenges, Ohio State University, September 1990.

28. Christopher Madison, "At Last, Peace in El Salvador," *National Journal,* 18 January 1992, p. 185.

29. Steve Hoadley, "The US Congress and the New Zealand Military Preference Elimination Bill," *Political Science* 43 (Summer 1991): 52.

30. Tierney, "Interest Group Involvement," pp. 95–96.

31. Cheney, "Congressional Overreaching," pp. 106–7, and Johnston and Wines, "Spying Data on Sandinistas."

32. Franck and Weisband, *Foreign Policy by Congress,* p. 27.

33. Robert G. Kaiser, "To Save SALT, Sen. Byrd Huddled in Secret with Soviet," *Washington Post,* 28 October 1979.

34. Arnson, *Crossroads,* p. 203, and Barry, *The Ambition and the Power,* pp. 309–23.

35. Mark G. McDonough, "Panama Canal Treaty Negotiations (B): Concluding a Treaty," Case C14-79-224, Harvard University, John F. Kennedy School of Government, 1979, pp. 11–12.

36. Stephen E. Ambrose, "The Presidency and Foreign Policy," *Foreign Affairs* 70 (Winter 1991/92): 125.

37. Anna Kasten Nelson, "John Foster Dulles and the Bipartisan Congress," *Political Science Quarterly* 102 (Spring 1987): 64.

38. Quoted in Smith, *Constitution and Foreign Policy,* p. 258.

39. Jeffrey A. Meyer, "Congressional Control of Foreign Assistance," *Yale Journal of International Law* 13 (Winter 1988): 86.

40. Lugar, *Letters to the Next President,* p. 48.

41. Quoted in Carroll J. Doherty, "Consultation on the Gulf Crisis Is Hit or Miss for Congress," *Congressional Quarterly Weekly Report,* 13 October 1990, p. 3441.

42. Carroll J. Doherty, "New Scene, Familiar Script," *Congressional Quarterly Weekly Report,* 23 October 1993, p. 2897.

43. Doherty, "Consultation on the Gulf Crisis," pp. 3440–41.

44. Carroll J. Doherty, "Members Rally around Flag As Bush Solicits Support," *Congressional Quarterly Weekly Report,* 1 September 1990, p. 2777.

45. Doherty, "Consultation on the Gulf Crisis," pp. 3440–41.

46. Carroll J. Doherty, "Uncertain Congress Confronts President's Gulf Strategy," *Congressional Quarterly Weekly Report,* 17 November 1990, p. 3880, and Christopher Madison, "Sideline Players," *National Journal,* 15 December 1990, p. 3025.

47. Malcolm E. Jewell, *Senatorial Politics and Foreign Policy* (Lexington: University of Kentucky Press, 1962), p. 158.

48. George Moffett III, *The Limits of Victory: The Ratification of the Panama Canal Treaties* (Ithaca, N.Y.: Cornell University Press, 1985), p. 85.

49. Alan Platt, "The Politics of Arms Control and the Strategic Balance," in *Rethinking the U.S. Strategic Posture,* ed. Barry M. Blechman (Cambridge, Mass.: Ballinger, 1982), pp. 169–70.

50. See Carroll J. Doherty, "Lawmakers Seek Political Cover As Israel Aid Delay Runs Out," *Congressional Quarterly Weekly Report,* 18 January 1992, pp. 118–23.

51. Quoted in John Felton, "Bush, Hill Agree to Provide Contras with New Aid," *Congressional Quarterly Weekly Report,* 25 March 1989, p. 655.

52. Woodrow Wilson, *Congressional Government: A Study in American Politics* (Gloucester, Mass.: Peter Smith, 1973), p. 195.

53. See Daniel Schorr, "Ten Days That Shook the White House," *Columbia Journalism Review,* July/August 1991, pp. 21–23.

54. In an earlier article I referred to congressional activities aimed at influencing public and elite opinion as "grandstanding." James M. Lindsay, "Congress and Foreign Policy: Why the Hill Matters," *Political Science Quarterly* 107 (Winter 1992–93): 622–26. I have adopted the term *framing* here to avoid the pejorative connotation usually associated with grandstanding.

55. David McCullough, *Truman* (New York: Simon and Schuster, 1992), p. 288.

56. Quoted in George C. Herring, "The Executive, Congress, and the Vietnam War, 1965–1975," in *Congress and United States Foreign Policy,* ed. Michael Barnhart (Albany: State University of New York, 1987), p. 179.

57. On the rise of outside strategies in Congress, see Smith, *The Power Game,* pp. 36–46 and 119–46.

58. Quoted in David S. Cloud, "China MFN Bill Going Nowhere As Adjournment Approaches," *Congressional Quarterly Weekly Report,* 16 November 1991, p. 3366.

59. See Dan Caldwell, *The Dynamics of Domestic Politics and Arms Control: The SALT II Treaty Ratification Debate* (Columbia: University of South Carolina Press, 1991), pp. 160–63.

60. See Barry Rubin, "The Media and the Neutron Warhead," *Washington Review of Strategic and International Studies* 1 (July 1978): 93.

61. Smith, *The Power Game,* p. 140.

62. Chuck Alston, "Solarz Looks Abroad to Find Election Cash at Home," *Congressional Quarterly Weekly Report,* 11 March 1989, p. 501.

63. See Timothy E. Cook, *Making Laws and Making News: Media Strategies in the U.S. House of Representatives* (Washington, D.C.: Brookings Institution, 1989).

64. E. E. Schattschneider, *The Semisovereign People* (New York: Holt and Rinehart, 1961), pp. 1–3.

65. Roger Hilsman recognized the virtue of simple appeals more than three decades ago. See Roger Hilsman, "Congressional-Executive Relations and the Foreign Policy Consensus," *American Political Science Review* 52 (September 1958): 737.

66. See Cook, *Making Laws and Making News,* pp. 62–65.

67. John Felton, "A Policy Confrontation on China," *Congressional Quarterly Weekly Report,* 24 June 1989, p. 1564.

68. Warner R. Schilling, "The Politics of National Defense: Fiscal 1950," in *Strategy, Politics, and Defense Budgets,* ed. Warner Schilling, Paul Y. Hammond, and Glenn H. Snyder (New York: Columbia University Press, 1962), p. 248.

69. Michael Barone and Grant Ujifusa, *The Almanac of American Politics, 1988* (Washington, D.C.: National Journal, 1987), p. 424.

70. Karen Wright, "Heating the Global Warming Debate," *New York Times Magazine,* 3 February 1991, p. 31.

71. Anna M. Warrock and Howard Husock, "Taking Toshiba Public," Case C15-88-858.0, Harvard University, John F. Kennedy School of Government, 1988, pp. 11–12.

72. R. W. Apple, Jr., "Bonn and Tokyo Are Criticized for Not Bearing More of Gulf Cost," *New York Times,* 13 September 1990.

73. John Tagliabue, "Kohl Vows to Widen Role in Gulf Effort," *New York Times,* 14 September 1990, and Steven R. Weisman, "Japan Defends Aid in Mideast Effort," *New York Times,* 15 September 1990.

74. See Jonathan Schell, *The Time of Illusion* (New York: Vintage Books, 1975).

75. Mark Hertsgaard, *On Bended Knee: The Press and the Reagan Presidency* (New York: Schocken Books, 1989), p. 115.

76. David E. Rosenbaum, "Talk about Tax Breaks Is . . . Just Talk," *New York Times,* 22 October 1991.

77. For examples see Hertsgaard, *On Bended Knee,* pp. 24–25 and 252.

CHAPTER 7. INFLUENCE

1. Quoted in Carroll J. Doherty, "The Reluctant Warriors," *Congressional Quarterly Weekly Report,* 13 February 1993, p. 323.

2. The distinction among crisis, strategic, and structural policy draws on the work of Samuel P. Huntington, *The Common Defense: Strategic Programs in National Politics* (New York: Columbia University Press, 1961), pp. 3–4; Theodore J. Lowi, "Making Democracy Safe for the World: National Politics and Foreign Policy," in *Domestic Sources of Foreign Policy,* ed. James N. Rosenau (New York: Free Press, 1967), pp. 324–25; and Randall B. Ripley and Grace A. Franklin, *Congress, the Bureaucracy, and Public Policy,* 5th ed. (Pacific Grove, Calif.: Brooks/Cole, 1991), pp. 22–24. The argument here expands the one presented in James M. Lindsay and Randall B. Ripley, "How Congress Influences Foreign

and Defense Policy," in *Congress Resurgent: Foreign and Defense Policy on Capitol Hill,* ed. Randall B. Ripley and James M. Lindsay (Ann Arbor: University of Michigan Press, 1993).

3. The term "two presidencies" was coined by Aaron Wildavsky in "The Two Presidencies," *Transaction* 4 (December 1966): 7–14. Wildavsky's article spawned a long line of research that has variously confirmed, modified, and challenged his original findings. Many of these studies are reprinted in Steven A. Shull, ed., *The Two Presidencies: A Quarter Century Assessment* (Chicago: Nelson-Hall, 1991). The relevance of these subsequent studies to the question of how presidential power varies across policy domains is limited, however. Because these studies analyze roll-call votes, they actually address the much narrower question of presidential success in Congress. See James M. Lindsay and Wayne P. Steger, "The 'Two Presidencies' in Future Research: Moving beyond Roll-Call Analysis," *Congress and the Presidency* 20 (Autumn 1993): 103–17.

4. Arthur M. Schlesinger, Jr., *The Imperial Presidency* (Boston: Houghton Mifflin, 1989), p. 420.

5. Quoted in Doherty, "Reluctant Warriors," p. 323.

6. I. M. Destler, Leslie H. Gelb, and Anthony Lake, *Our Own Worst Enemy: The Unmaking of American Foreign Policy* (New York: Simon and Schuster, 1984), p. 150.

7. Schlesinger, *Imperial Presidency,* p. 420.

8. See David Gray Adler, "The Constitution and Presidential Warmaking: The Enduring Debate," *Political Science Quarterly* 103 (Spring 1988): 8–13; Alexander Hamilton, "Federalist No. 69," in Alexander Hamilton, James Madison, and John Jay, *The Federalist Papers,* ed. Garry Wills (New York: Bantam Books, 1982); and Louis Henkin, *Foreign Affairs and the Constitution* (Mineola, N.Y.: Foundation Press, 1972), pp. 50–51.

9. Woodrow Wilson, *Constitutional Government in the United States* (New York: Columbia University Press, 1961), p. 139.

10. Loch K. Johnson, "Covert Action and Accountability: Decision-Making for America's Secret Foreign Policy," *International Studies Quarterly* (March 1989): 99.

11. U.S. Congress, House Committee on Armed Services, *Department of Defense Authorization for Appropriations for Fiscal Year 1975,* 93d Cong., 2d sess., 1974, p. 3583. On the Defense Department's penchant for manipulating the information it gives to Congress, see Les Aspin, "Games the Pentagon Plays," *Foreign Policy* 11 (Summer 1973): 80–92; J. Ronald Fox, *Arming America: How the U.S. Buys Weapons* (Cambridge: Harvard University Press, 1974), pp. 136–40; and Hedrick Smith, *The Power Game: How Washington Works* (New York: Random House, 1988), pp. 163–73.

12. See, for example, U.S. Congress, General Accounting Office, "State Department's Commitment to Accurate Reporting Has Increased," GAO/NSIAD-90-224, September 1990.

13. Quoted in Jean E. Smith, *The Constitution and American Foreign Policy* (St. Paul, Minn.: West Publishing, 1989), pp. 8–9.

14. For scholarly commentary on the *Curtiss-Wright* case, see Adler, "The Constitution and Presidential Warmaking," pp. 29–36; David M. Levitan, "The Foreign Relations Power: An Analysis of Mr. Justice Sutherland's Theory," *Yale Law Journal* 55 (April 1946): 467–97; and Charles Lofgren, "*United States v. Curtiss-Wright Export Corporation:* An Historical Reassessment," *Yale Law Journal* 83 (November 1973): 1–32.

15. *Japan Whaling Association v. American Cetacean Society,* 478 U.S. 221 (1986), p. 187.

16. The doctrine of political questions is discussed in Thomas M. Franck, "Courts and Foreign Policy," *Foreign Policy* 83 (Summer 1991): 66–86; Thomas M. Franck, *Political Questions/Judicial Answers: Does the Rule of Law Apply to Foreign Affairs?* (Princeton: Princeton University Press, 1992); Michael J. Glennon, *Constitutional Diplomacy* (Princeton: Princeton University Press, 1990), pp. 314–42; Louis Henkin, *Constitutionalism, Democracy, and Foreign Affairs* (New York: Columbia University Press, 1990), pp. 69–91; and Harold Hongju Koh, *The National Security Constitution: Sharing Power after the Iran-Contra Affair* (New Haven: Yale University Press, 1990), pp. 134–49.

17. Smith, *Constitution and Foreign Policy*, p. 136.

18. *Goldwater v. Carter*, 444 U.S. 996 (1979), p. 1002.

19. Joseph White, "Decision Making in the Appropriations Subcommittees on Defense and Foreign Operations," in Ripley and Lindsay, *Congress Resurgent*, p. 192 (emphasis in the original).

20. See James M. Lindsay, "Congressional Oversight of the Department of Defense: Reconsidering the Conventional Wisdom," *Armed Forces and Society* 17 (Fall 1990): 16–18.

21. David C. Jones, "What's Wrong with Our Defense Establishment," in *The Domestic Sources of American Foreign Policy*, ed. Charles W. Kegley, Jr., and Eugene R. Wittkopf (New York: St. Martin's Press, 1988), p. 195.

22. See Theodore A. Postol, "Lessons of the Gulf War Experience with Patriot," *International Security* 16 (Winter 1991/92): 74–118; Theodore A. Postol, "Patriot Experience in the Gulf War," *International Security* 17 (Summer 1992): 225–40; and Robert M. Stein, "Patriot Experience in the Gulf War," *International Security* 17 (Summer 1992): 199–225.

23. Quoted in Schlesinger, *Imperial Presidency*, p. 401.

24. For discussions of the war power, see Adler, "The Constitution and Presidential Warmaking," pp. 3–17; John Hart Ely, *War and Responsibility: Constitutional Lessons of Vietnam and Its Aftermath* (Princeton: Princeton University Press, 1993); Charles Lofgren, "War-Making under the Constitution," *Yale Law Journal* 81 (March 1972): 672–702; Schlesinger, *Imperial Presidency*, esp. chaps. 3–7; Robert Scigliano, "Politics, the Constitution, and the President's War Power," in *The New Politics of American Foreign Policy*, ed. David A. Deese (New York: St. Martin's Press, 1994); J. Gregory Sidak, "To Declare War," *Duke Law Journal* 41 (September 1991): 27–121; Abraham D. Sofaer, *War, Foreign Affairs, and Constitutional Power: The Origins* (Cambridge, Mass.: Ballinger, 1976); and Francis D. Wormuth and Edwin Firmage, *To Chain the Dog of War: The War Power of Congress in History and Law* (Dallas, Tex.: Southern Methodist University Press, 1986).

25. Adler, "The Constitution and Presidential Warmaking," p. 4.

26. Dean Acheson, *Present at the Creation: My Years in the State Department* (New York: Norton, 1987), pp. 413–14.

27. Although few members of Congress anticipated a wider war in Vietnam when they voted for the Gulf of Tonkin Resolution, the floor managers for the bill emphasized during the debates that the resolution gave President Johnson authority to wage a large-scale war in Southeast Asia. See Ely, *War and Responsibility*, pp. 16–19.

28. Quoted in Smith, *Constitution and Foreign Policy*, p. 258.

29. Schlesinger, *Imperial Presidency*, p. 433.

30. "Congress Approves Aid for Lebanon . . . But Demands Role in Troop Deci-

sion," *Congressional Quarterly Almanac, 1983* (Washington, D.C.: Congressional Quarterly, 1984), pp. 116–17.

31. "Joint Resolution to Keep Marines in Lebanon," *Congressional Quarterly Weekly Report*, 8 October 1983, p. 2101.

32. Clifford A. Krauss, "House Vote Urges Clinton to Limit U.S. Somalia Role," *New York Times*, 29 September 1993, and Elizabeth A. Palmer, "Senate Demands Voice in Policy but Shies Away from Confrontation," *Congressional Quarterly Weekly Report*, 11 September 1993, p. 2399.

33. For evaluations of the War Powers Resolution, see Ely, *War and Responsibility*, pp. 48–67; Michael J. Glennon, "The Gulf War and the Constitution," *Foreign Affairs* 70 (Spring 1991): 84–101; Robert A. Katzmann, "War Powers: Toward a New Accommodation," in *A Question of Balance: The President, the Congress, and Foreign Policy*, ed. Thomas E. Mann (Washington, D.C.: Brookings Institution, 1990); Marc E. Smyrl, *Conflict or Codetermination? Congress, the President, and the Power to Make War* (Cambridge, Mass.: Ballinger, 1988); and Gerald Felix Warburg, *Conflict and Consensus: The Struggle between Congress and the President over Foreign Policymaking* (New York: Harper and Row, 1989), pp. 119–51.

34. Katzmann, "War Powers," p. 57.

35. "Resolution on Lebanon Signed into Law," *Congressional Quarterly Weekly Report*, 15 October 1983, p. 2142.

36. *Lowry v. Reagan*, 676 F. Supp. 333 (D.D.C. 1987), p. 339.

37. *Dellums v. Bush*, 752 F. Supp. 1141 (D.D.C. 1990), p. 1151.

38. *Congressional Record*, 101st Cong., 1st sess., 1989, 135, pt. 1:465–66.

39. See Doherty, "Reluctant Warriors," p. 323.

40. Quoted in ibid., p. 323.

41. See Ely, *War and Responsibility*, pp. 21–23.

42. Quoted in Walter LaFeber, *America, Russia, and the Cold War, 1945–1971*, 2d ed. (New York: Wiley, 1972), p. 60.

43. See Carroll J. Doherty, "Both Chambers Craft Resolutions Backing Bush's Gulf Policy," *Congressional Quarterly Weekly Report*, 29 September 1990, pp. 3140–42, and Carroll J. Doherty, "Congress Cautiously Supports Bush's Past Gulf Actions," *Congressional Quarterly Weekly Report*, 6 October 1990, p. 3240.

44. Quoted in Carroll J. Doherty, "Uncertain Congress Confronts President's Gulf Strategy," *Congressional Quarterly Weekly Report*, 17 November 1990, p. 3881.

45. See Paul N. Stockton, "Congress and the Making of National Security Strategy for the Post–Cold War Era," in Ripley and Lindsay, *Congress Resurgent*.

46. U.S. Congress, House Committee on Armed Services, *The Fading Threat: Soviet Conventional Military Power in Decline* (Washington, D.C.: U.S. Government Printing Office, 1990), p. 12.

47. U.S. Congress, House Committee on Appropriations, *Foreign Assistance and Related Programs Appropriations for 1988*, pt. 4, 100th Cong., 1st sess., 1987, p. 529.

48. Tanya Broder and Bernard D. Lambek, "Military Aid to Guatemala: The Failure of U.S. Human Rights Legislation," *Yale Journal of International Law* 13 (Winter 1988): 130.

49. See Stockton, "Congress and the Making of National Security Strategy," pp. 256–57.

50. John Lehman, *Making War: The 200-Year-Old Battle between the President and Congress over How America Goes to War* (New York: Scribner, 1992), p. 254.

51. Ibid., p. 270.

52. See Barry M. Blechman, *The Politics of National Security: Congress and U.S. Defense Policy* (New York: Oxford University Press, 1990), and James M. Lindsay, *Congress and Nuclear Weapons* (Baltimore: Johns Hopkins University Press, 1991).

53. Ripley and Franklin, *Congress, the Bureaucracy, and Public Policy*, pp. 152–53.

54. White, "Decision Making in the Appropriations Subcommittees," pp. 204–5.

55. Alexander Hamilton, "Federalist No. 70," in Hamilton, Madison, and Jay, *Federalist Papers*, p. 356.

CHAPTER 8. VICES AND VIRTUES

1. For positive assessments of Congress's role in foreign policy, see Eileen Burgin, "Congress and Foreign Policy: The Misperceptions," in *Congress Reconsidered*, 5th ed., ed. Lawrence C. Dodd and Bruce I. Oppenheimer (Washington, D.C.: CQ Press, 1993); Alton Frye, "Congress: The Virtues of Its Vices," *Foreign Policy* 3 (Summer 1971): 108–25; Stanley J. Heginbotham, "Congress and Defense Policymaking: Toward Realistic Expectations in a System of Countervailing Parochialisms," in *National Security Policy: The Decision-Making Process*, ed. Robert L. Pfaltzgraff, Jr., and Uri Ra'anan (Hamden, Conn.: Archon Books, 1984); Stanley J. Heginbotham, "Dateline Washington: The Rules of the Game," *Foreign Policy* 53 (Winter 1983–84): 157–72; Miroslav Nincic, *Democracy and Foreign Policy: The Fallacy of Political Realism* (New York: Columbia University Press, 1992), pp. 58–89; and Robert A. Pastor, "Congress and U.S. Foreign Policy: Comparative Advantage or Disadvantage?" *Washington Quarterly* 14 (Autumn 1991): 101–14.

2. Eugene V. Rostow, *President, Prime Minister, or Constitutional Monarch?* McNair Papers, no. 3 (Washington, D.C.: National Defense University, 1989), p. 7.

3. I. M. Destler, Leslie H. Gelb, and Anthony Lake, *Our Own Worst Enemy: The Unmaking of American Foreign Policy* (New York: Simon and Schuster, 1984), p. 129 (emphasis in the original).

4. Alexis de Tocqueville, *Democracy in America* (Garden City, N.Y.: Anchor Books, 1969), pp. 228–29.

5. George F. Kennan, *American Diplomacy, 1900–1950* (Chicago: University of Chicago Press, 1951), p. 66.

6. Robert A. Dahl, *Congress and Foreign Policy* (New York: Harcourt, Brace, 1950), p. 169.

7. John Lehman, *Making War: The 200-Year-Old Battle between the President and Congress over How America Goes to War* (New York: Scribner, 1992), p. xii.

8. Bruce W. Jentleson, "American Diplomacy: Around the World and along Pennsylvania Avenue," in *A Question of Balance: The President, the Congress, and Foreign Policy*, ed. Thomas E. Mann (Washington, D.C.: Brookings Institution, 1990), p. 184.

9. Pamela Fessler, "Complaints Are Stacking Up As Hill Piles on Reports," *Congressional Quarterly Weekly Report*, 7 September 1991, p. 2566. Cheney's views on congressional micromanagement are contained in "White Paper on the Department of Defense and Congress," Report to the President by the Secretary of Defense, January 1990.

10. Among others see L. Gordon Crovitz, "Micromanaging Foreign Policy," *Public*

Interest 100 (Summer 1990): 102–15; I. M. Destler, "Executive-Congressional Conflict in Foreign Policy: Explaining It, Coping with It," in *Congress Reconsidered,* 3d ed., ed. Lawrence C. Dodd and Bruce I. Oppenheimer (Washington, D.C.: CQ Press, 1985); Jentleson, "American Diplomacy," p. 177; Mackubin Thomas Owens, "Micromanaging the Defense Budget," *Public Interest* 100 (Summer 1990): 131–46; and Howard J. Wiarda, *Foreign Policy without Illusion: How Foreign Policy-Making Works and Fails to Work in the United States* (Glenview, Ill.: Scott, Foresman/Little, Brown, 1990), pp. 219–20.

11. See, for example, the remarks by Sen. Sam Nunn in *Congressional Record,* 99th Cong., 1st sess., 1985, 131, pt. 18:25350-54, and U.S. Congress, Senate Committee on Armed Services, *Defense Organization: The Need for Change,* 99th Cong., 1st sess., S. Prt. 99–86, 1985.

12. Quoted in John Felton, "'Earmark' Tradition Shows Staying Power on Hill," *Congressional Quarterly Weekly Report,* 22 April 1989, p. 904.

13. See Jacques S. Gansler, *Affording Defense* (Cambridge: MIT Press, 1989), p. 108, and Kenneth R. Mayer, "Policy Disputes As a Source of Administrative Controls: Congressional Micromanagement of the Department of Defense," *Public Administration Review* 53 (July/August 1993): 294.

14. Quoted in Murray Weidenbaum, "The Pentagon's Fruitcake Rules," *New York Times,* 5 January 1992.

15. Jentleson, "American Diplomacy," p. 173.

16. Ibid.

17. Robert J. Art, "Congress and the Defense Budget: Enhancing Policy Oversight," *Political Science Quarterly* 100 (Summer 1985): 238, and James M. Lindsay, *Congress and Nuclear Weapons* (Baltimore: Johns Hopkins University Press, 1991), p. 87.

18. Personal communication from Leonard G. Campbell, director for Plans and Systems, Office of the Comptroller of the Department of Defense, 12 February 1992.

19. Fessler, "Complaints Are Stacking Up," pp. 2565–66.

20. U.S. Congress, House Committee on Foreign Affairs, *Required Reports to Congress on Foreign Policy* (Washington, D.C.: U.S. Government Printing Office, 1988), pp. 8 and 23. See also U.S. Congress, House Committee on Foreign Affairs, *Foreign Assistance Reporting Requirements* (Washington, D.C.: U.S. Government Printing Office, 1989).

21. Jeffrey T. Bergner, "Organizing Congress for National Security," *Comparative Strategy* 6 (1987): 303.

22. Wiarda, *Foreign Policy without Illusion,* p. 219.

23. J. William Fulbright, "The Legislator as Educator," *Foreign Affairs* 57 (Spring 1979): 726.

24. See Mayer, "Policy Disputes," pp. 293–301.

25. Foreign aid legislation has drawn particular criticism for its complexity. See Felton, "'Earmark' Tradition," pp. 903–4; Christopher Madison, "Foreign Aid Follies," *National Journal,* 1 June 1991, pp. 1288–91; and U.S. Congress, House Committee on Foreign Affairs, *Report of the Task Force on Foreign Assistance* (Washington, D.C.: U.S. Government Printing Office, 1989).

26. See Carroll J. Doherty, "Support for Foreign Aid Wilting under Glare of Domestic Woes," *Congressional Quarterly Weekly Report,* 16 May 1992, p. 1357; Felton, "'Earmark' Tradition," p. 903; and Fessler, "Complaints Are Stacking Up," pp. 2562 and 2566.

27. See James M. Lindsay, "Congress and the Defense Budget," *Washington Quarterly*

11 (Winter 1988): 59–60; Frank J. Smist, Jr., *Congress Oversees the United States Intelligence Community, 1947–1989* (Knoxville: University of Tennessee Press, 1990), pp. 106–7; and Pat Towell, "Defense Bill Moves On to Bush after Final Power Struggle," *Congressional Quarterly Weekly Report,* 30 November 1991, p. 3538.

28. Carroll J. Doherty, "Foreign Aid's Maze," *Congressional Quarterly Weekly Report,* 16 May 1992, p. 1357.

29. James Brooke, "U.S. Delegation in Rio Strained and Divided over Policy," *New York Times,* 12 June 1992.

30. See Joseph White, "Decision Making in the Appropriations Subcommittees on Defense and Foreign Operations," in *Congress Resurgent: Foreign and Defense Policy on Capitol Hill,* ed. Randall B. Ripley and James M. Lindsay (Ann Arbor: University of Michigan Press, 1993), p. 196.

31. John W. Finney, "Halt of Sentinel Is Traced to a Ten-Month-Old Memo," *New York Times,* 9 February 1969.

32. Thomas McNaugher, *New Weapons, Old Politics: America's Military Procurement Muddle* (Washington, D.C.: Brookings Institution, 1989), p. 9.

33. See Elaine Sciolino, "Iraq Policy Still Bedevils Bush As Congress Asks: Were Crimes Committed?" *New York Times,* 9 August 1992.

34. See James Madison, "Federalist No. 51," in Alexander Hamilton, James Madison, and John Jay, *The Federalist Papers,* ed. Garry Wills (New York: Bantam Books, 1982), p. 262.

35. Richard Spohn and Charles McCollum, *The Revenue Committees: A Study of the House Ways and Means and Senate Finance Committees and the House and Senate Appropriations Committees* (New York: Grossman, 1975), pp. 221–22.

36. Tocqueville, *Democracy in America,* p. 229.

37. Quoted in Charles W. Kegley, Jr., and Eugene R. Wittkopf, *American Foreign Policy: Patterns and Process,* 4th ed. (New York: St. Martin's Press, 1991), pp. 420–21.

38. Kenneth R. Mayer, "Patterns of Congressional Influence in Defense Contracting," in *Arms, Politics, and the Economy: Historical and Contemporary Perspectives,* ed. Robert Higgs (New York: Holmes and Meier, 1990), and Kenneth R. Mayer, *The Political Economy of Defense Contracting* (New Haven: Yale University Press, 1991).

39. James M. Lindsay, "Congress and the Defense Budget: Parochialism or Policy?" in Higgs, *Arms, Politics, and the Economy,* and Lindsay, *Congress and Nuclear Weapons,* pp. 123–43.

40. Eileen Burgin, "Representatives' Decisions on Participation in Foreign Policy Issues," *Legislative Studies Quarterly* 4 (November 1991): 521–46, and Eileen Burgin, "The Influence of Constituents: Congressional Decision Making on Issues of Foreign and Defense Policy," in Ripley and Lindsay, *Congress Resurgent.*

41. See Mohammed E. Ahrari, ed., *Ethnic Groups and U.S. Foreign Policy* (New York: Greenwood Press, 1987); Irving Louis Horowitz, "Ethnic Politics and U.S. Foreign Policy," in *Ethnicity and U.S. Foreign Policy,* ed. Abdul Aziz Said (New York: Praeger, 1977); John T. Tierney, "Congressional Activism in Foreign Policy: Its Varied Forms and Stimuli," in *The New Politics of American Foreign Policy,* ed. David A. Deese (New York: St. Martin's Press, 1994); John T. Tierney, "Interest Group Involvement in Congressional Foreign and Defense Policy," in Ripley and Lindsay, *Congress Resurgent;* and Eric Uslaner, "A Tower of Babel on Foreign Policy?" in *Interest Group Politics,* 3d ed., ed. Allan J. Cigler and Burdett A. Loomis (Washington, D.C.: CQ Press, 1991). For a skeptical assessment

of the power of the Greek lobby, see Ellen Laipson, *Congressional-Executive Relations and the Turkish Arms Embargo,* U.S. Congress, House Committee on Foreign Affairs (Washington, D.C.: U.S. Government Printing Office, 1981).

42. Pietro Nivola, "Trade Policy: Refereeing the Playing Field," in Mann, *Question of Balance,* p. 227.

43. Among others see Graham T. Allison, *Essence of Decision: Explaining the Cuban Missile Crisis* (Boston: Little, Brown, 1971); Morton H. Halperin, *Bureaucratic Politics and Foreign Policy* (Washington, D.C.: Brookings Institution, 1974); and Samuel P. Huntington, *The Common Defense: Strategic Programs in National Politics* (New York: Columbia University Press, 1961).

44. See Miroslav Nincic, "U.S.-Soviet Policy and the Electoral Connection," *World Politics* 42 (April 1990): 370–96; Charles W. Ostrom, Jr., and Brian Job, "The President and the Political Use of Force," *American Political Science Review* 80 (June 1986): 541–66; William B. Quandt, "The Electoral Cycle and the Conduct of American Foreign Policy," *Political Science Quarterly* 101 (1986): 825–37; and Richard J. Stoll, "The Guns of November: Presidential Elections and the Use of Force," *Journal of Conflict Resolution* 28 (June 1984): 231–46. For a study that found only muted links between presidential decision making on foreign policy and public opinion, see James M. Lindsay, Lois W. Sayrs, and Wayne P. Steger, "The Determinants of Presidential Foreign Policy Choice," *American Politics Quarterly* 20 (January 1992): 3–25.

45. Hamilton Jordan, *Crisis: The Last Year of the Carter Presidency* (New York: Putnam, 1982), p. 36. See also John Spanier and Eric M. Uslaner, *American Foreign Policy Making and the Democratic Dilemmas,* 5th ed. (Pacific Grove, Calif.: Brooks/Cole, 1989), p. 197.

46. See Mark Hertsgaard, *On Bended Knee: The Press and the Reagan Presidency* (New York: Schocken Books, 1989), esp. chap. 9.

47. Madison, "Federalist No. 51," p. 263.

48. Kenneth R. Mayer, "Problem? What Problem? Congressional Micromanagement of the Department of Defense," Paper presented at the 1991 annual meeting of the American Political Science Association, Washington, D.C., p. 14. See also "The Best Weapons," *U.S. News and World Report,* 10 July 1989, p. 27, and Richard Stubbing with Richard A. Mendel, *The Defense Game: An Insider Explores the Astonishing Realities of America's Defense Establishment* (New York: Harper and Row, 1986), p. 142.

49. Quoted in Andrew Weinschenk, "A Congressional Add-On Shines in the Persian Gulf," *Defense Week,* 5 August 1991.

50. For statistical evidence on this point, see James D. Morrow, "Electoral and Congressional Incentives and Arms Control," *Journal of Conflict Resolution* 35 (June 1991): 245–65.

51. Studies of decision making during crises find that leaders exaggerate the unity of their opponents. See Robert Jervis, *Perception and Misperception in International Politics* (Princeton: Princeton University Press, 1976), pp. 319–42. At the same time, leaders of authoritarian governments often display considerable ignorance of American politics. For some examples, see Jentleson, "American Diplomacy," pp. 153–54; John R. MacArthur, *Second Front: Censorship and Propaganda in the Gulf War* (New York: Hill and Wang, 1992), pp. 130–31; and Robert Wiener, *Live from Baghdad: Gathering News at Ground Zero* (New York: Doubleday, 1992), p. 70.

52. See Mark G. McDonough, "Panama Canal Treaty Negotiations (A)," Case C14-79-223, Harvard University, John F. Kennedy School of Government, 1979, and

Mark G. McDonough, "Panama Canal Treaty Negotiations (B): Concluding a Treaty," Case C14-79-224, Harvard University, John F. Kennedy School of Government, 1979.

53. For two examples, see Edward A. Gargan, "A 'Chastened' Pakistan: Peace with U.S. Is Aim," *New York Times,* 19 February 1992, and John Lehman, *The Executive, Congress, and Foreign Policy: Studies of the Nixon Administration* (New York: Praeger, 1976), pp. 89 and 103.

54. Quoted in William Safire, *Before the Fall* (New York: Belmont Tower Books, 1975), p. 505.

55. Robert A. Pastor, *Congress and the Politics of U.S. Foreign Economic Policy, 1929–1976* (Berkeley: University of California Press, 1980), p. 193.

56. Steve Hoadley, "The US Congress and the New Zealand Military Preference Elimination Bill," *Political Science* 43 (June 1991): 47–60.

57. McDonough, "Panama Canal Treaty Negotiations (B)," pp. 8–11.

58. Richard L. Siegel, *Evaluating the Results of Foreign Policy: Soviet and American Efforts in India,* University of Denver Monograph Series in World Affairs, vol. 6, monograph no. 4, p. 35.

59. See, for example, Cynthia J. Arnson, *Crossroads: Congress, the Reagan Administration, and Central America* (New York: Pantheon Books, 1989), pp. 131 and 141.

60. Lee H. Hamilton, "Congress and the Presidency in American Foreign Policy," *Presidential Studies Quarterly* 18 (Summer 1988): 508.

61. For an eloquent discussion of why open debate encourages policy innovation, see John Stuart Mill, "Representative Government," in *Utilitarianism, Liberty, and Representative Government* (London: Dent, 1910), esp. chap. 3.

62. Paul N. Stockton, "Congress and Defense Policymaking for the Post–Cold War Era," in Ripley and Lindsay, *Congress Resurgent,* p. 244.

63. Arnson, *Crossroads,* p. 131.

64. Alexander Hamilton, "Federalist No. 70," in Hamilton, Madison, and Jay, *Federalist Papers,* p. 358.

65. See Dahl, *Congress and Foreign Policy,* pp. 103–4; Robert Dahl, *Controlling Nuclear Weapons: Democracy versus Guardianship* (Syracuse, N.Y.: Syracuse University Press, 1985), pp. 43–46; and Huntington, *The Common Defense,* pp. 130–31.

66. Quoted in Arthur M. Schlesinger, Jr., *The Imperial Presidency* (Boston: Houghton Mifflin, 1989), p. 15.

67. On the frequency with which the executive branch leaks information, see Elie Abel, *Leaking: Who Does It? Who Benefits? At What Cost?* (New York: Priority Press, 1987); Hertsgaard, *On Bended Knee,* pp. 140–47; Martin Linsky, *Impact: How the Press Affects Federal Policymaking* (New York: Norton, 1986); and David C. Morrison, "Blabbermouths," *National Journal,* 1 August 1987, p. 2002.

68. *The Tower Commission Report: The Full Text of the President's Special Review Board* (New York: Bantam Books/Times Books, 1987), p. 98.

69. On the neutron bomb, see Barry Rubin, "The Media and the Neutron Warhead," *Washington Review of Strategic and International Studies* 1 (July 1978): 90–94, and Deborah Shapely, "The Media and National Security," *Daedalus* 111 (Fall 1982): 199–209. On the Soviet brigade, see Dan Caldwell, *The Dynamics of Domestic Politics and Arms Control: The SALT II Treaty Ratification Debate* (Columbia: University of South Carolina Press, 1991), pp. 155–69, and Gloria Duffy, "Crisis Mangling and the Cuban Brigade," *International Security* 8 (Summer 1983): 67–87.

70. Pastor, "Congress and U.S. Foreign Policy," p. 103.

71. On Congress as educator, see Fulbright, "Legislator as Educator," pp. 719–32.

72. Michael Walzer, "Deterrence and Democracy," *New Republic,* 2 July 1984, p. 19.

73. Richard E. Neustadt, *Presidential Power and the Modern Presidents: The Politics of Leadership from Roosevelt to Reagan* (New York: Free Press, 1990), p. 29.

INDEX

Library of Congress Cataloging-in-Publication Data

Lindsay, James M., 1959–
    Congress and the politics of U.S. foreign policy / James M. Lindsay.
    p.   cm.
    Includes bibliographical references and index.
    ISBN 0-8018-4881-4 (hc : acid-free paper). — ISBN 0-8018-4882-2
(pbk : acid-free paper)
    1. United States. Congress.   2. United States–Foreign relations—
1945–1989.   3 United States—Foreign relations—1989–   4. United
States—Military policy.   I. Title.   II. Title: Congress and the politics of
US foreign policy.
    JK1081.L56   1994
    328.73'0746—dc20   94-1246